PRISON PIT

BOOK 3

JOHNNY RYAN

FANTAGRAPHICS BOOKS, INC.

TAGRAPHICS BOOKS, 7563 Lake City Way NE, Seattle WA 98115. All contents © Johnny Ryan. Juction: Paul Baresh. Associate Publisher: Eric Reynolds. Published by Gary Groth & Kim Thompson. First on: July, 2011. ISBN: 978-1-60669-497-9. Printed in Singapore.

3

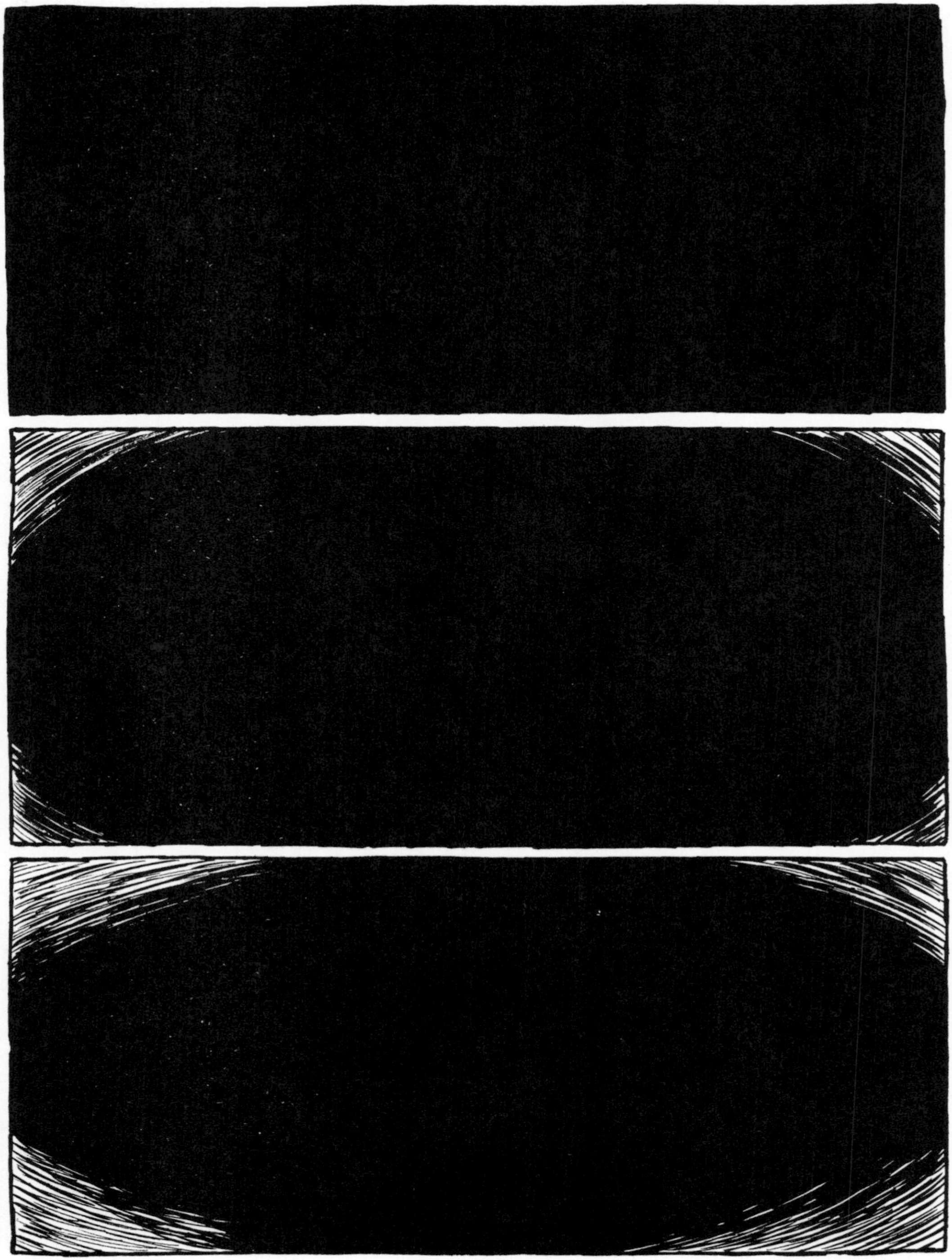

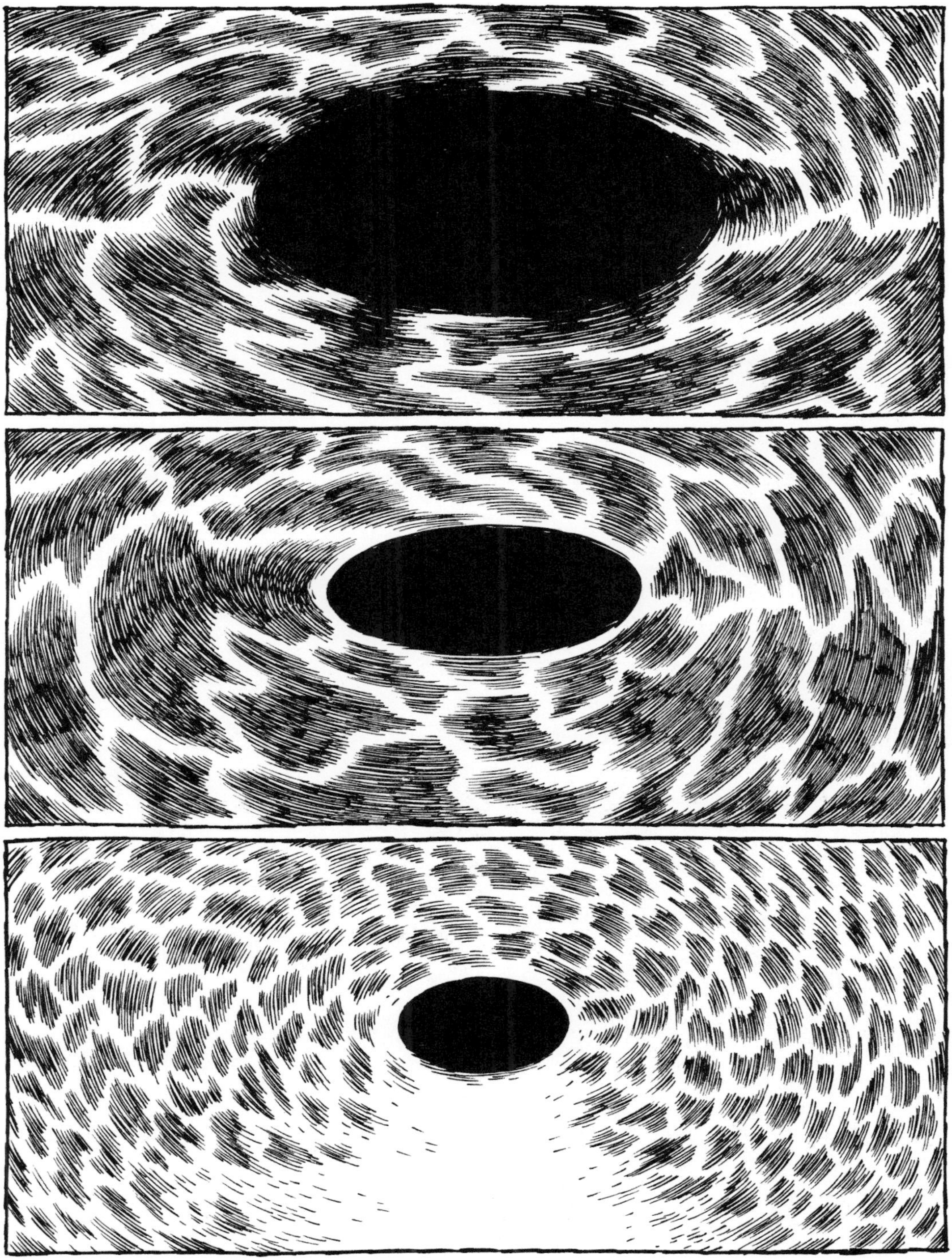

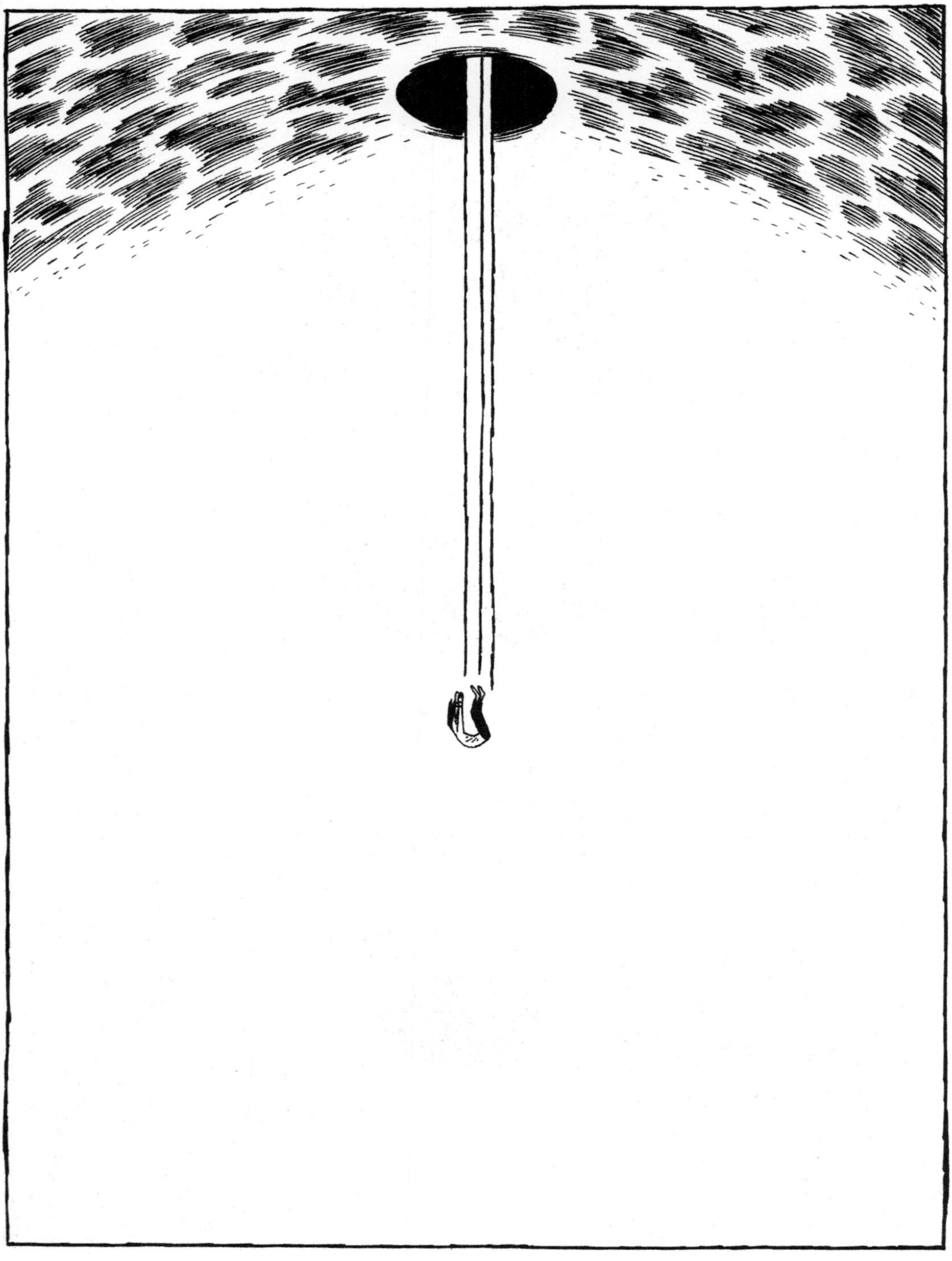

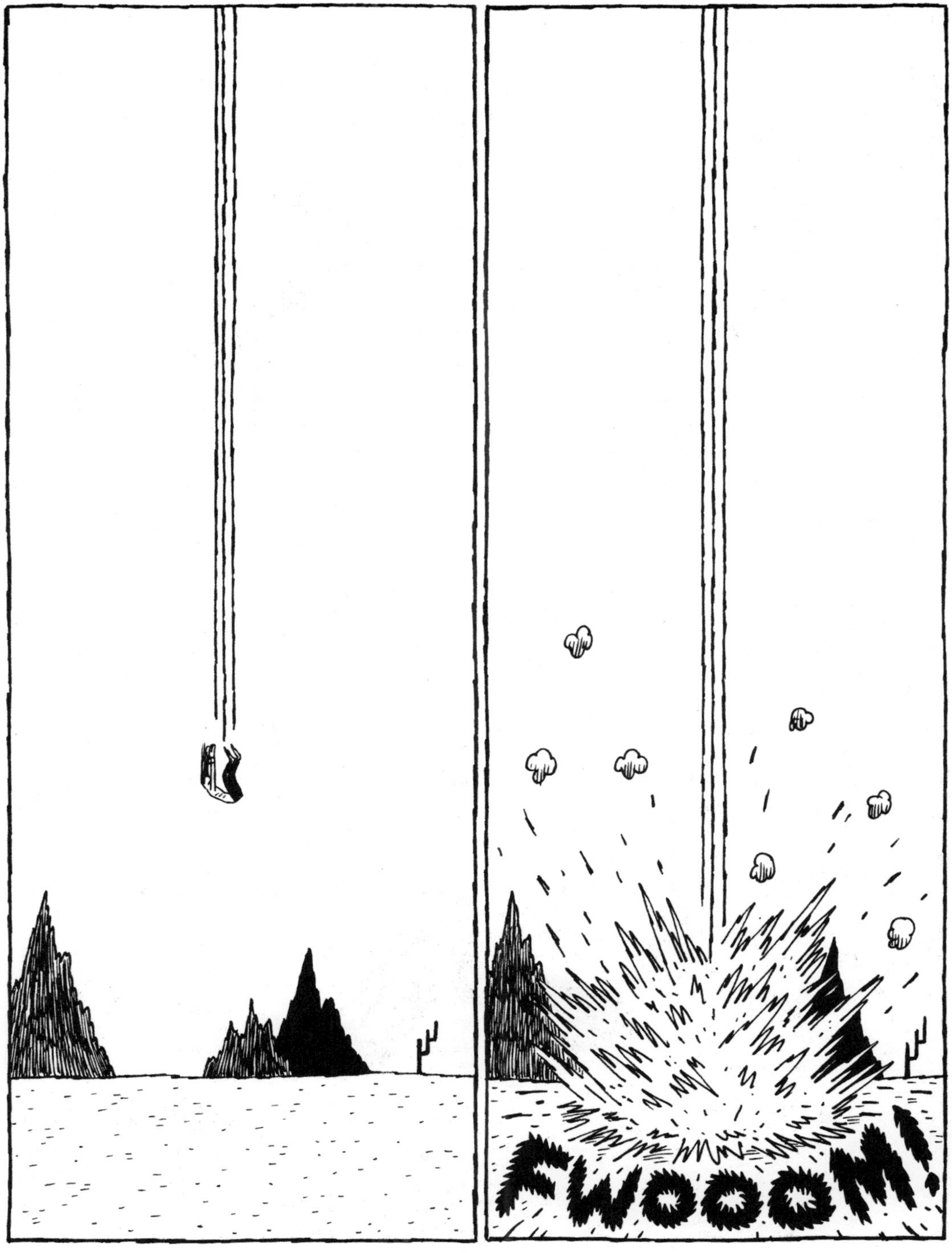
FWOOOM!

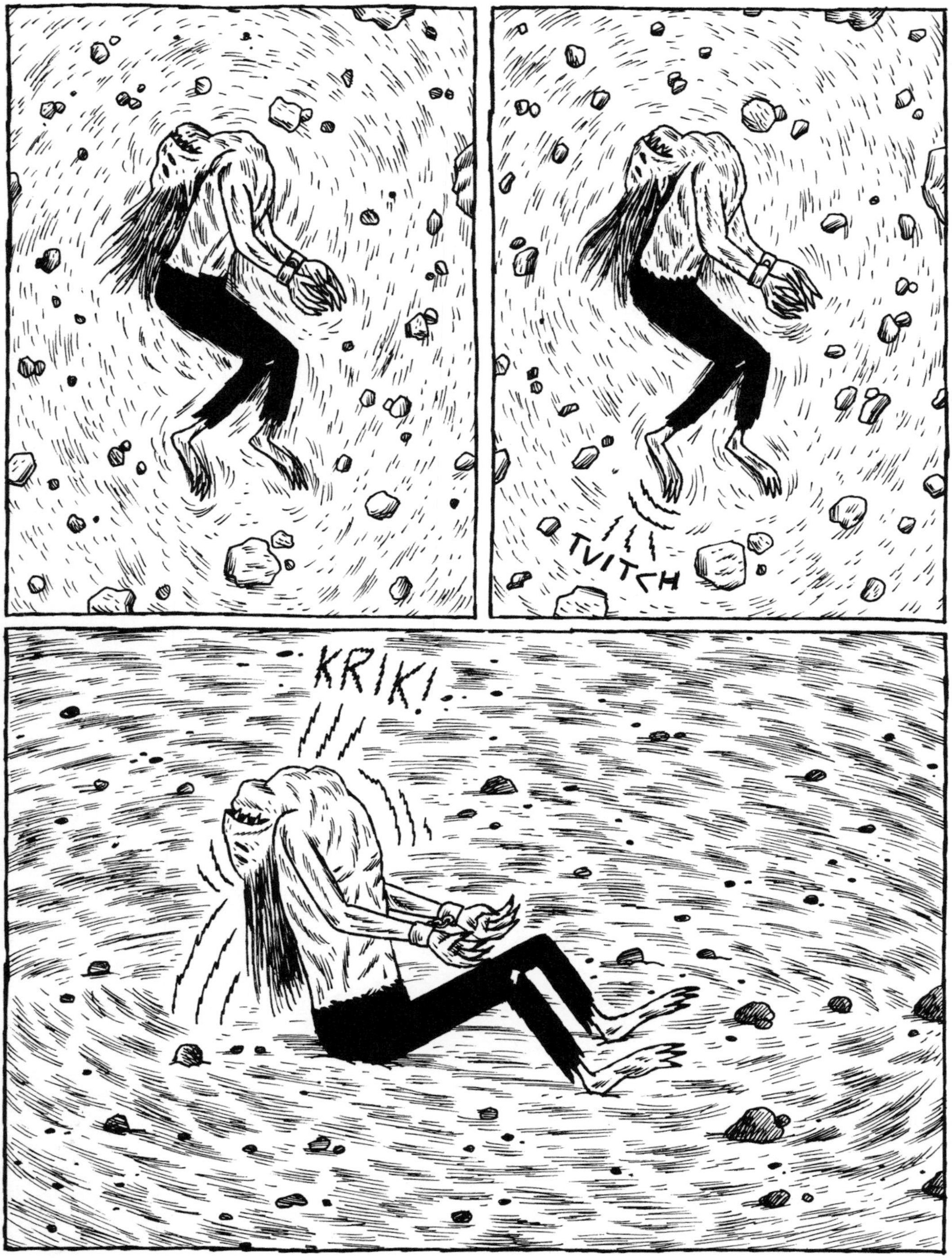
TWITCH
KRIK!

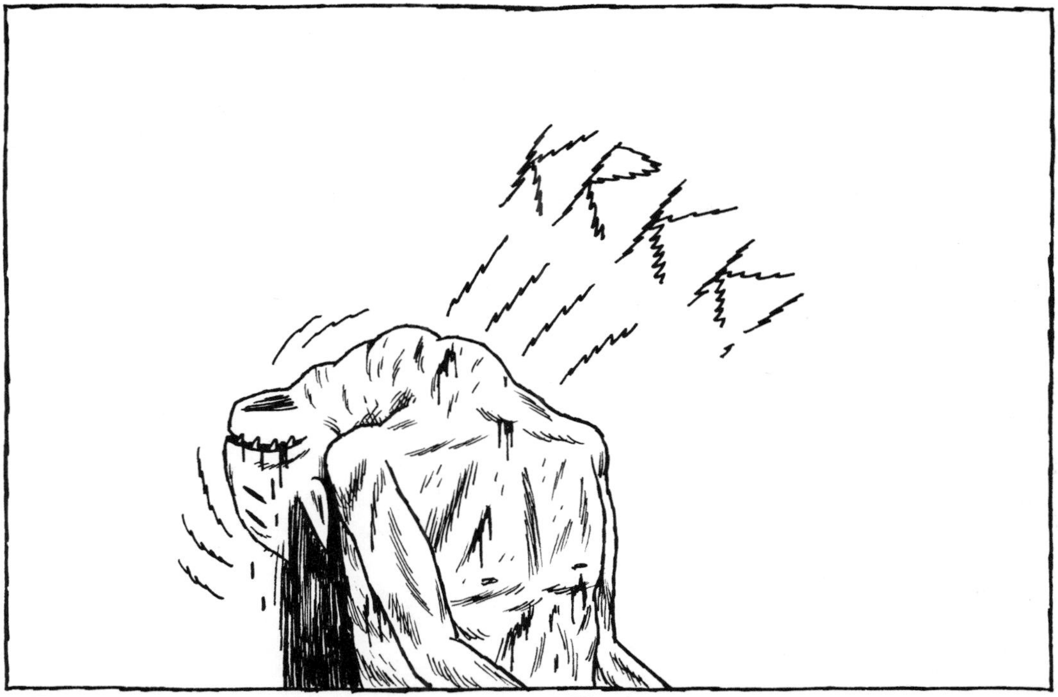
KRK!

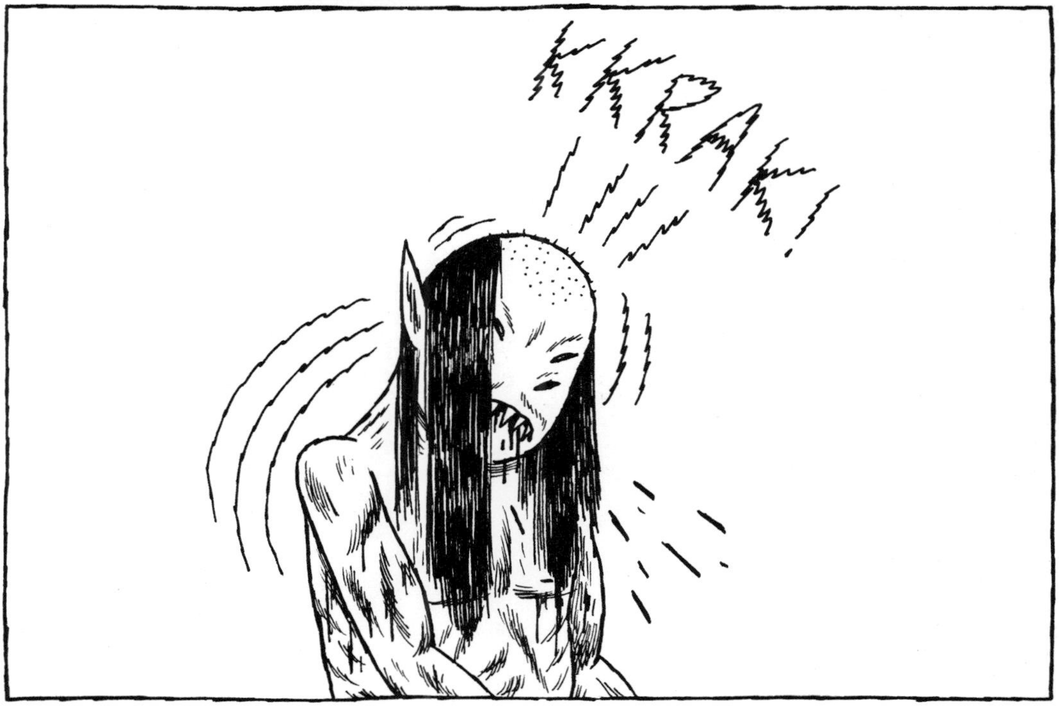
KKRAK!

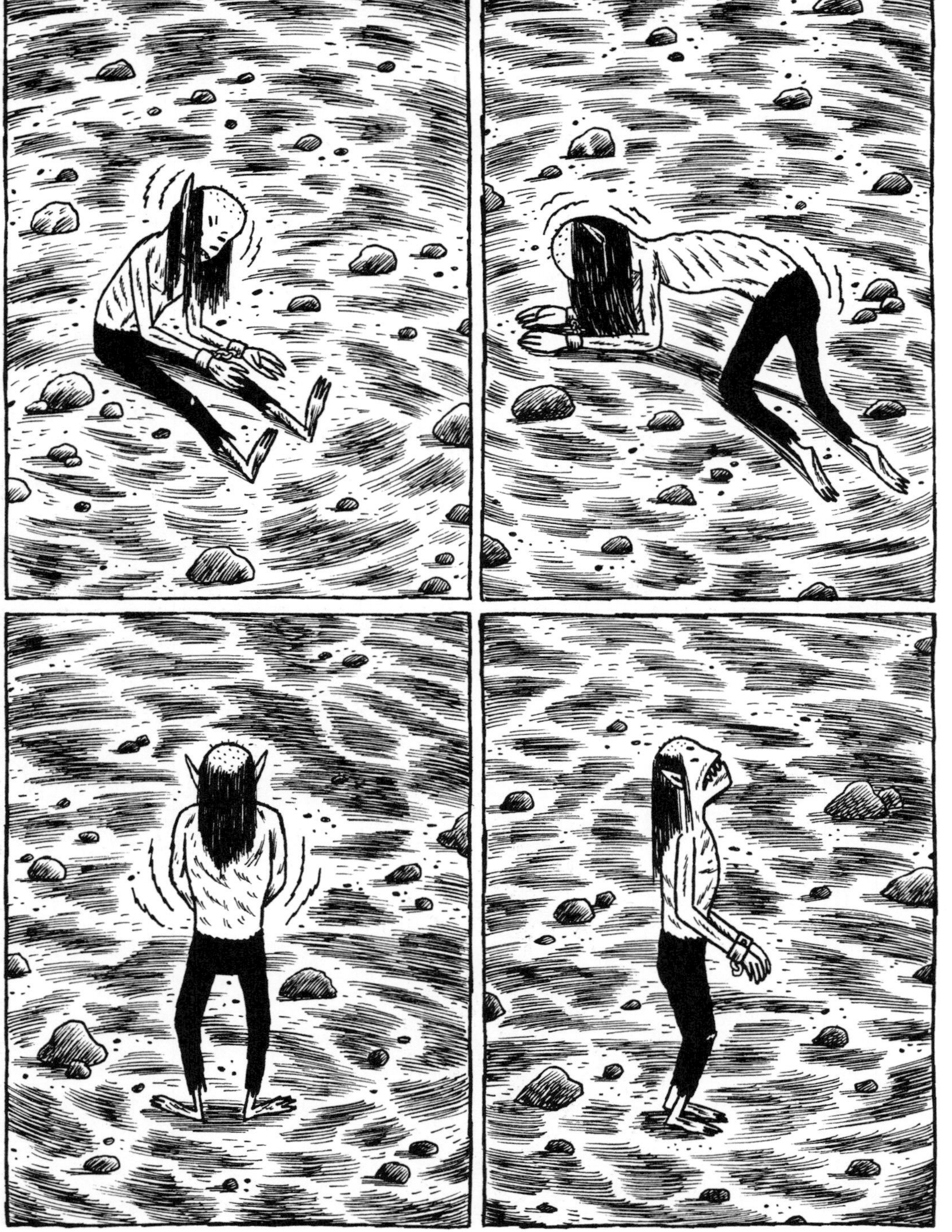

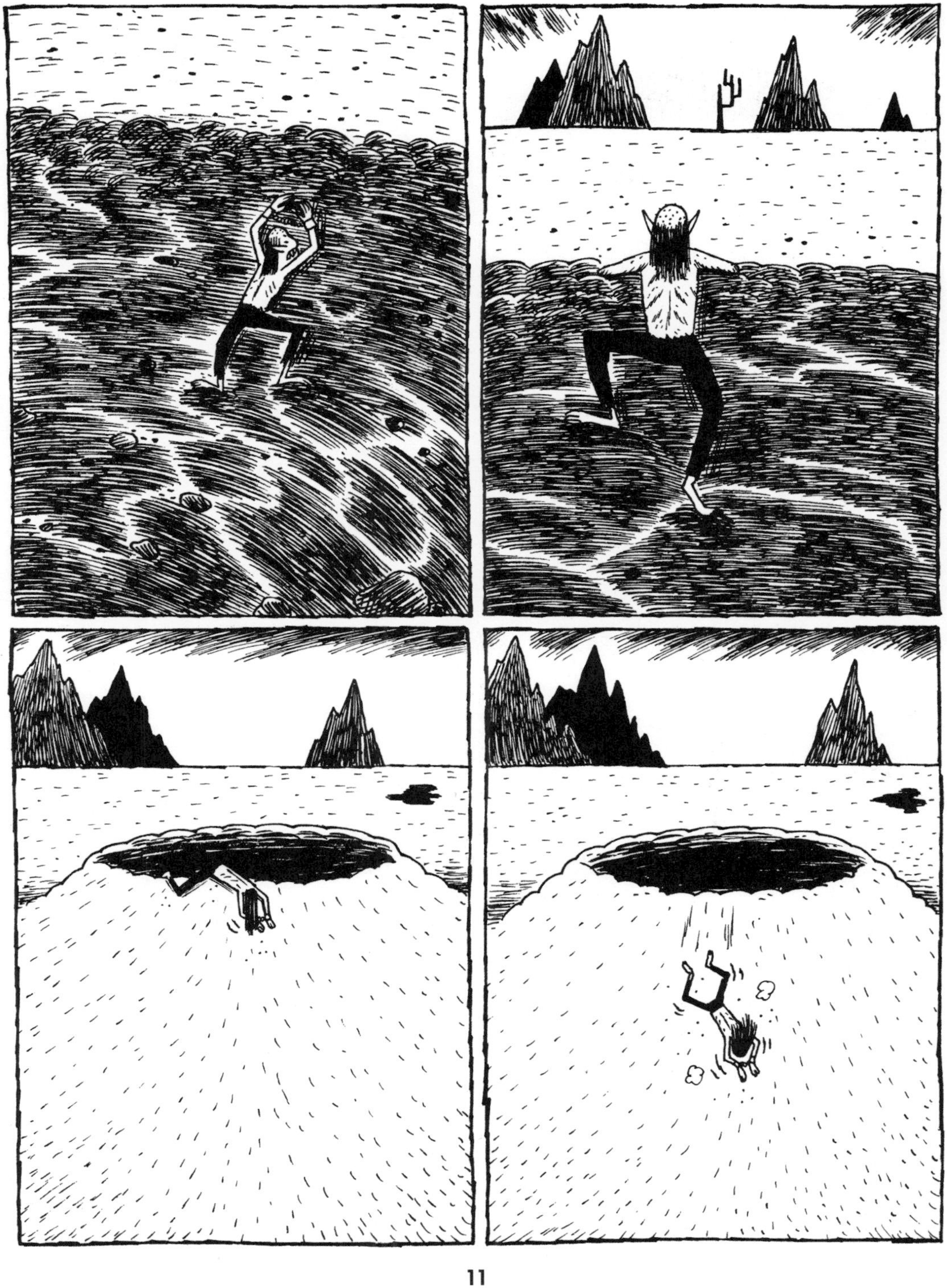

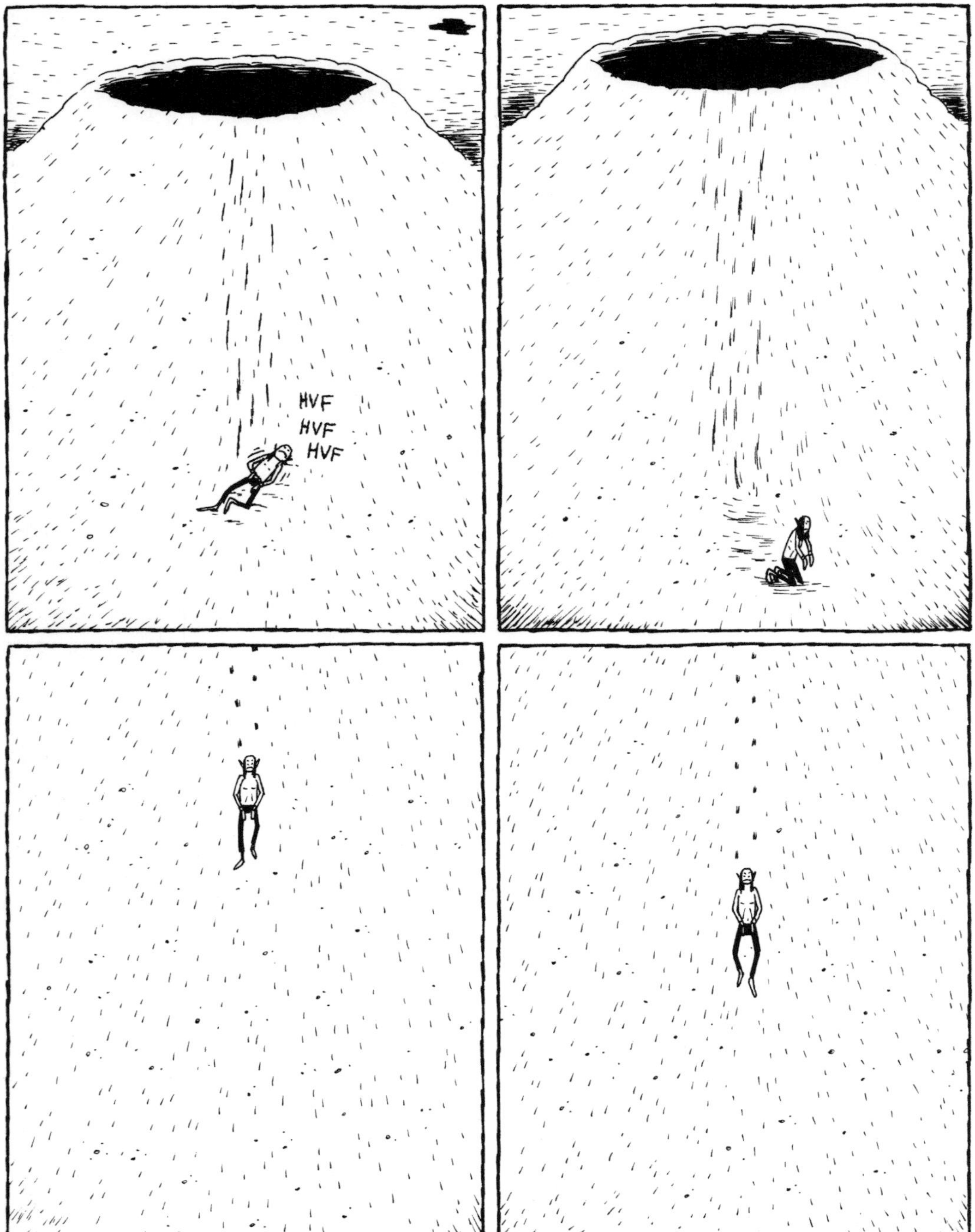
HVF
HVF
HVF

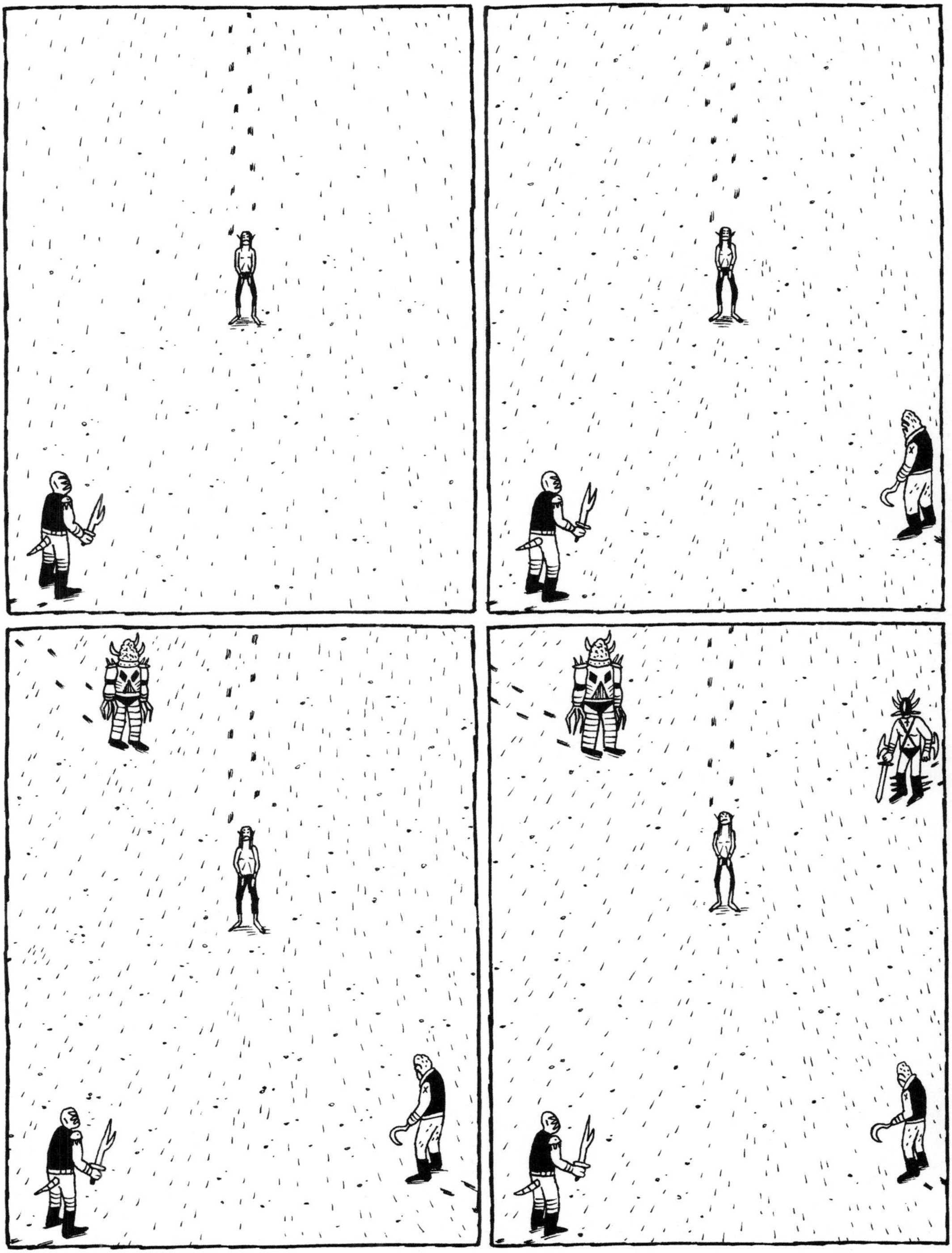

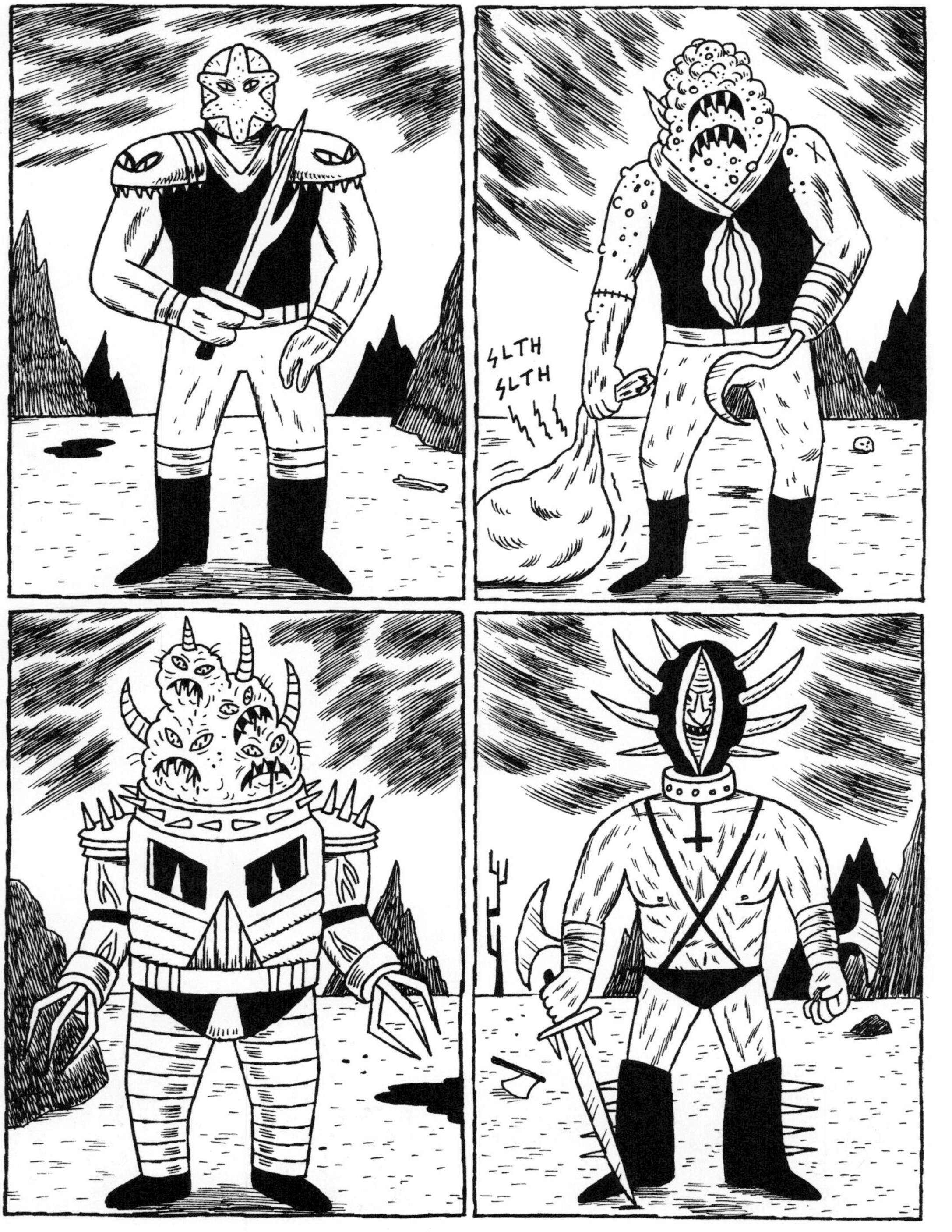
SLTH
SLTH

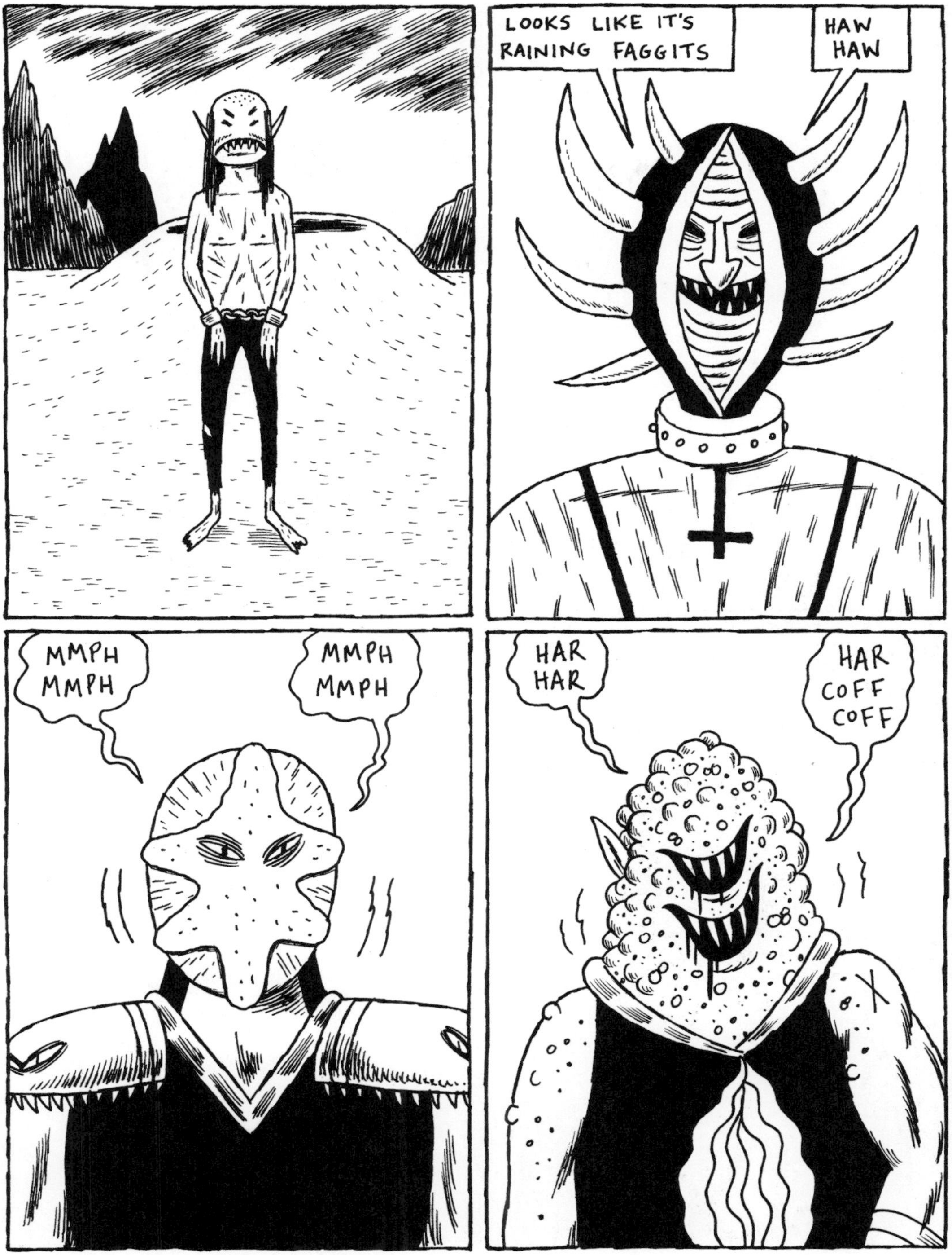

LOOKS LIKE IT'S RAINING FAGGITS
HAW HAW
MMPH MMPH
MMPH MMPH
HAR HAR
HAR COFF COFF

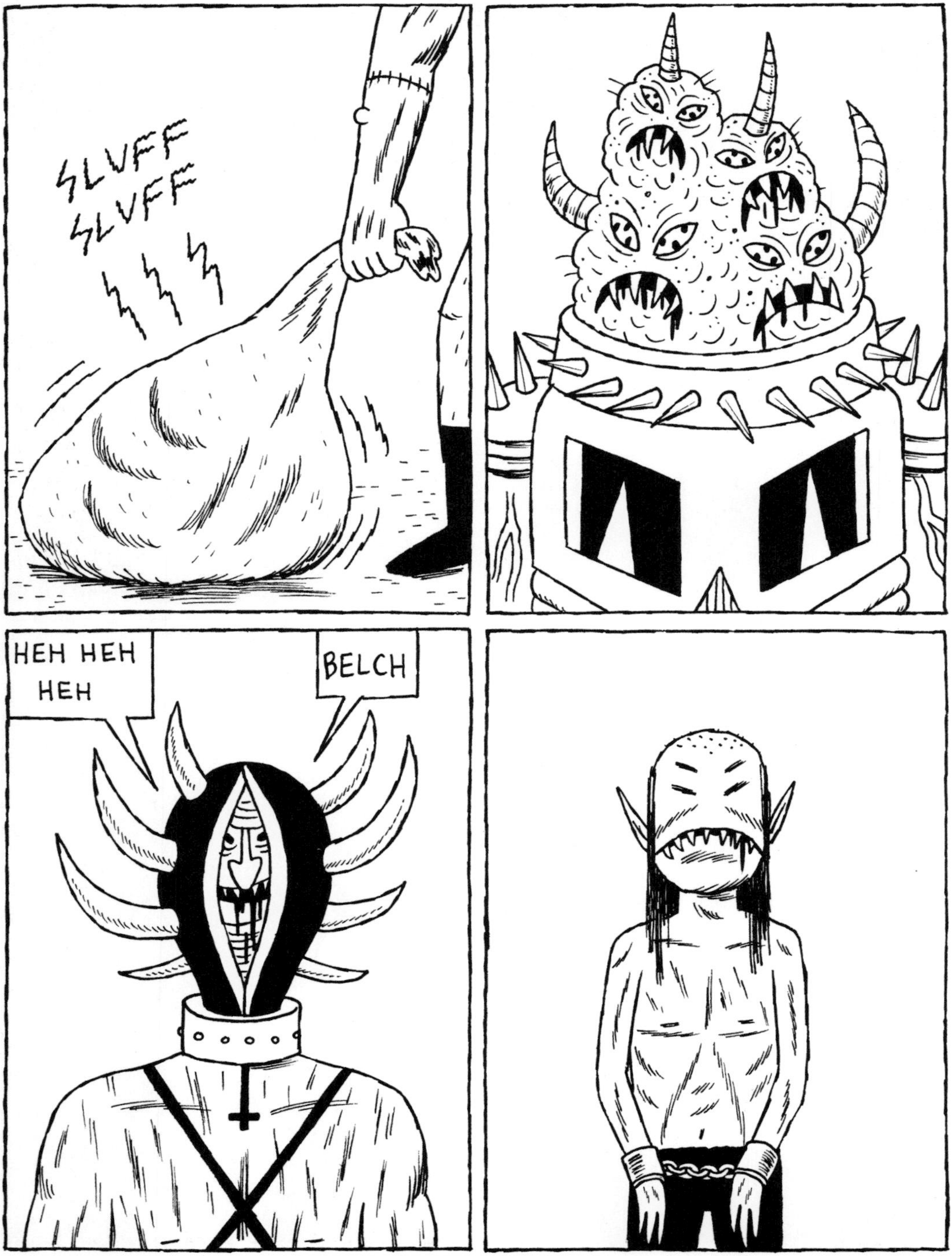
SLUFF
SLUFF
HEH HEH HEH
BELCH

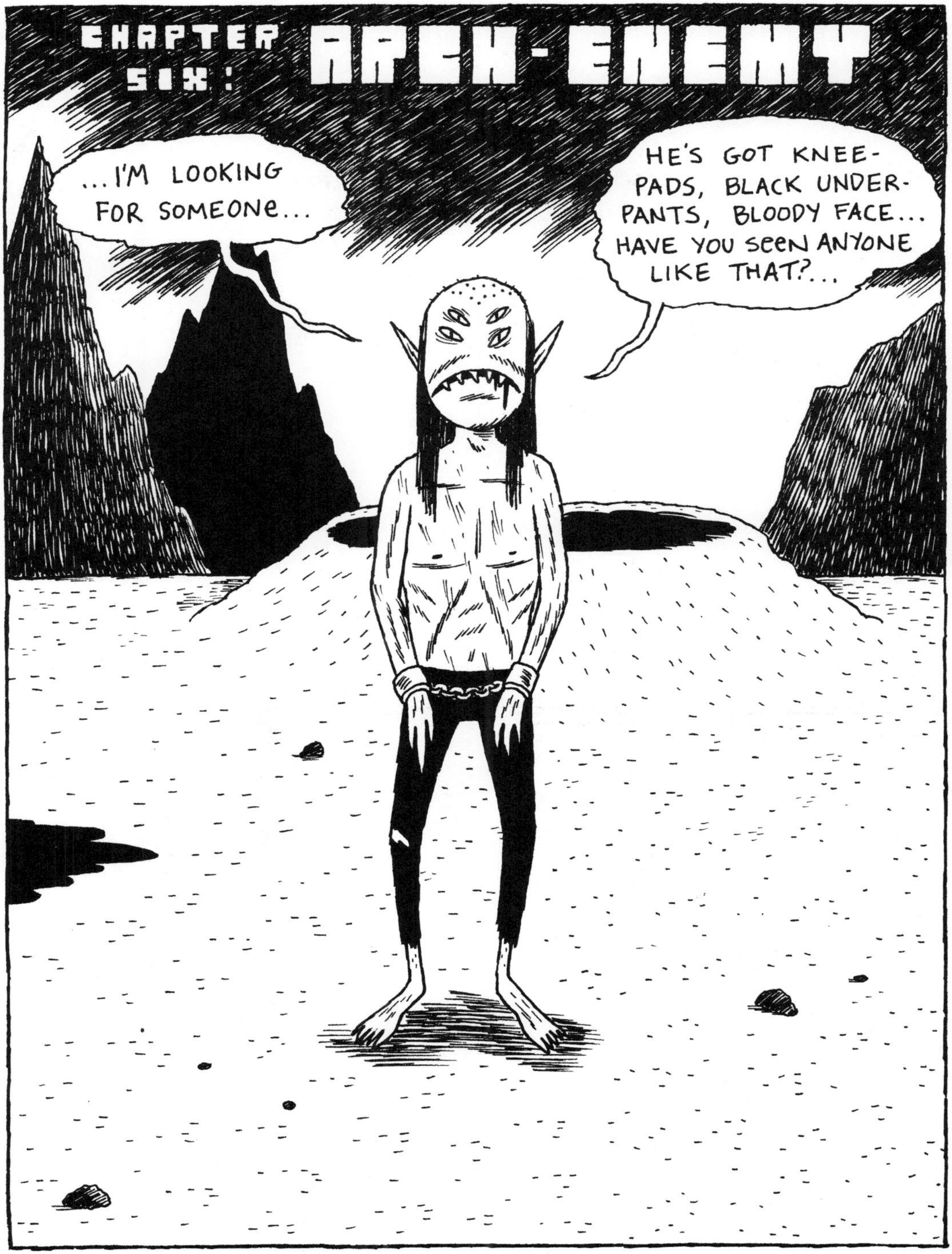
CHAPTER SIX: ARCH-ENEMY
...I'M LOOKING FOR SOMEONE...
HE'S GOT KNEE-PADS, BLACK UNDER-PANTS, BLOODY FACE... HAVE YOU SEEN ANYONE LIKE THAT?...

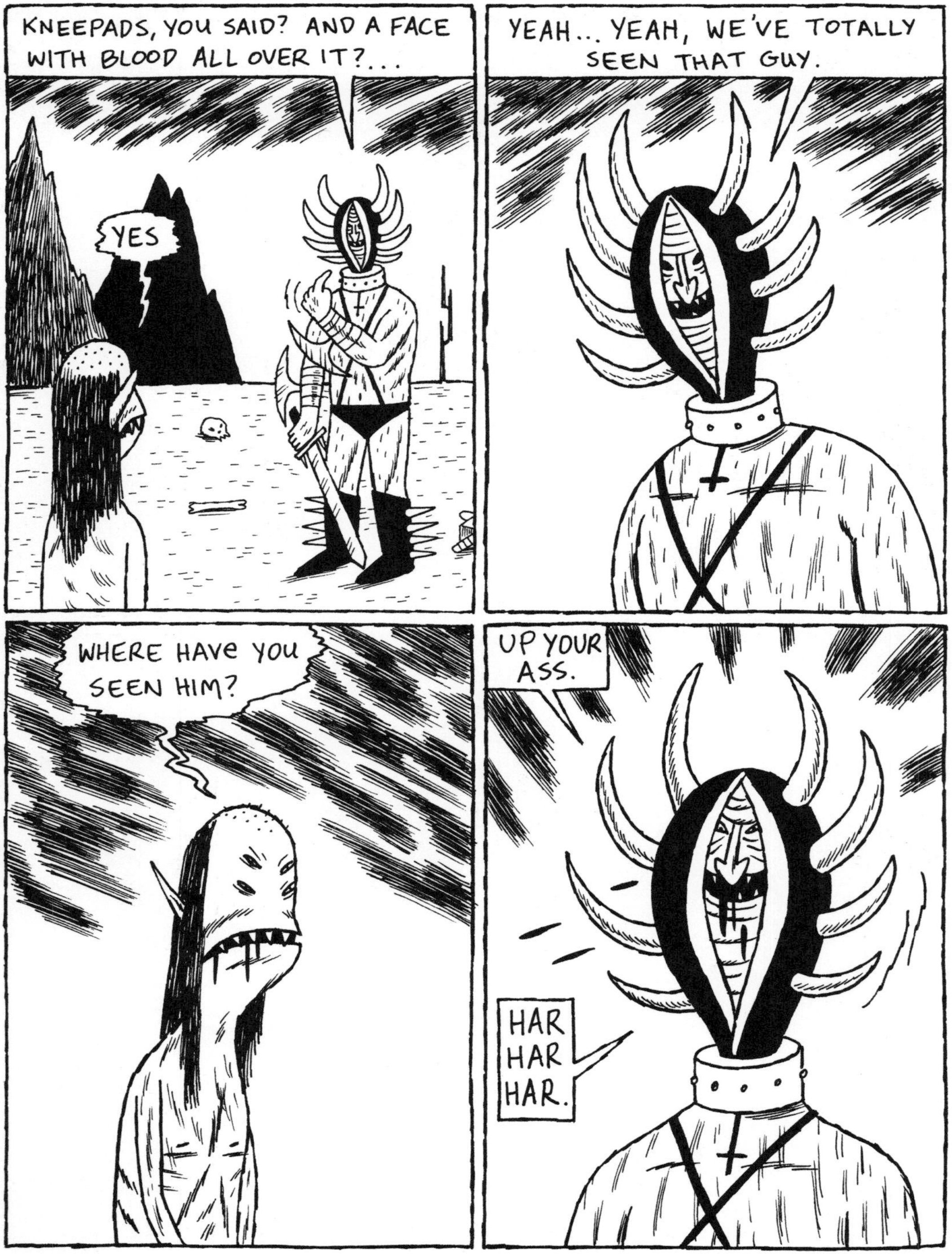
KNEEPADS, YOU SAID? AND A FACE WITH BLOOD ALL OVER IT?...
YES
YEAH... YEAH, WE'VE TOTALLY SEEN THAT GUY.
WHERE HAVE YOU SEEN HIM?
UP YOUR ASS.
HAR HAR HAR.

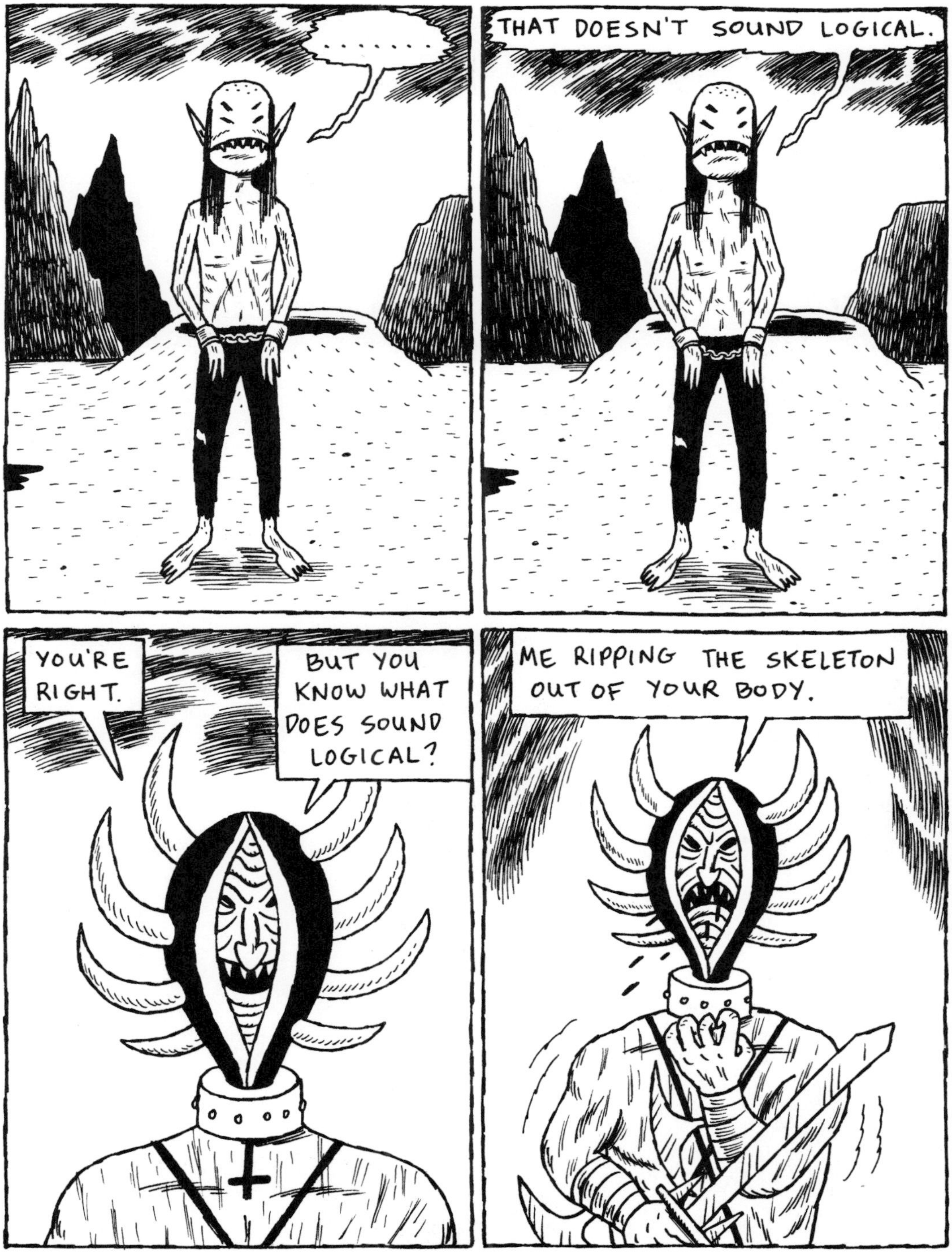
. . . .
THAT DOESN'T SOUND LOGICAL.
YOU'RE RIGHT.
BUT YOU KNOW WHAT DOES SOUND LOGICAL?
ME RIPPING THE SKELETON OUT OF YOUR BODY.

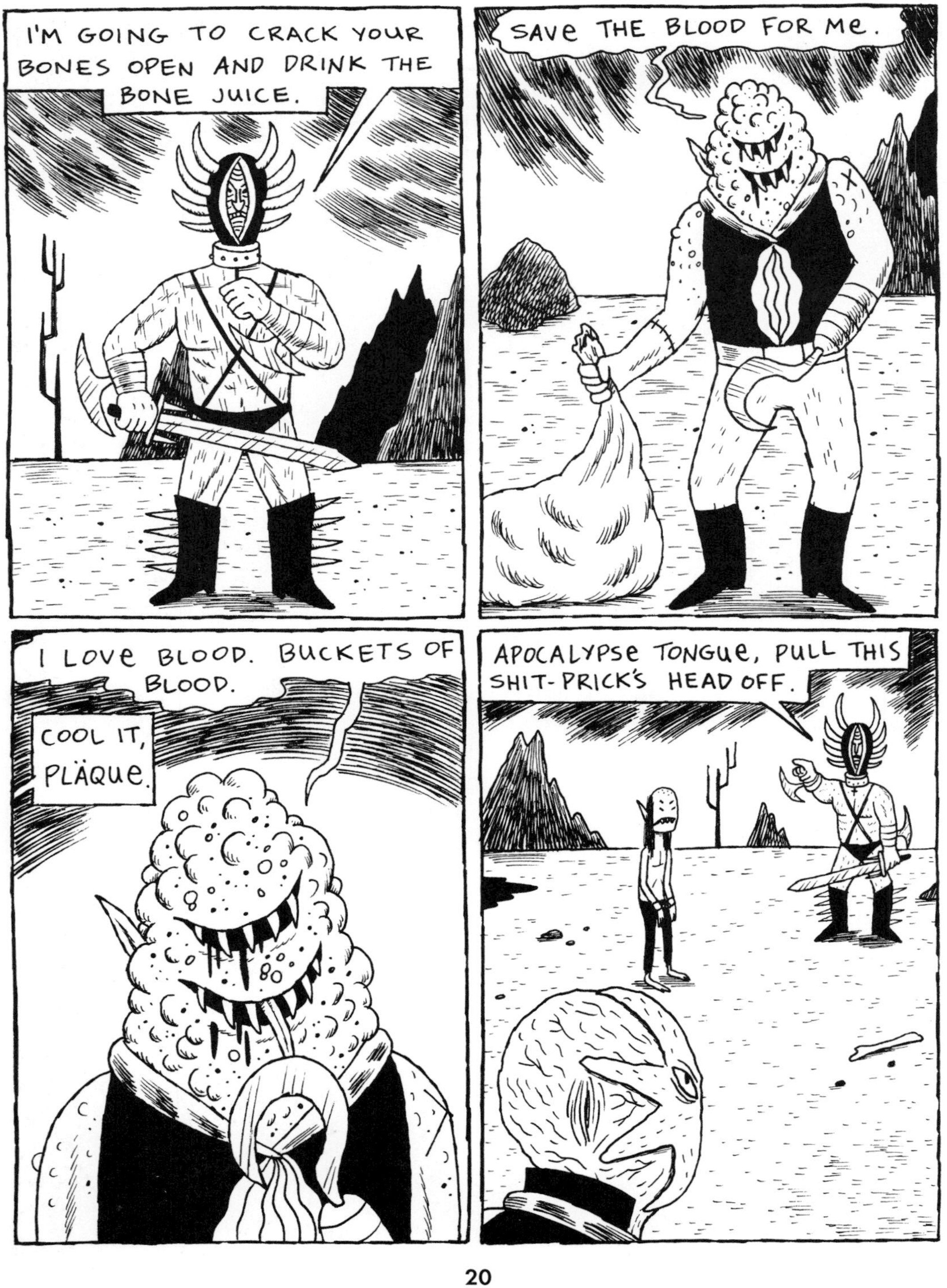
I'M GOING TO CRACK YOUR BONES OPEN AND DRINK THE BONE JUICE.
SAVE THE BLOOD FOR ME.
I LOVE BLOOD. BUCKETS OF BLOOD.
COOL IT, PLÄQUE.
APOCALYPSE TONGUE, PULL THIS SHIT-PRICK'S HEAD OFF.

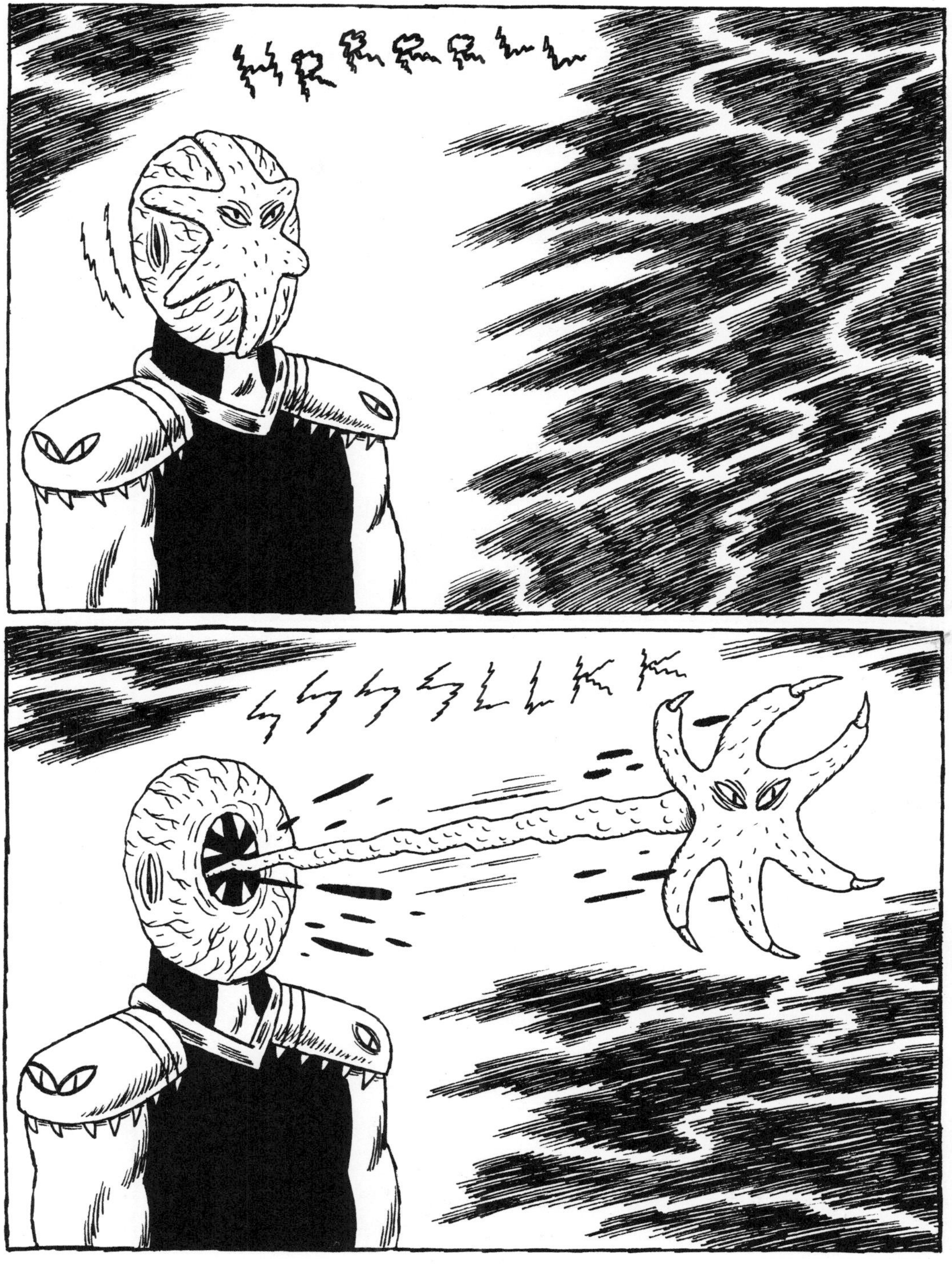
HRRRRLL
SSSSLLKK

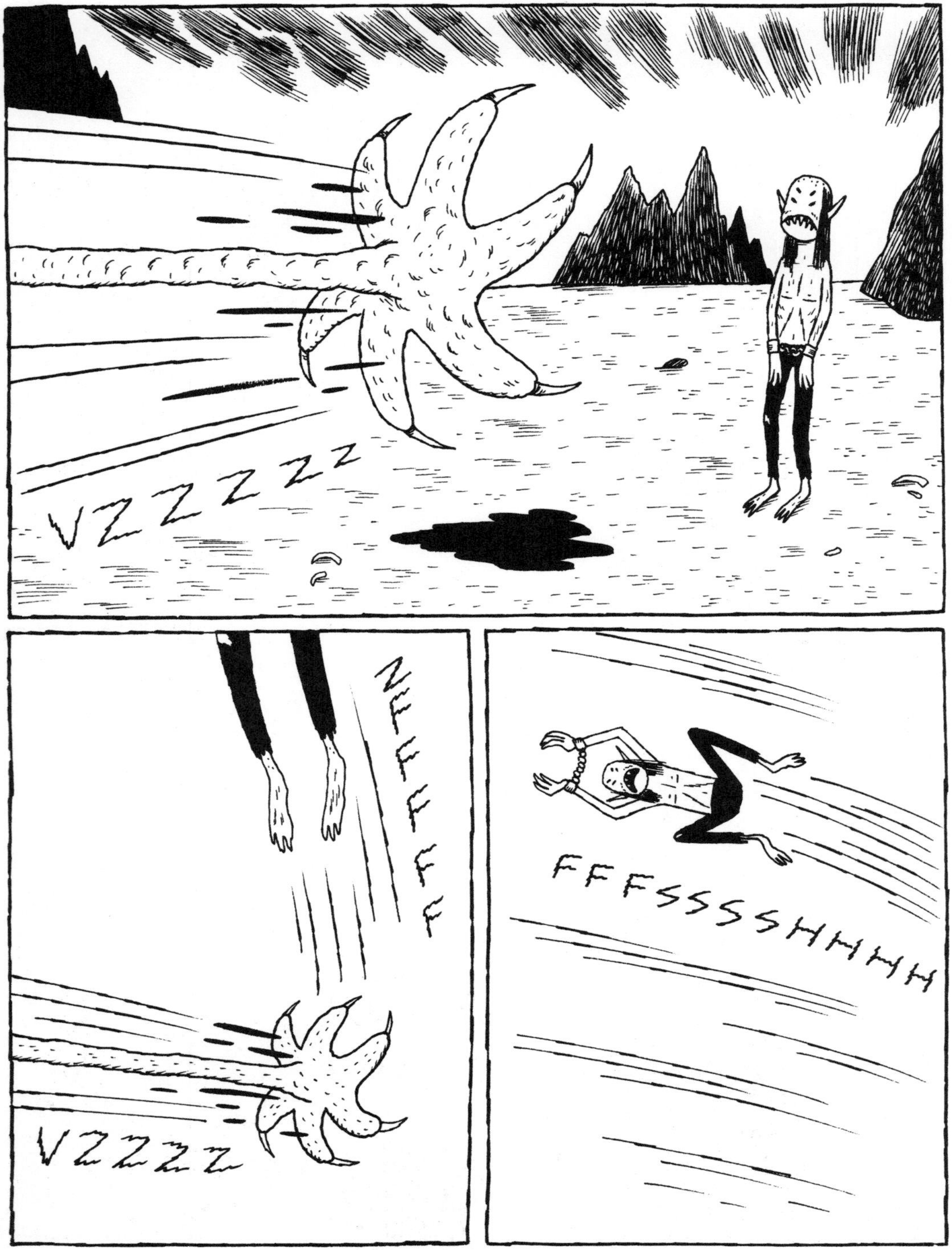
VZZZZZ
ZFFFFF
VZZZZ
FFFSSSSHHHHH

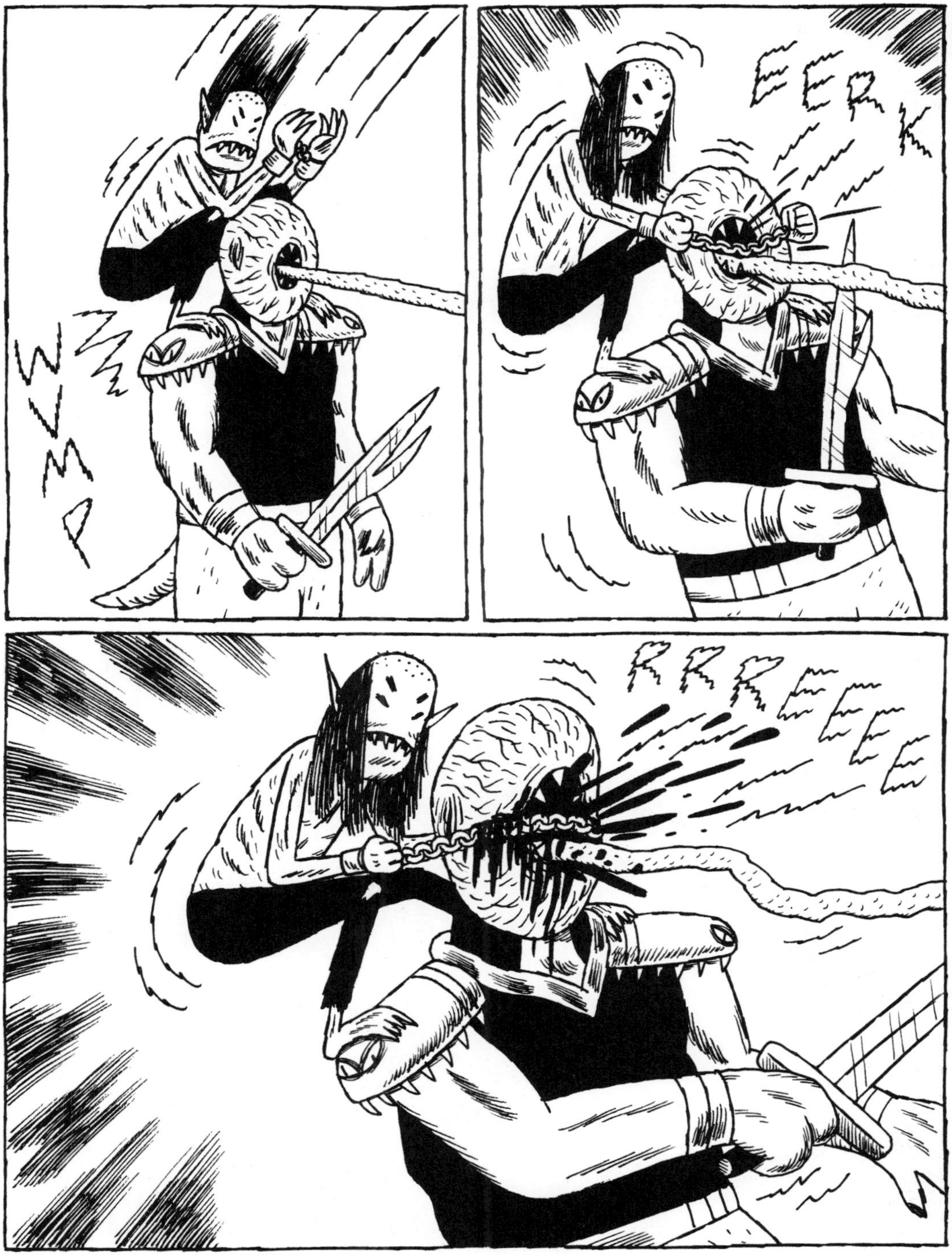
EERK
RRREEEE

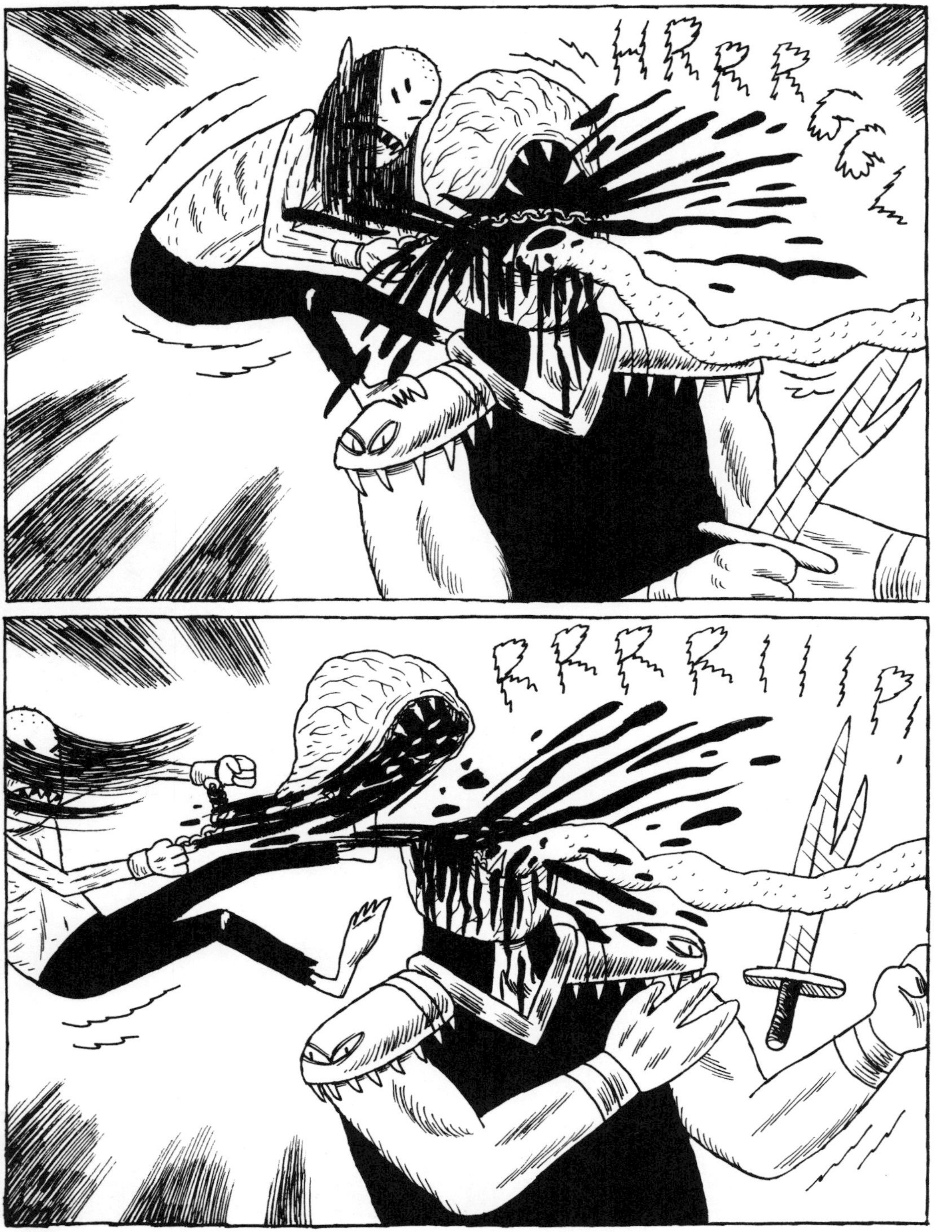
HRRRGGH
RRRRIIIP

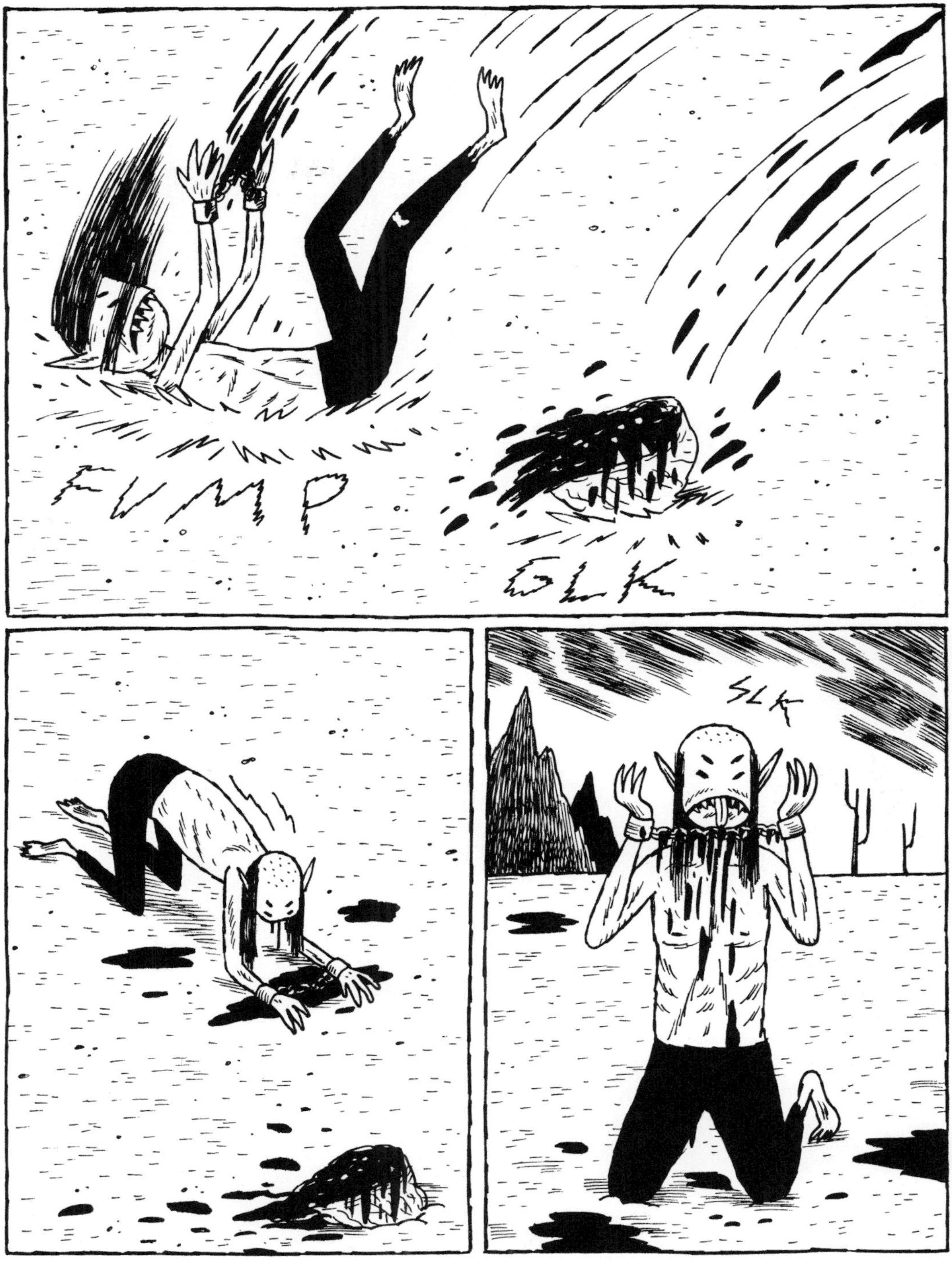
FUMP
GLK
SLK

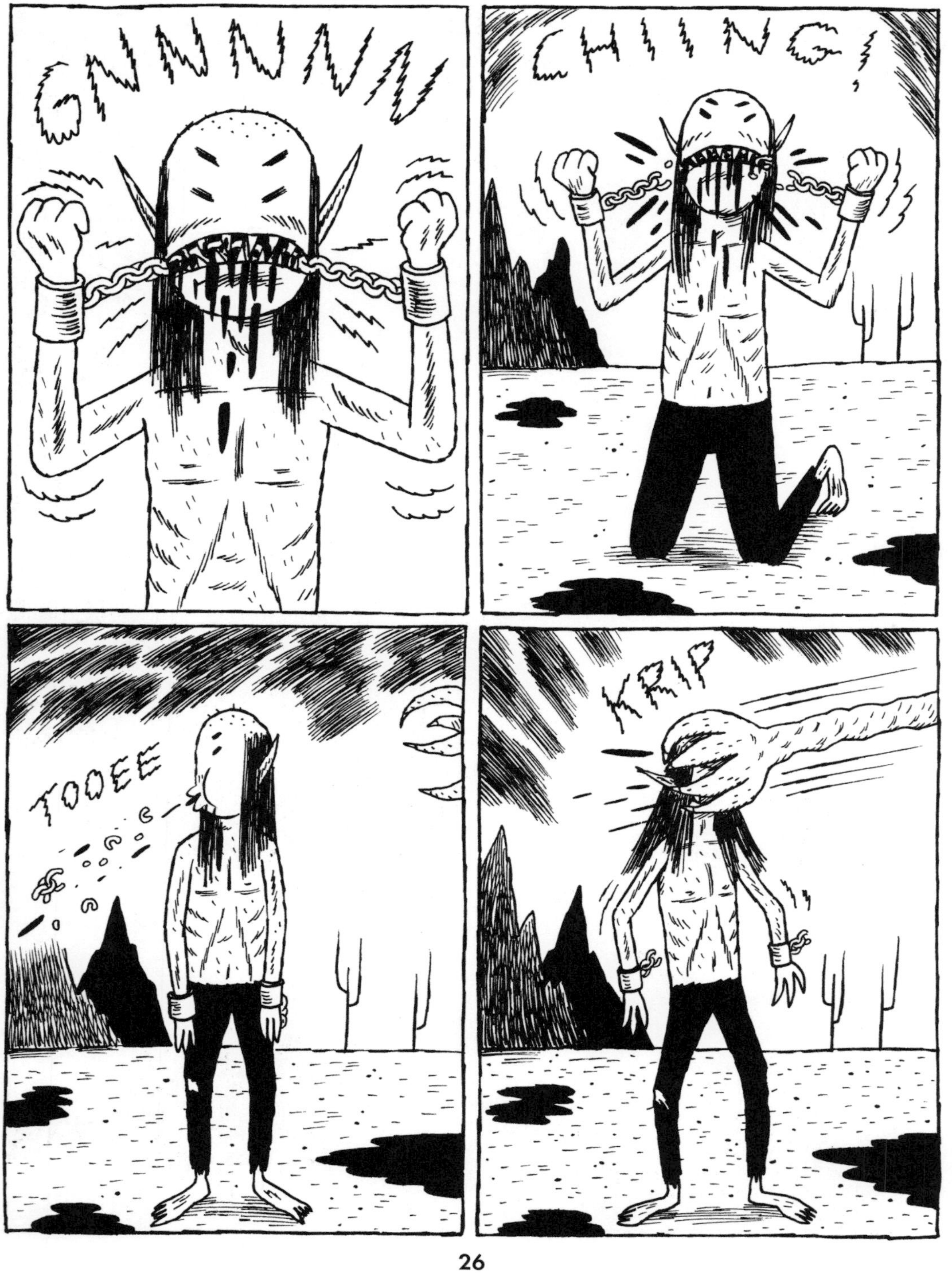
GNNNNN
CHIING!
TOOEE
KRIP

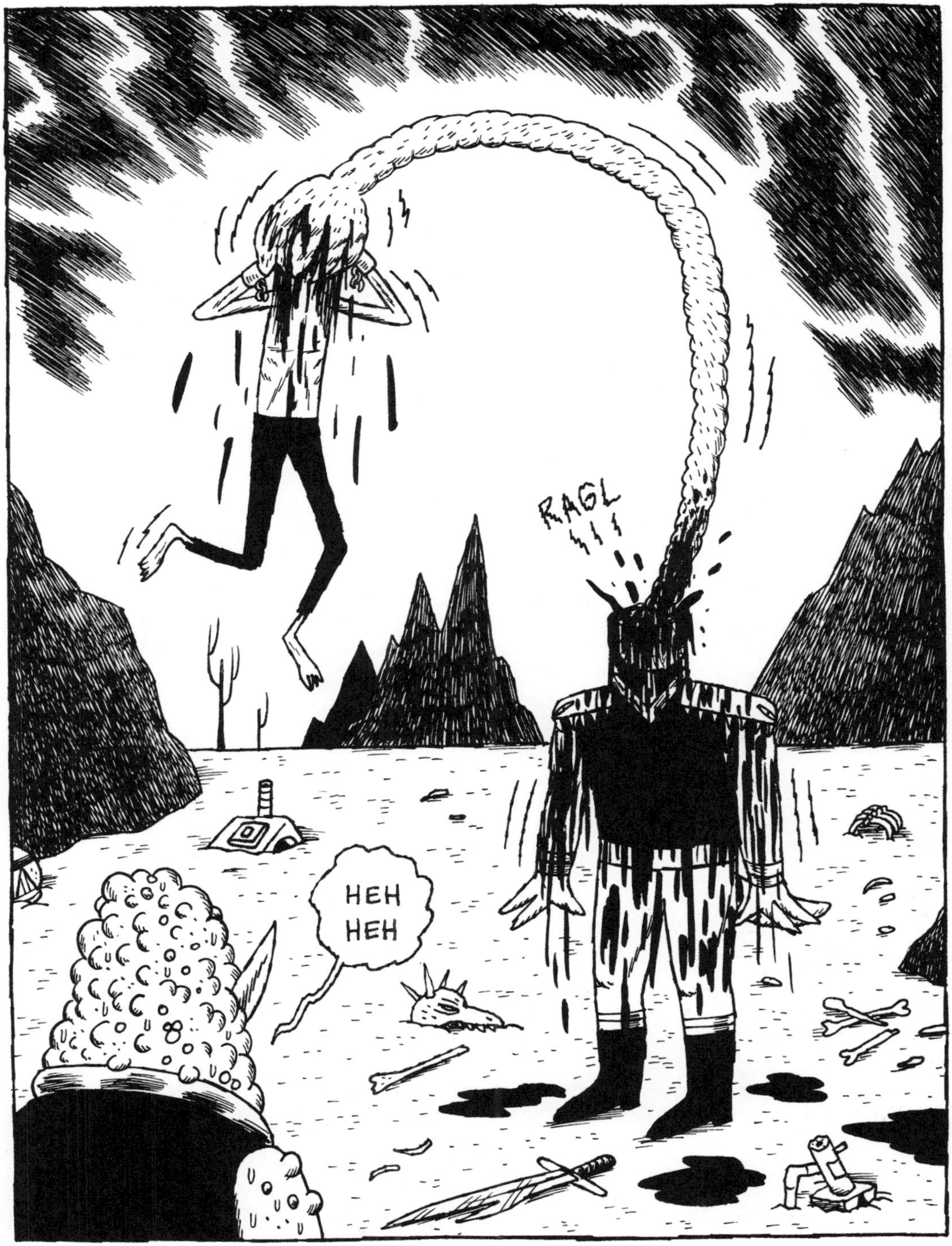
RAGL
HEH HEH

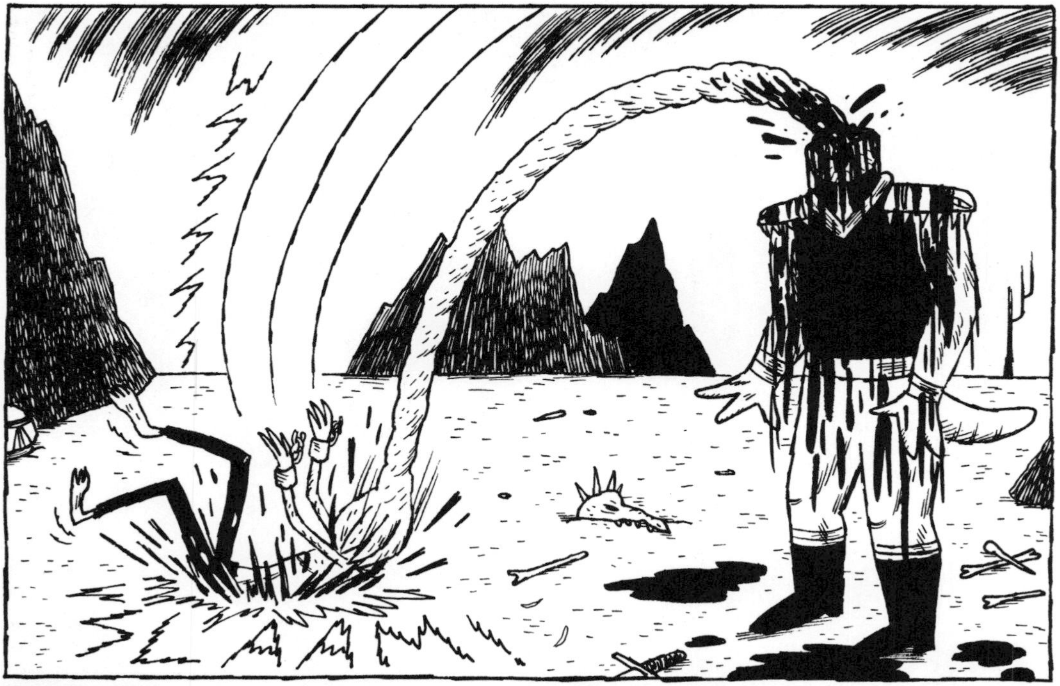
WSSSSSS
SLAAM.

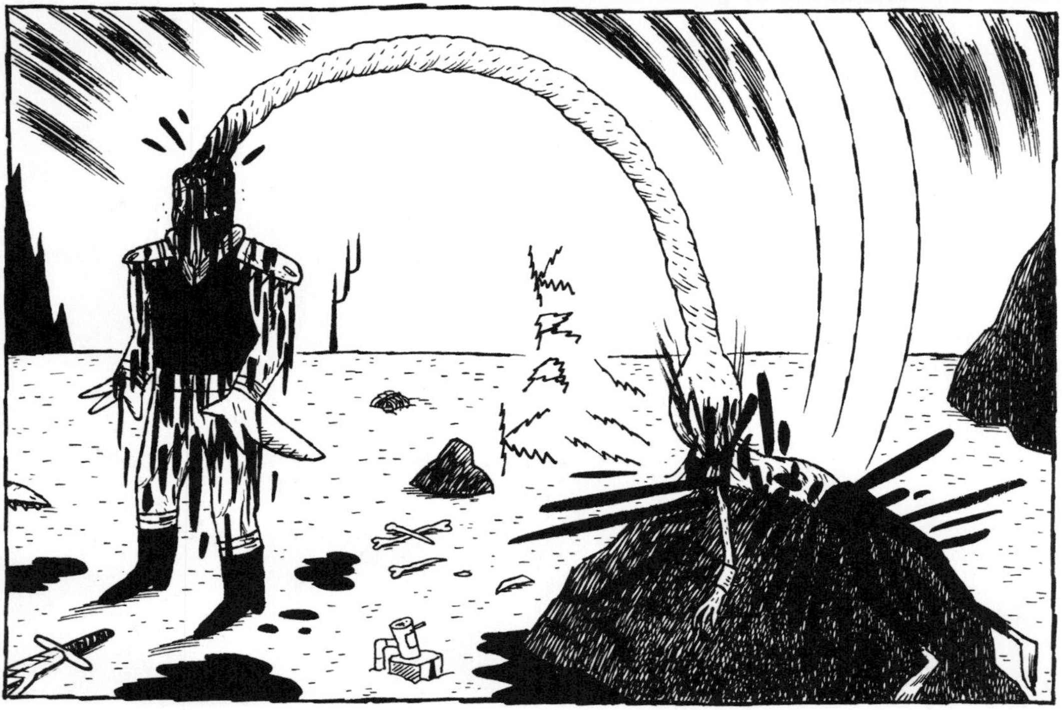
KRAK

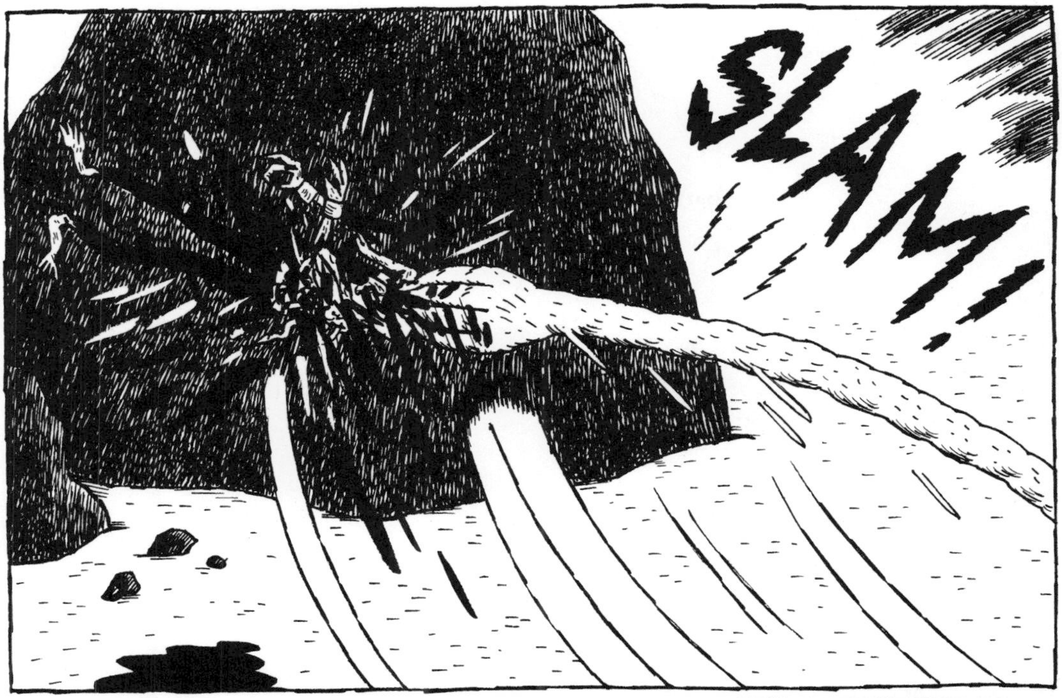
SLAM!!

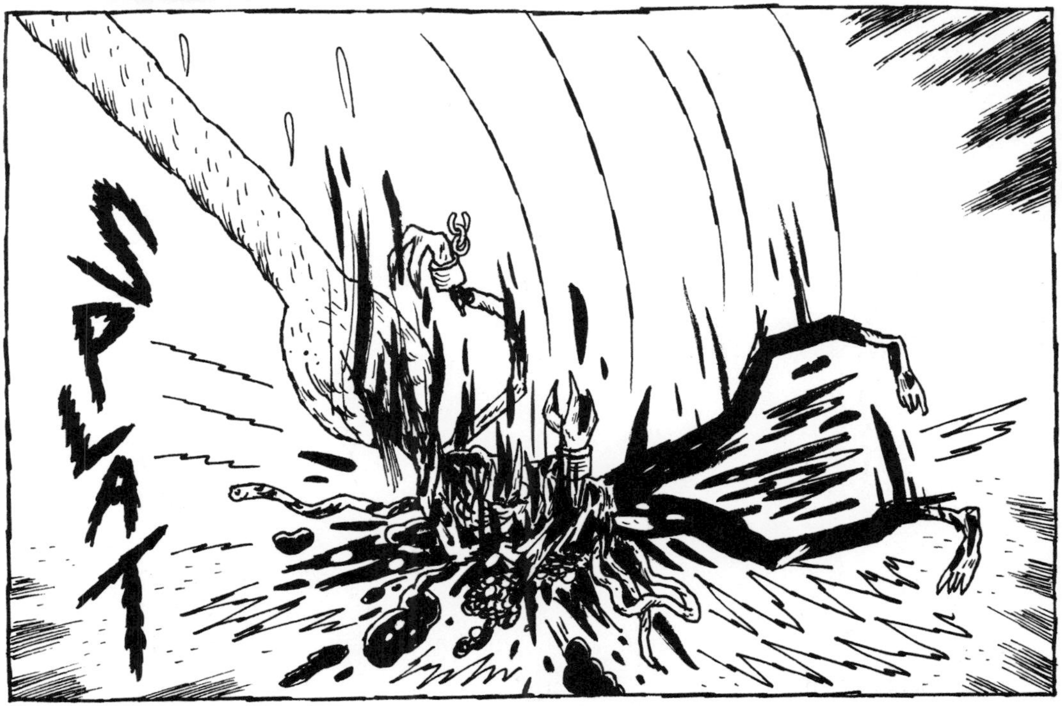
SPLAT

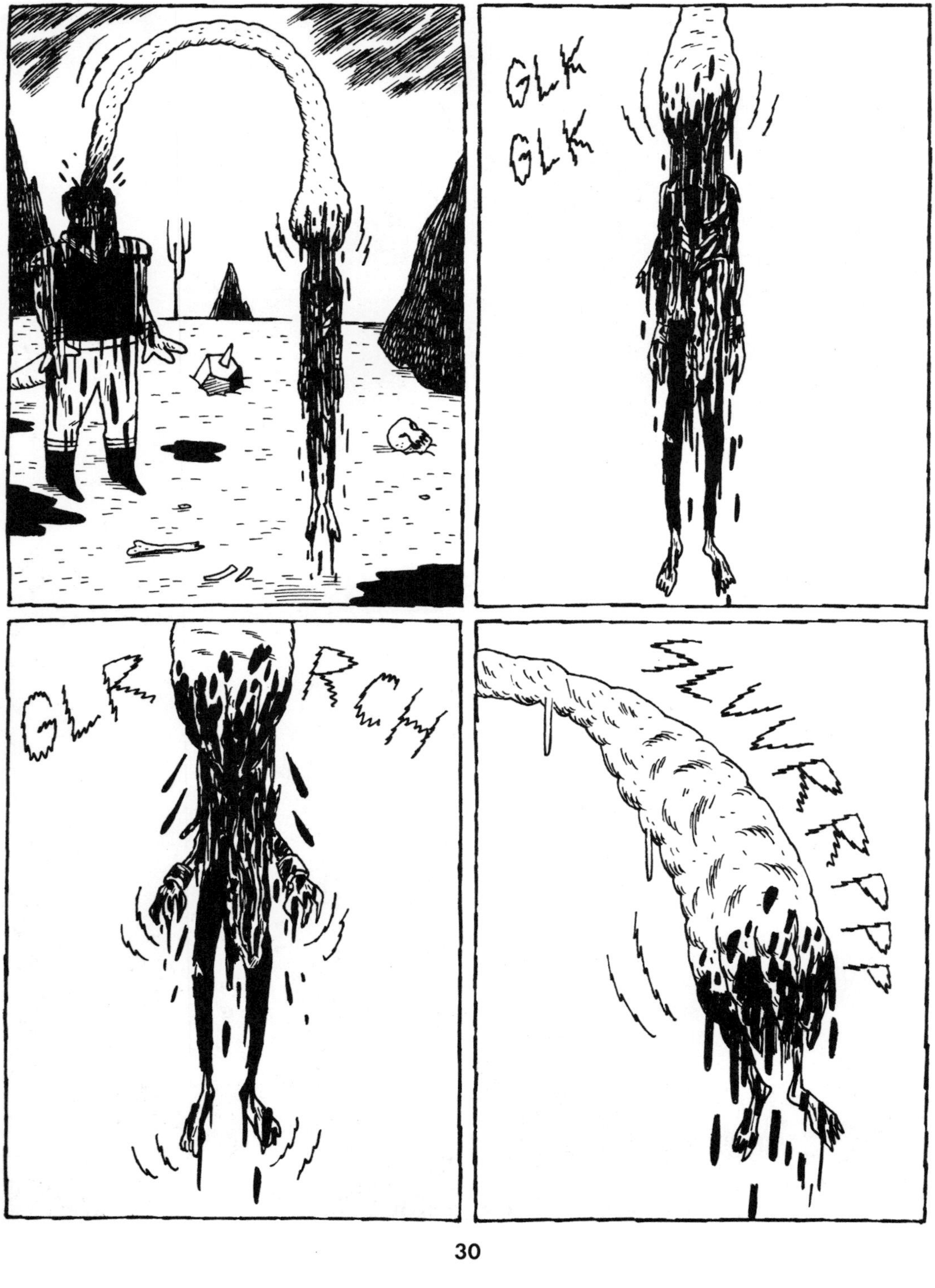
GLK
GLK
GLRRCH
SLUURRPPP

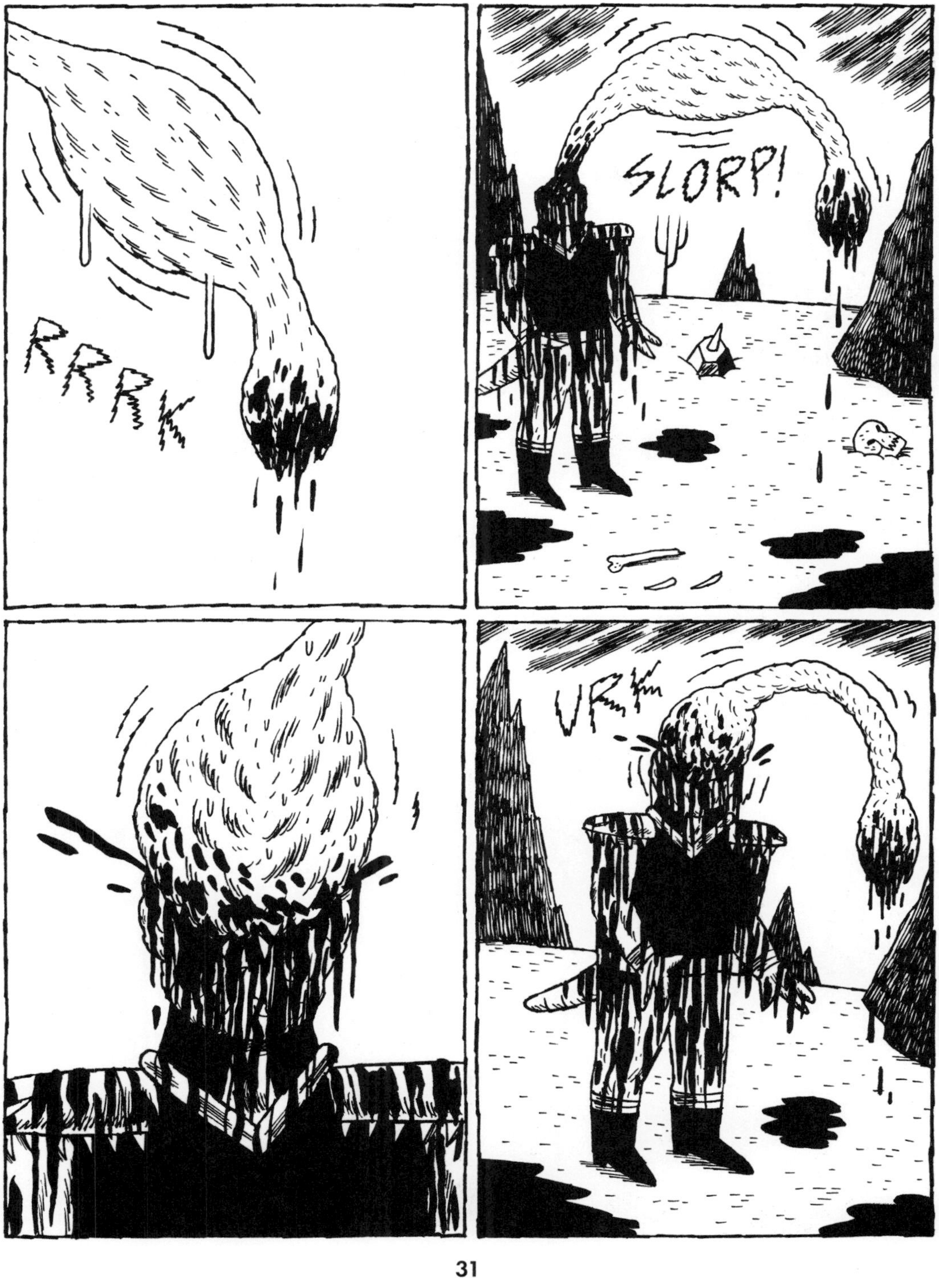
RRRK
SLORP!
URK

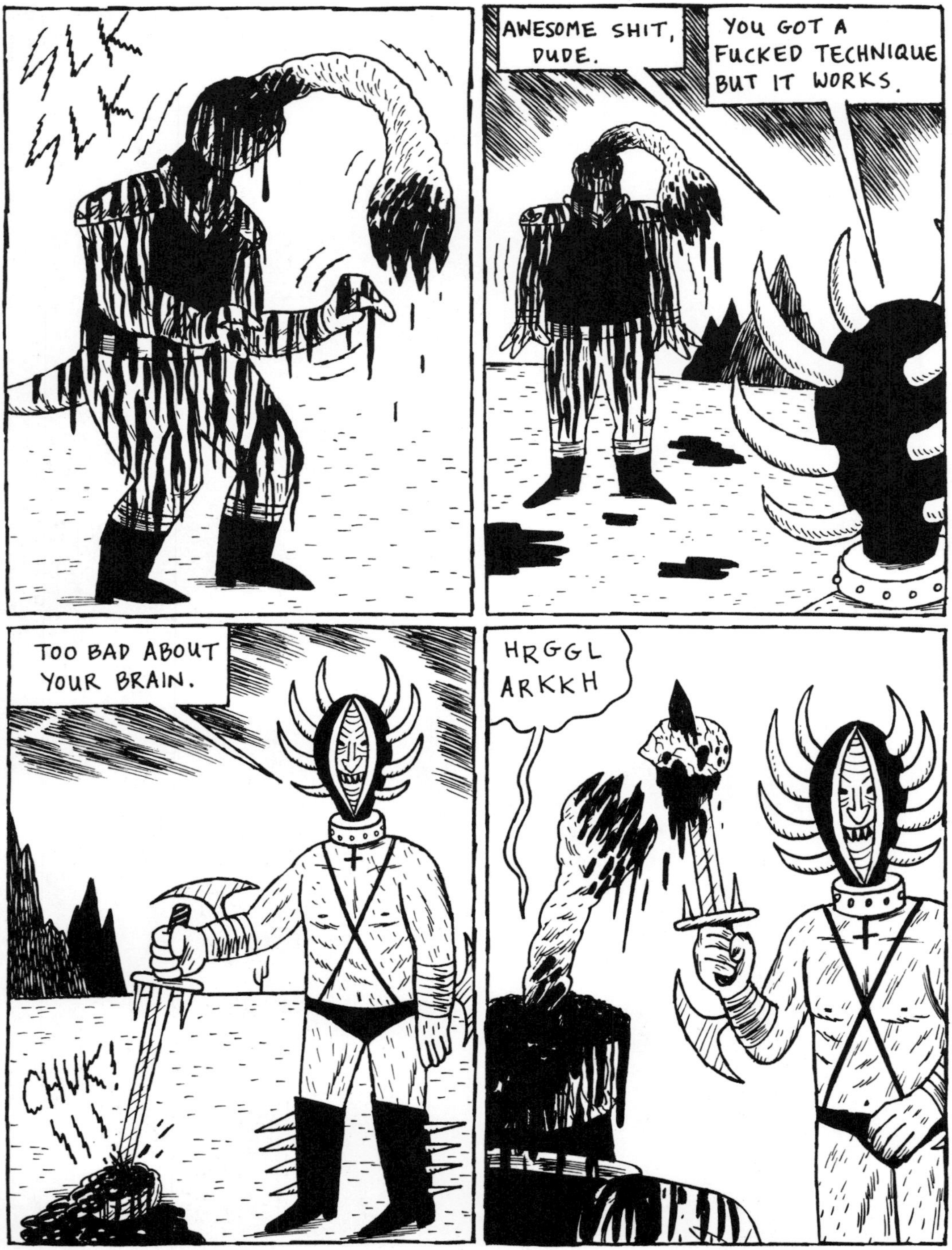
SLK SLK
AWESOME SHIT, DUDE.
YOU GOT A FUCKED TECHNIQUE BUT IT WORKS.
TOO BAD ABOUT YOUR BRAIN.
CHUK!
HRGGL ARKKH

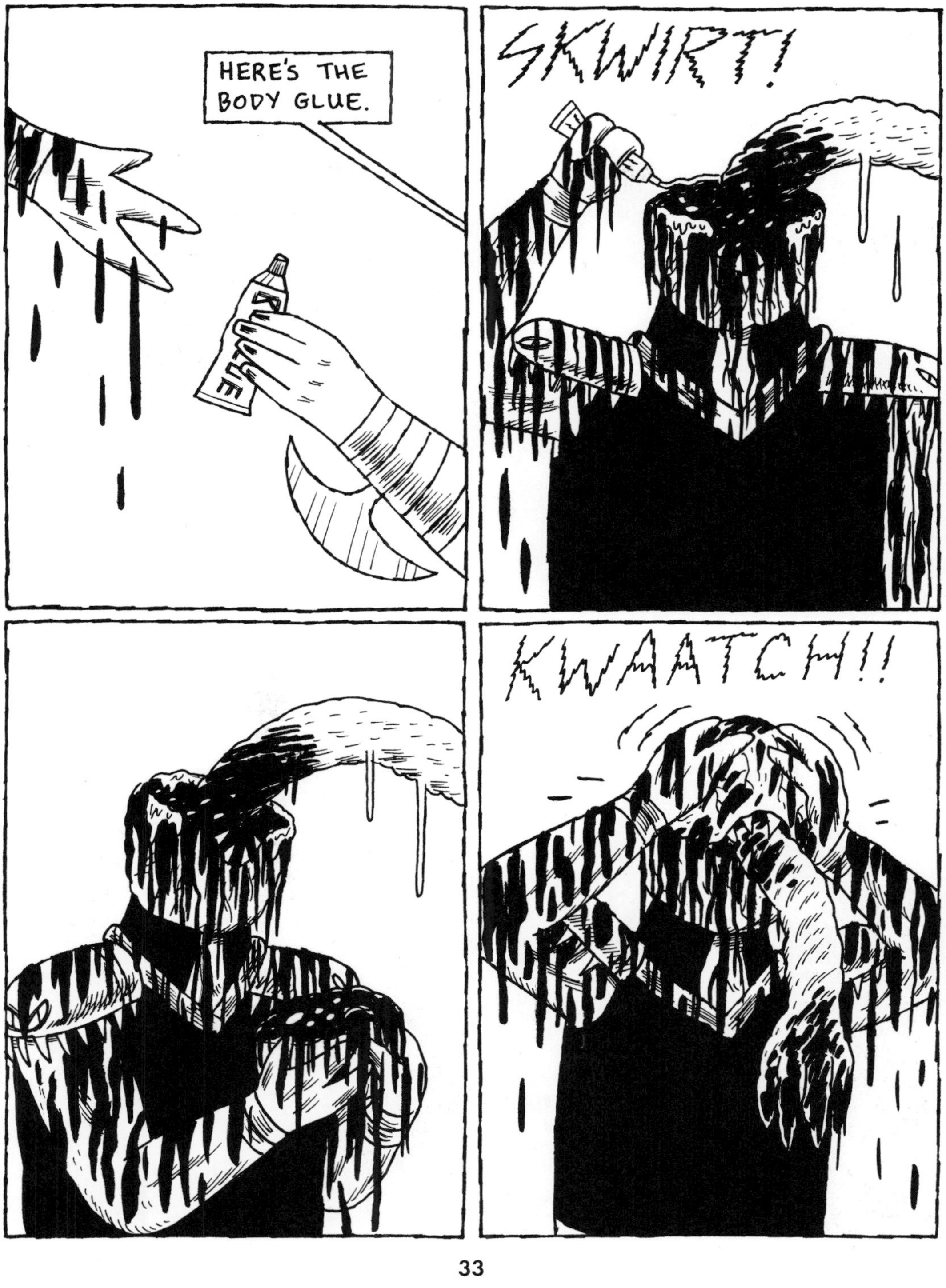
HERE'S THE BODY GLUE.
BODY GLUE
SKWIRT!
KWAATCH!!

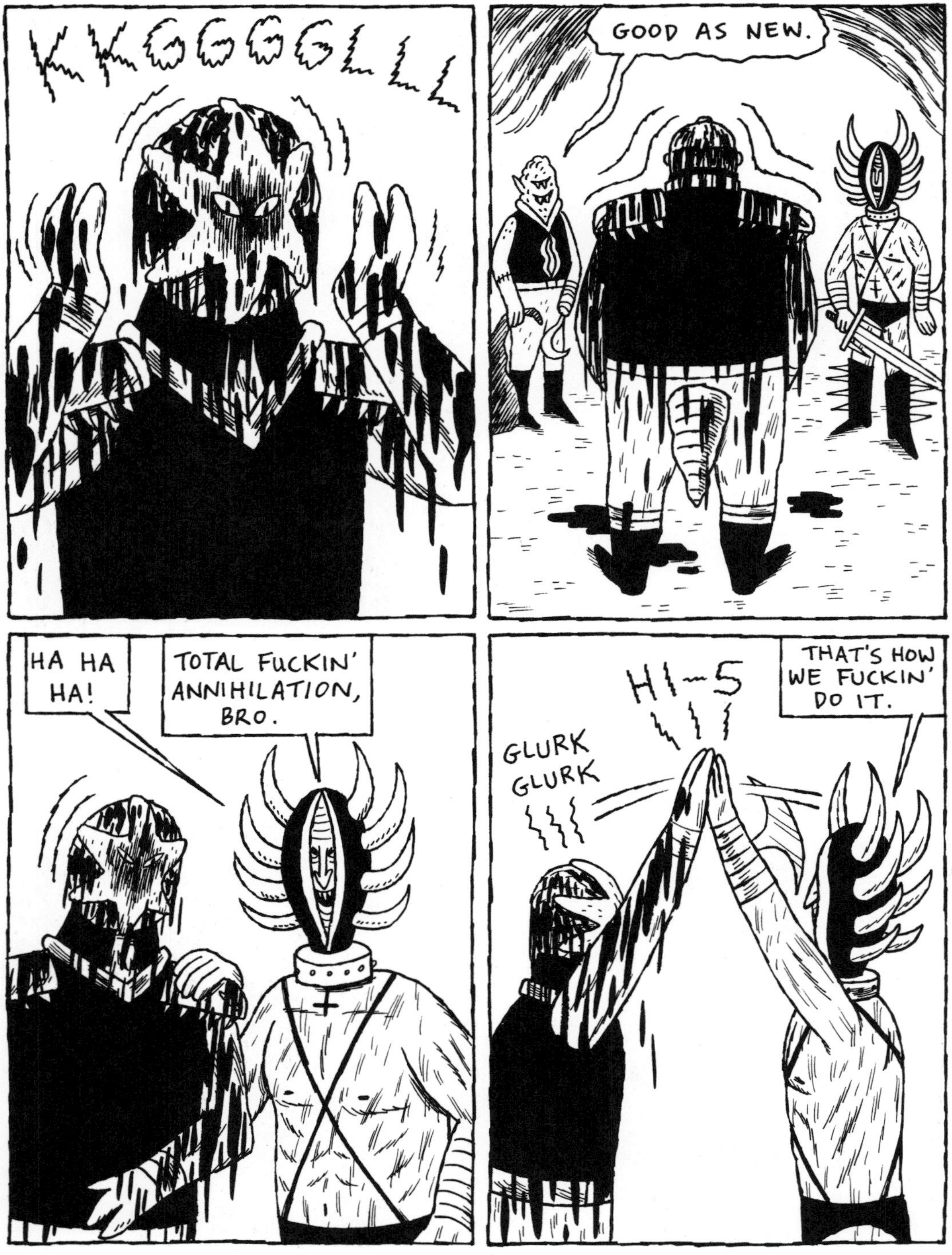
KKGGGGLLL
GOOD AS NEW.
HA HA HA!
TOTAL FUCKIN' ANNIHILATION, BRO.
GLURK GLURK
HI-5
THAT'S HOW WE FUCKIN' DO IT.

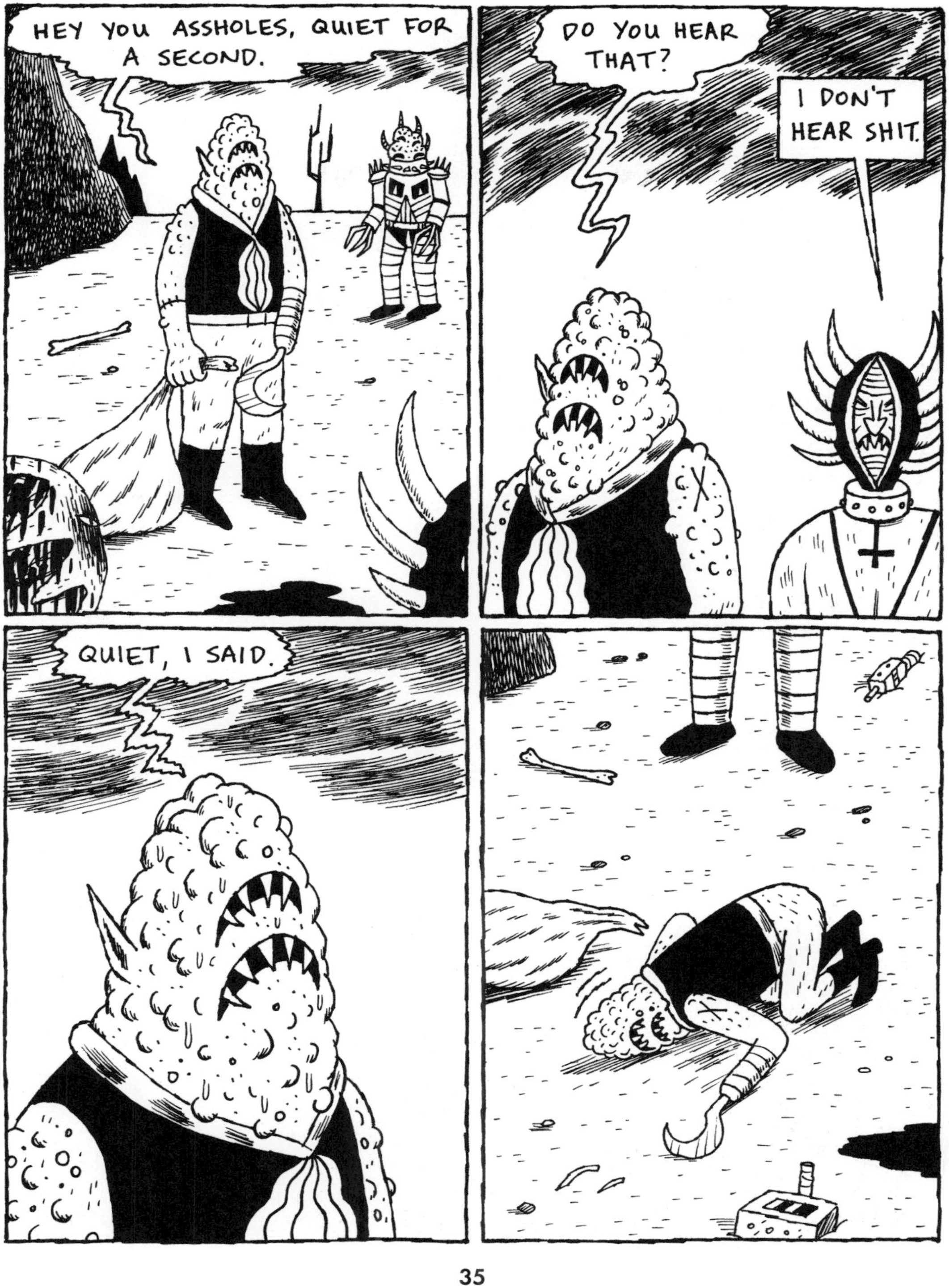
HEY YOU ASSHOLES, QUIET FOR A SECOND.
DO YOU HEAR THAT?
I DON'T HEAR SHIT.
QUIET, I SAID.

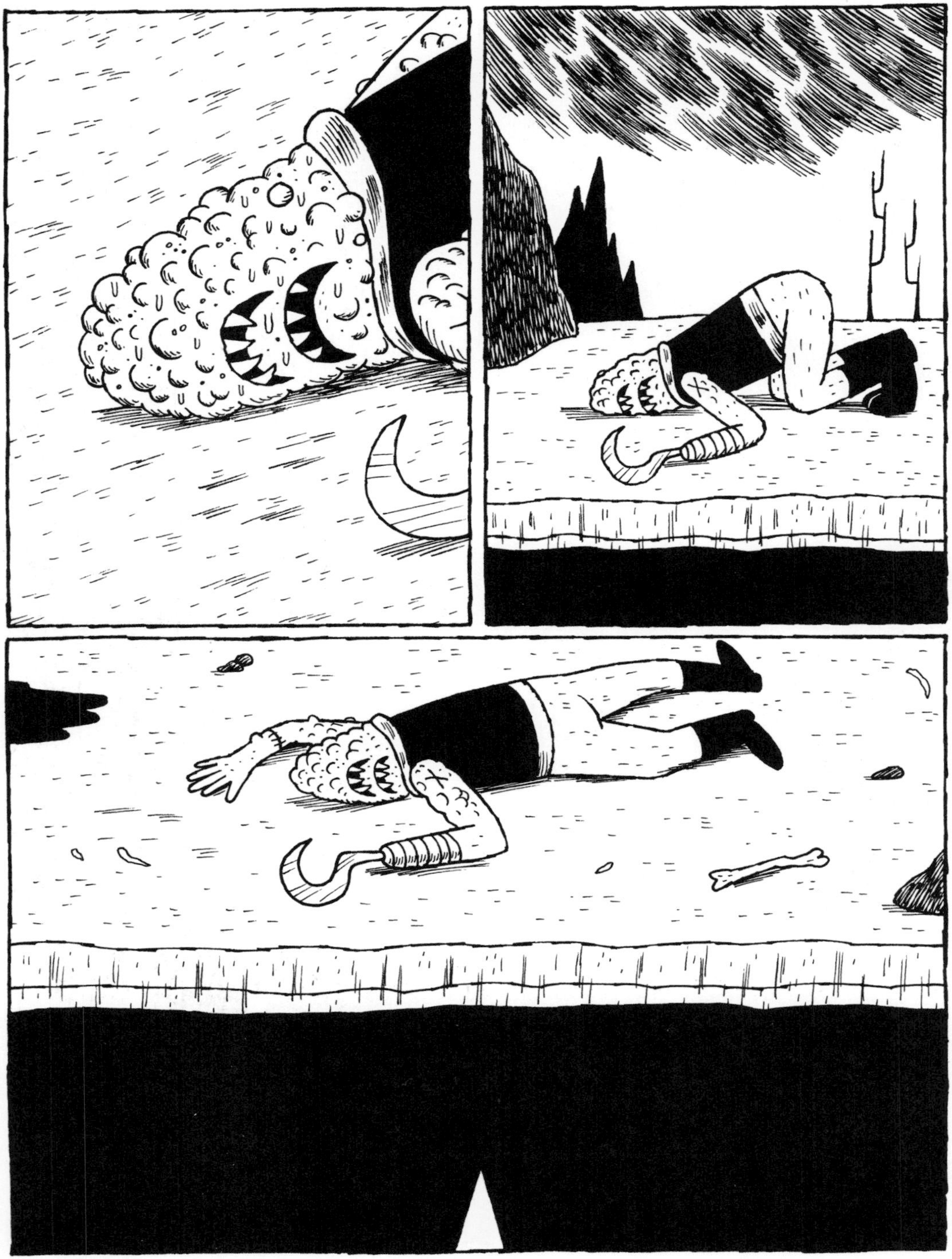

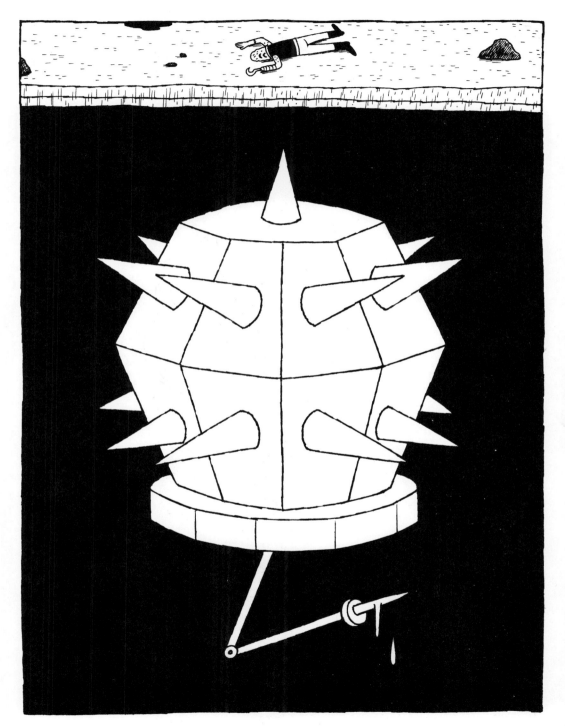

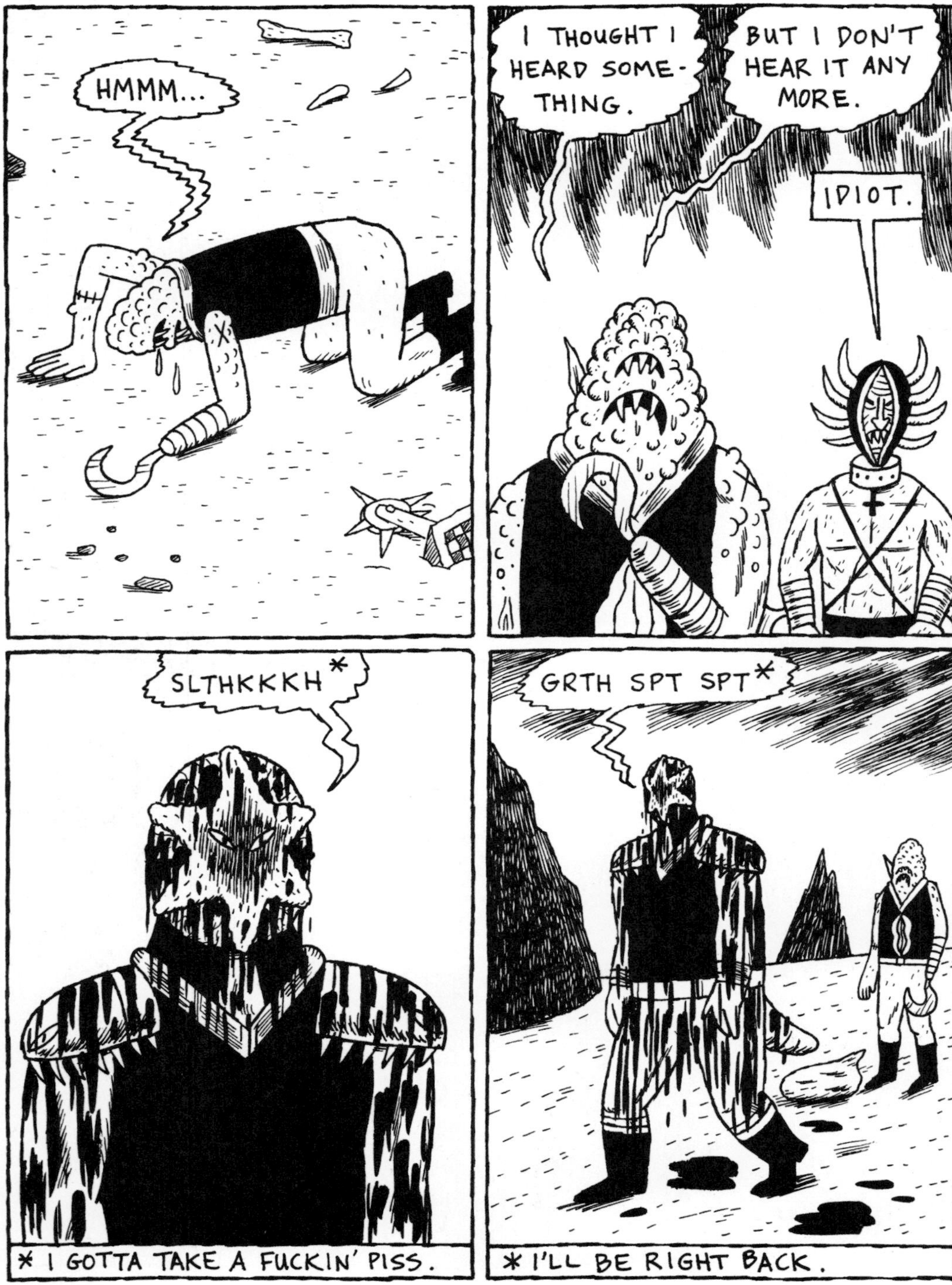
HMMM...
I THOUGHT I HEARD SOME-THING.
BUT I DON'T HEAR IT ANY MORE.
IDIOT.
SLTHKKKH*
* I GOTTA TAKE A FUCKIN' PISS.
GRTH SPT SPT*
* I'LL BE RIGHT BACK.

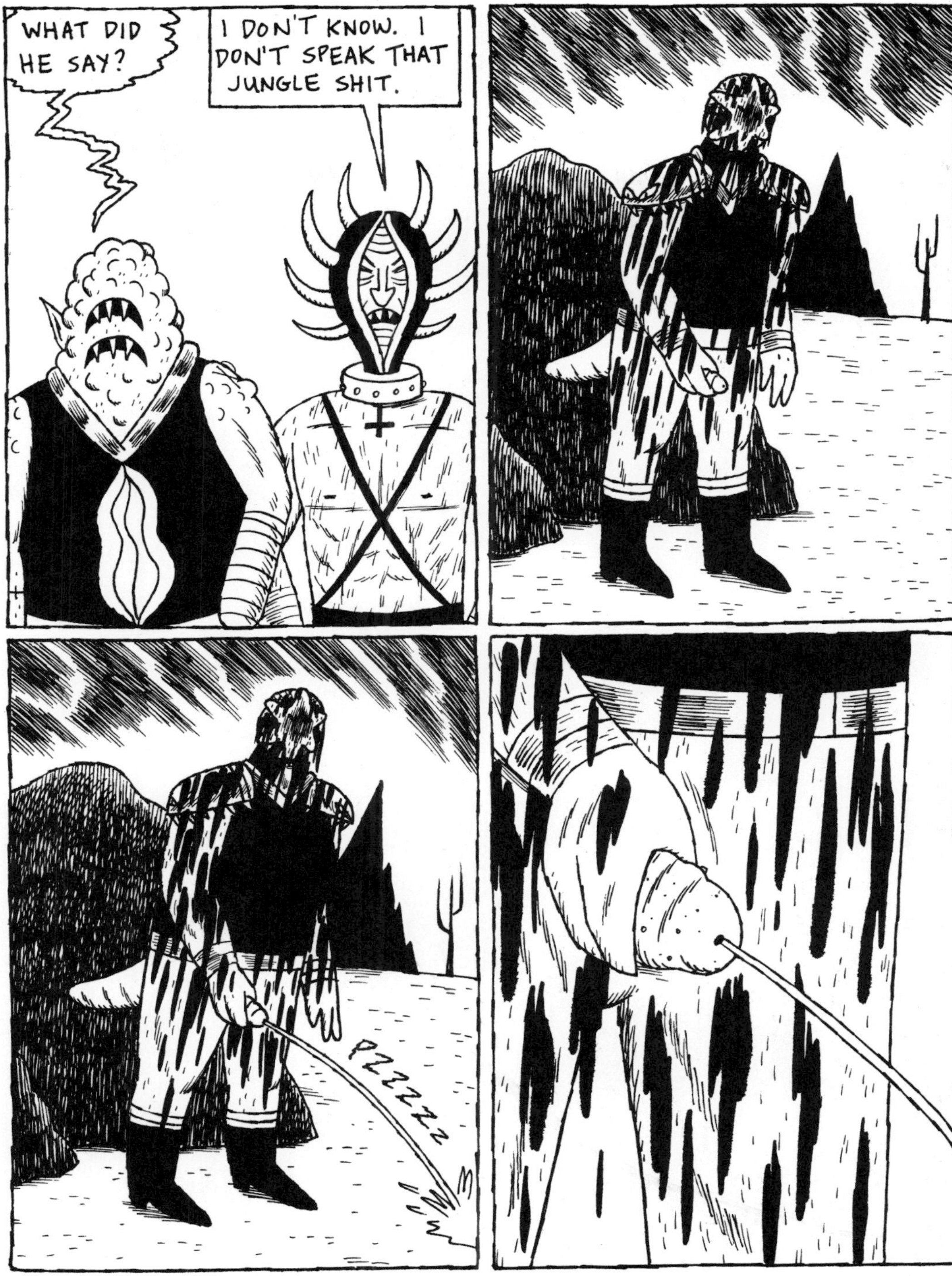
WHAT DID HE SAY?
I DON'T KNOW. I DON'T SPEAK THAT JUNGLE SHIT.
PZZZZZZ

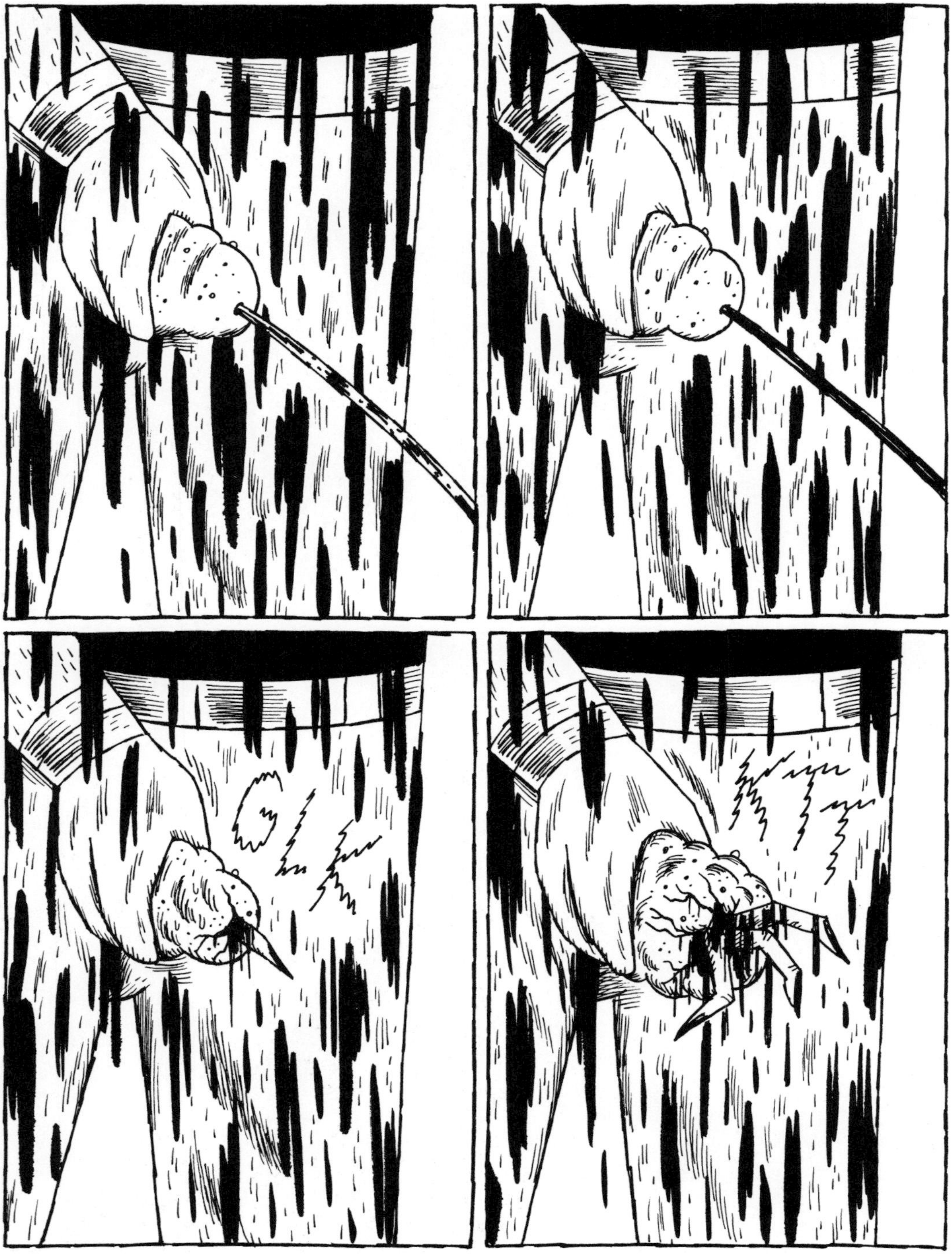

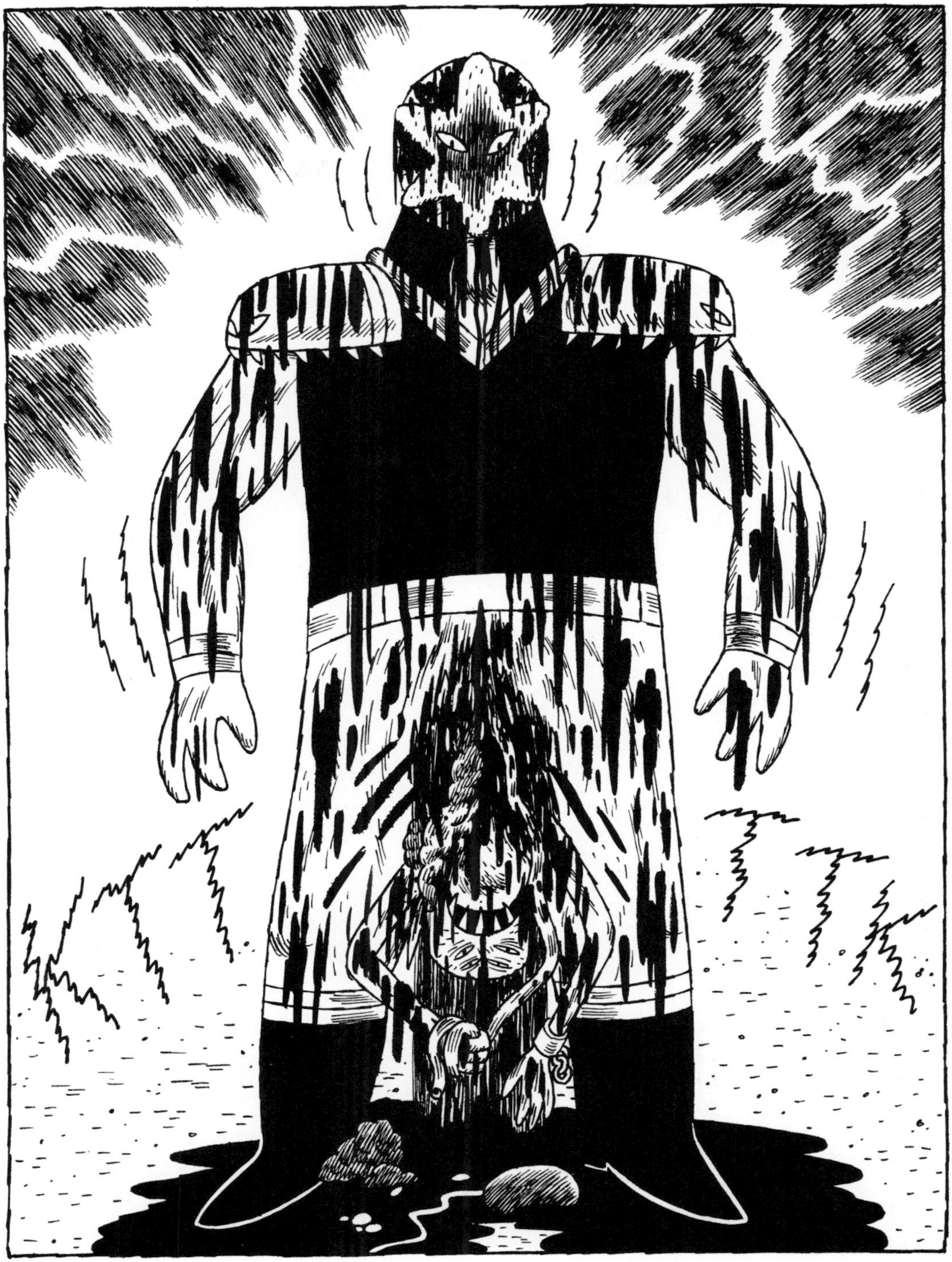

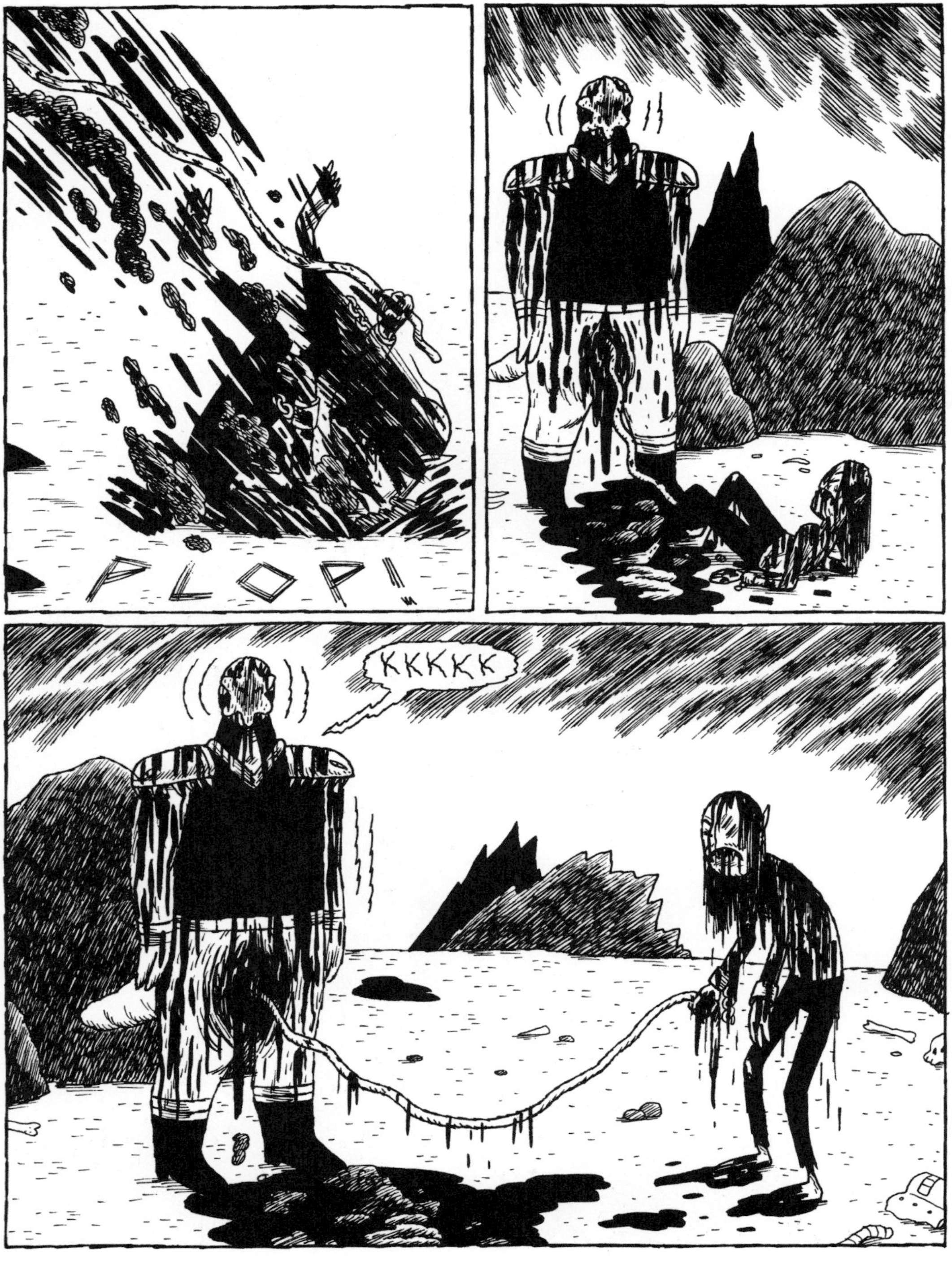
PLOP!
KKKKK

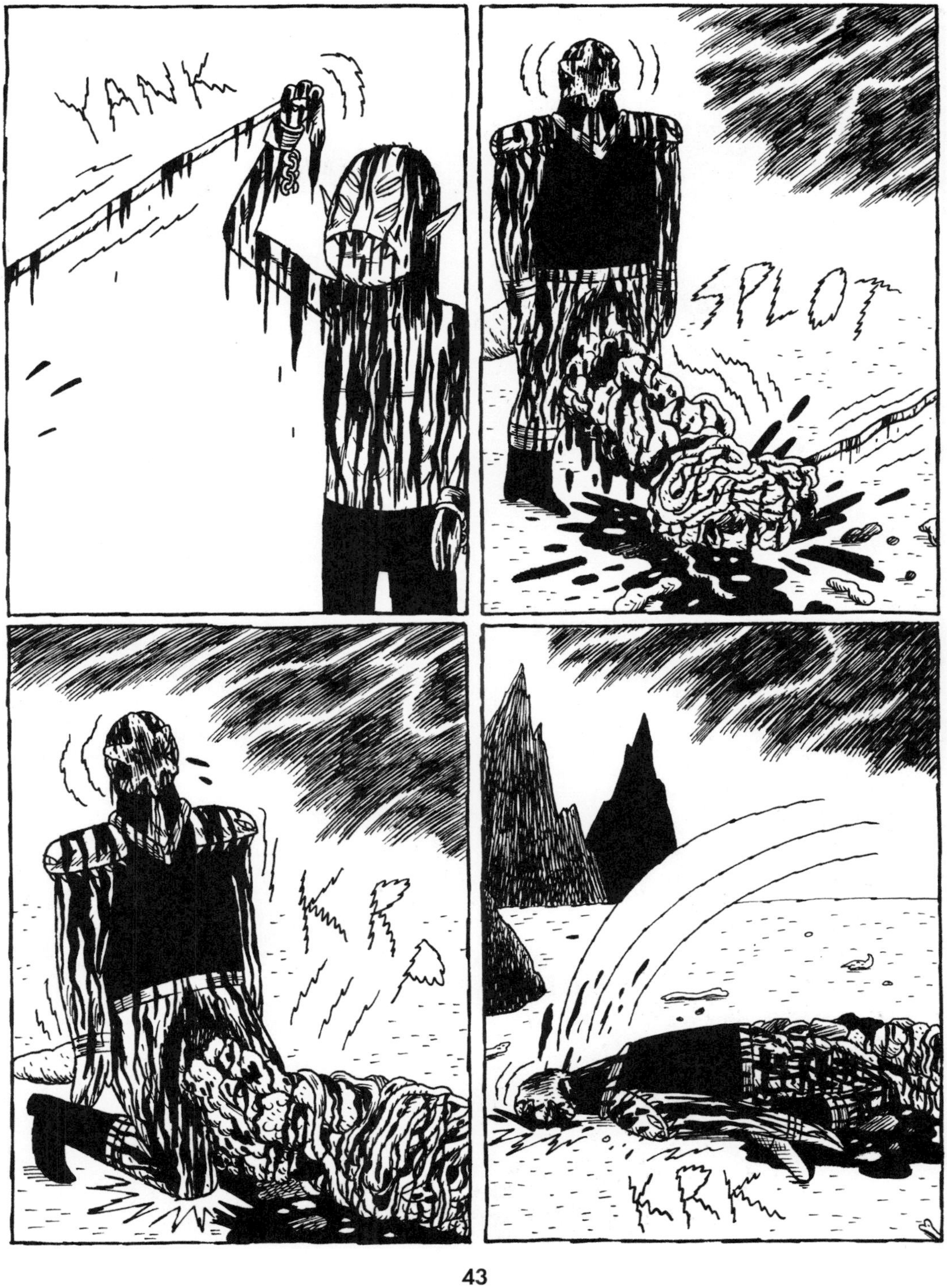
YANK
SPLOT
KR
KRK

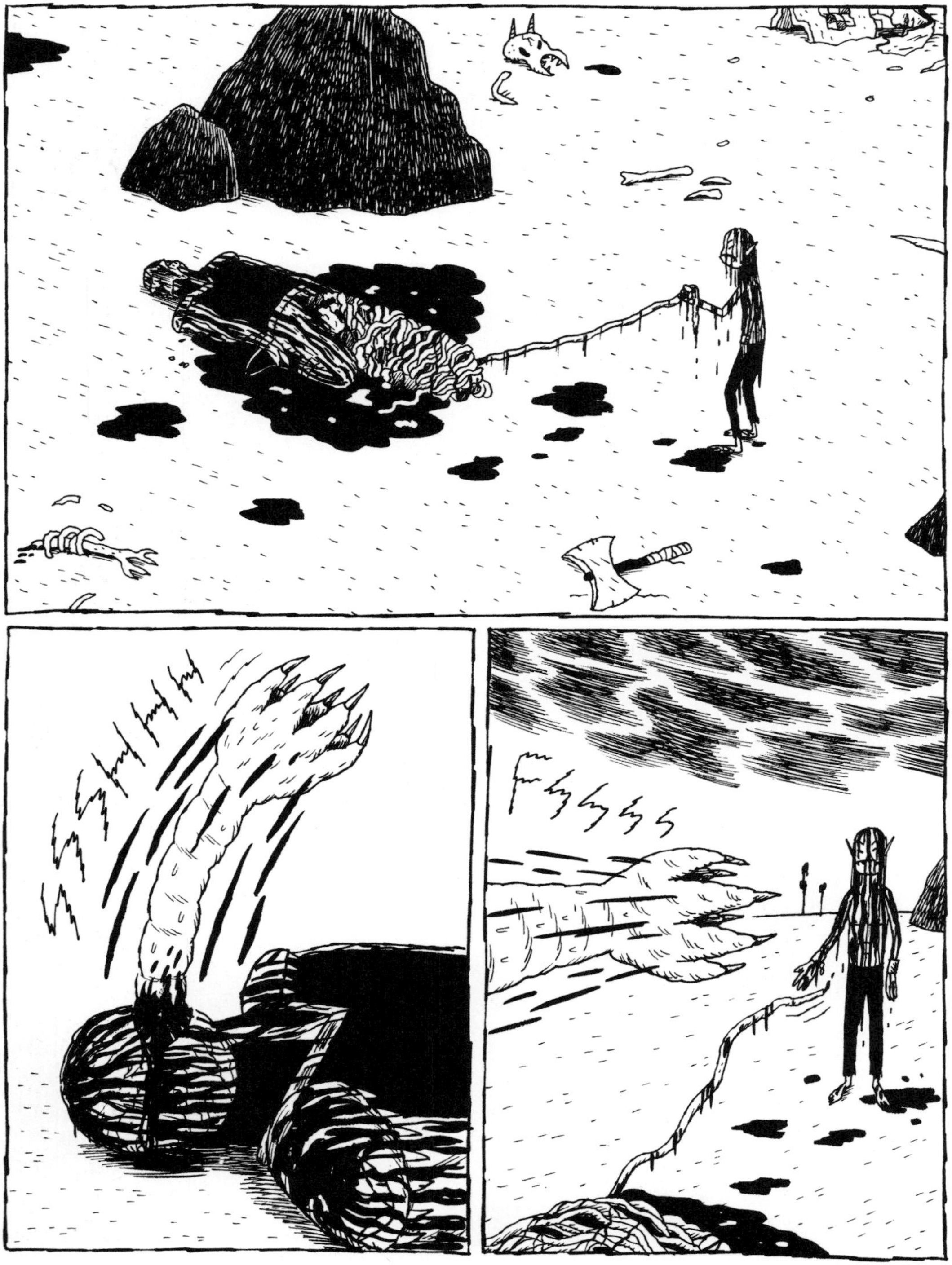

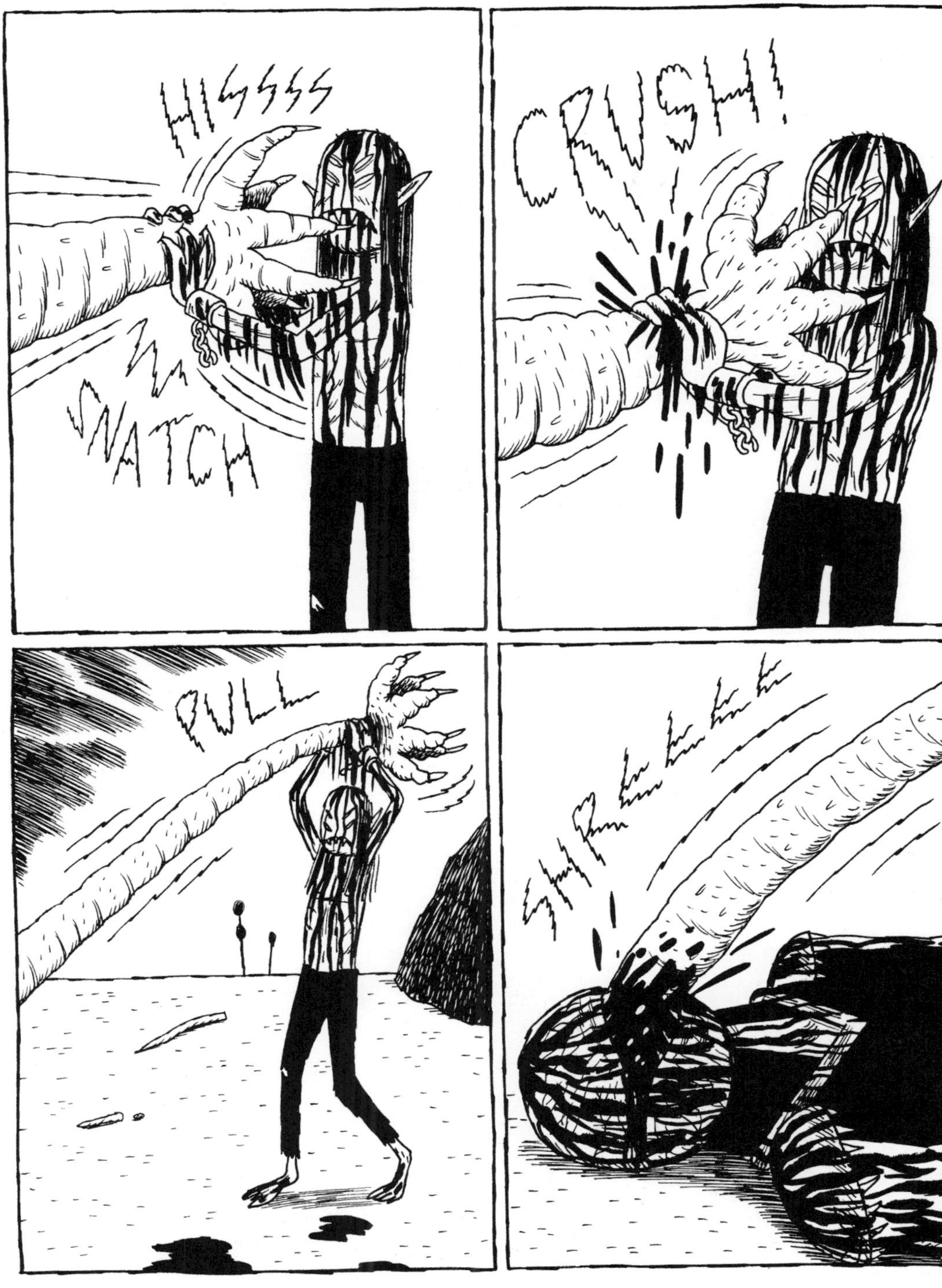
HISSSS
SNATCH
CRUSH!
PULL

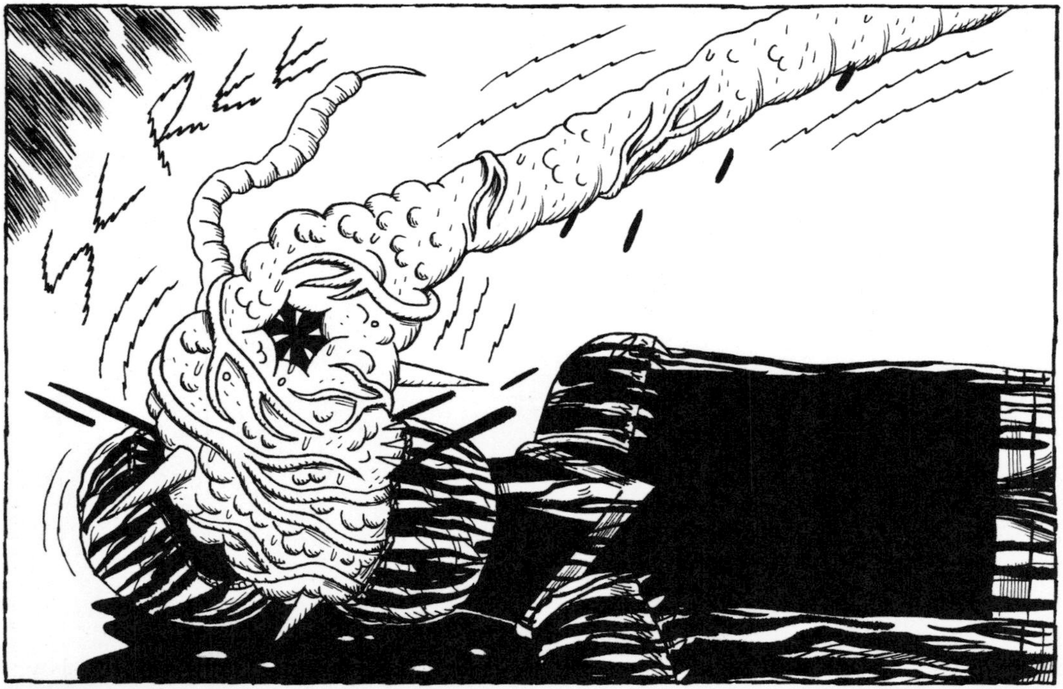

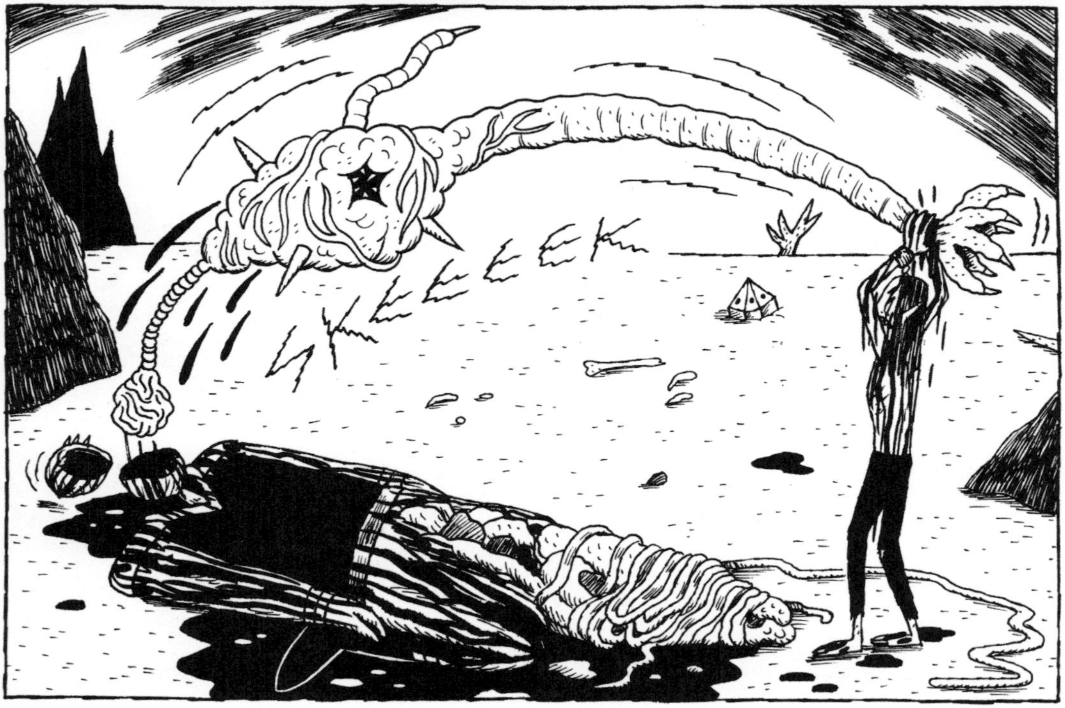
SKEEEEK

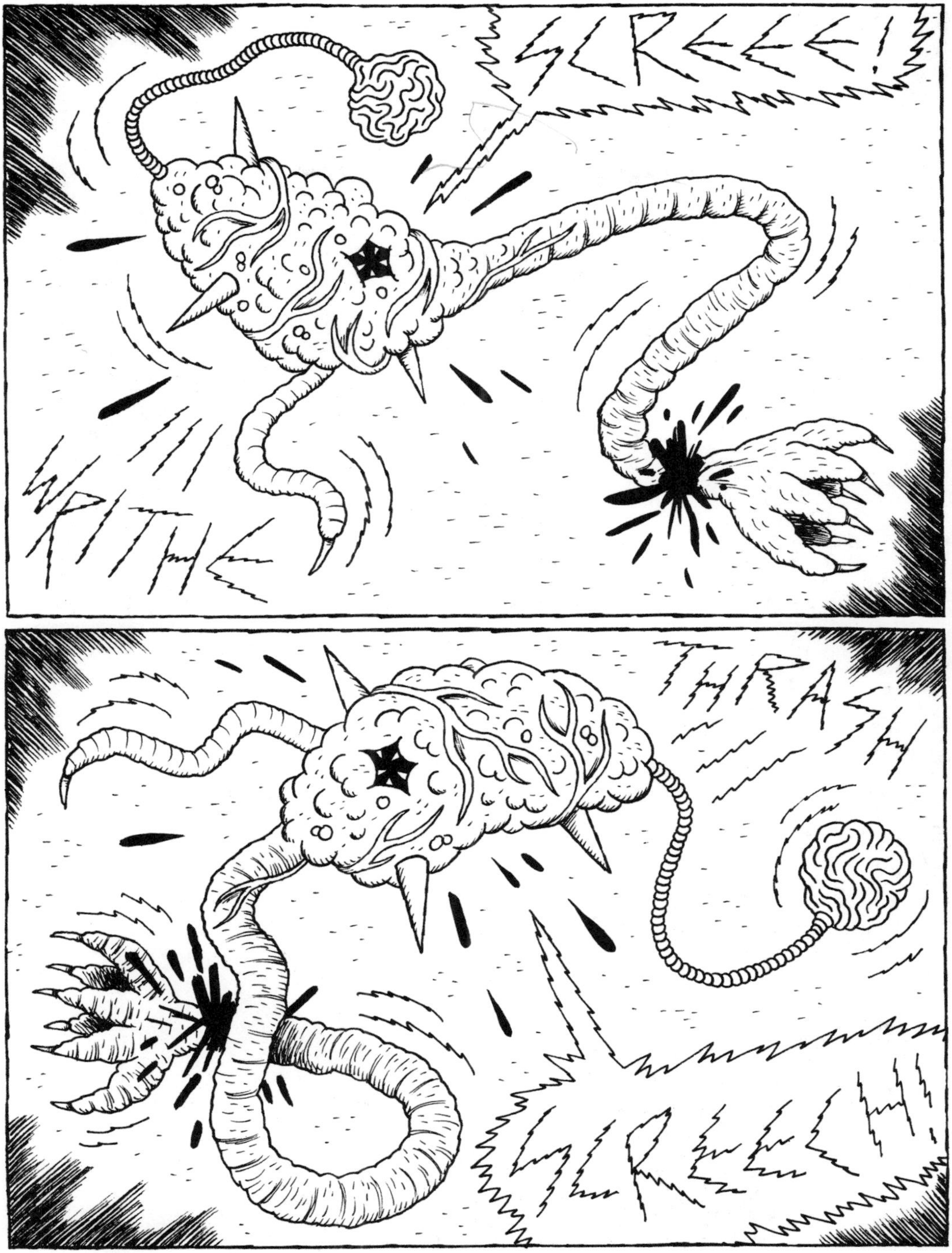
SCREEE!
WRITHE
THRASH
SCREECH

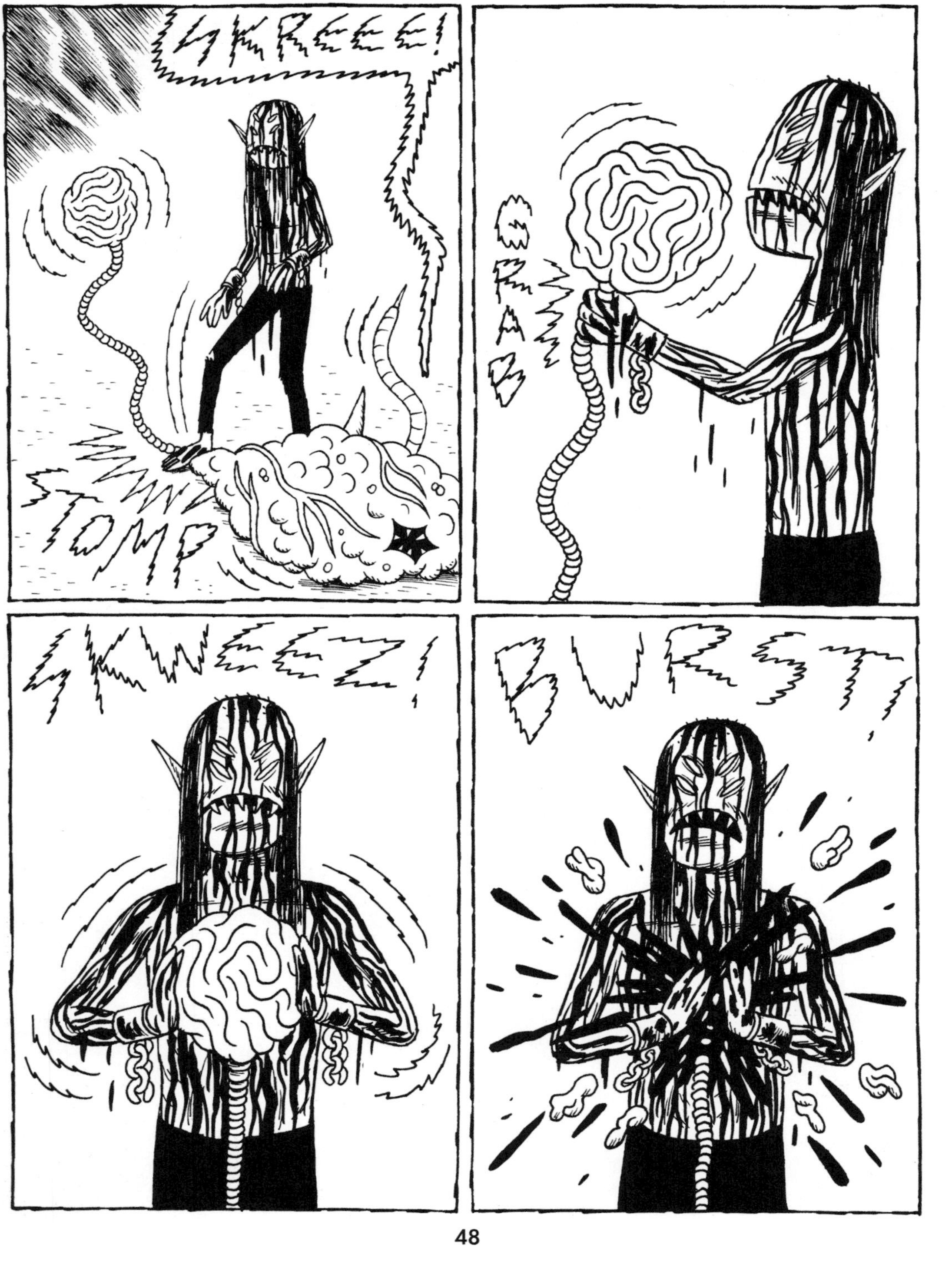
SKREEE!
STOMP
GRAB
SKWEEZ!
BURST!

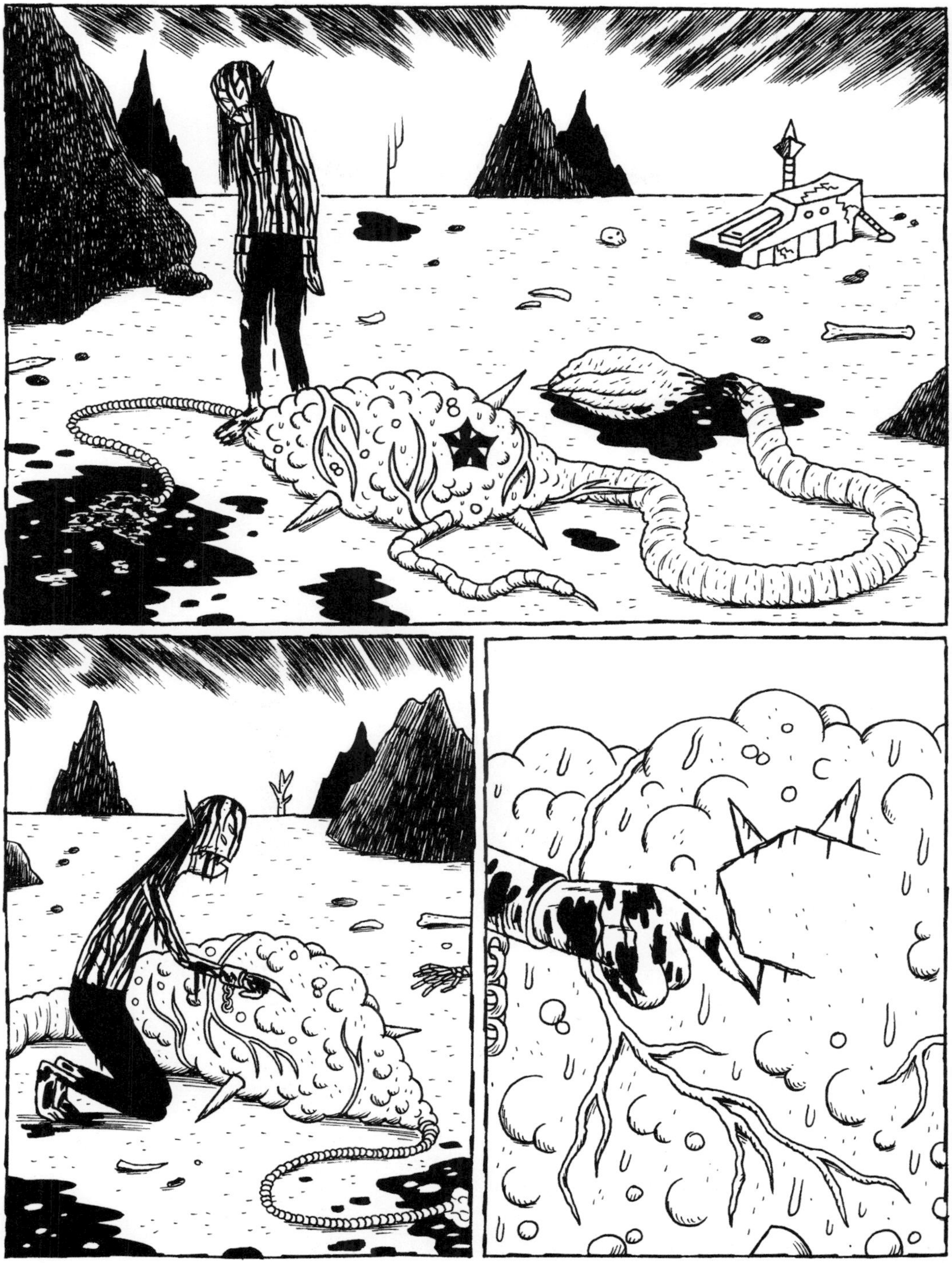

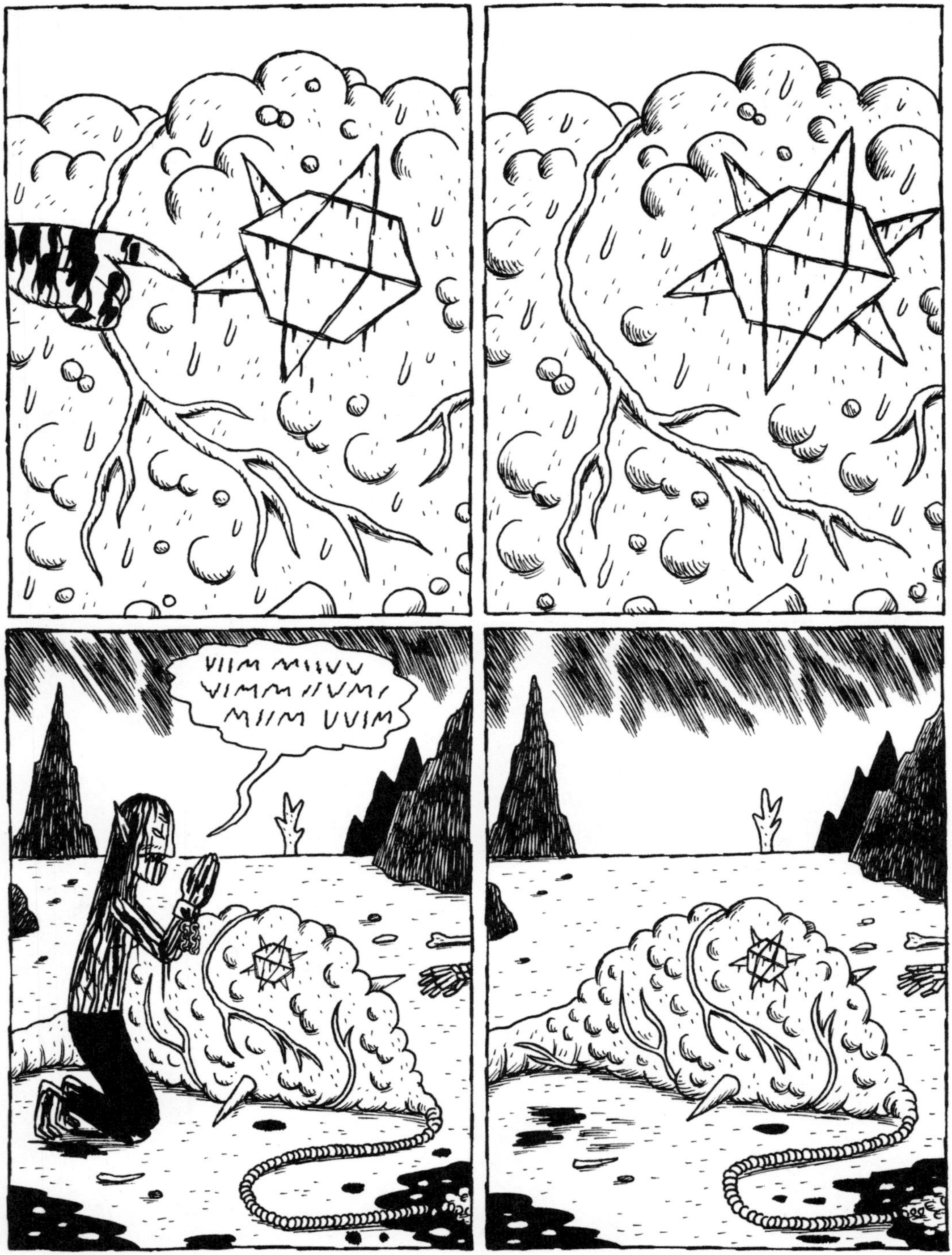
VIIM MIIVV
VIMM IIVMI
MIIM VVIM

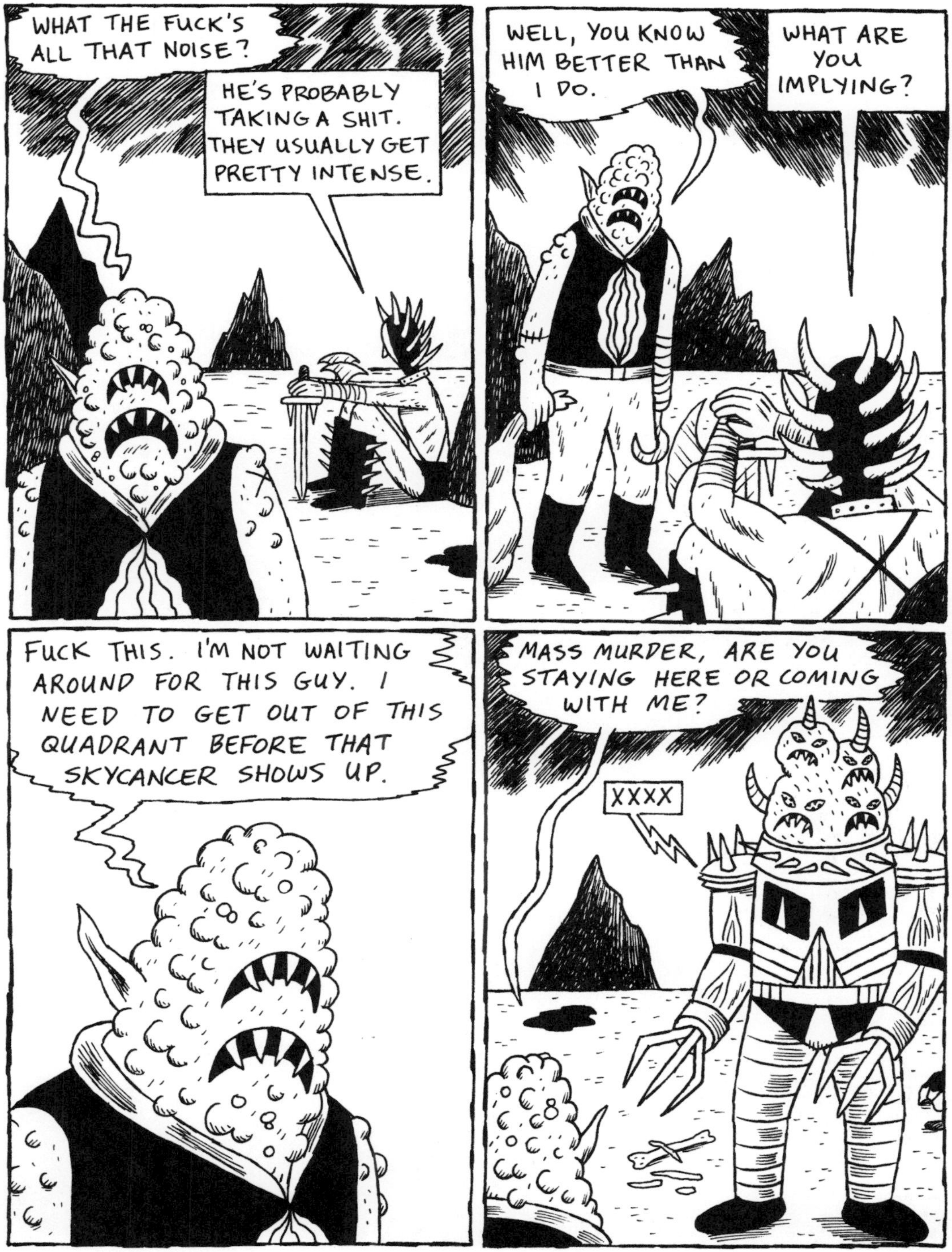

WHAT THE FUCK'S ALL THAT NOISE?
HE'S PROBABLY TAKING A SHIT. THEY USUALLY GET PRETTY INTENSE.
WELL, YOU KNOW HIM BETTER THAN I DO.
WHAT ARE YOU IMPLYING?
FUCK THIS. I'M NOT WAITING AROUND FOR THIS GUY. I NEED TO GET OUT OF THIS QUADRANT BEFORE THAT SKYCANCER SHOWS UP.
MASS MURDER, ARE YOU STAYING HERE OR COMING WITH ME?
XXXX

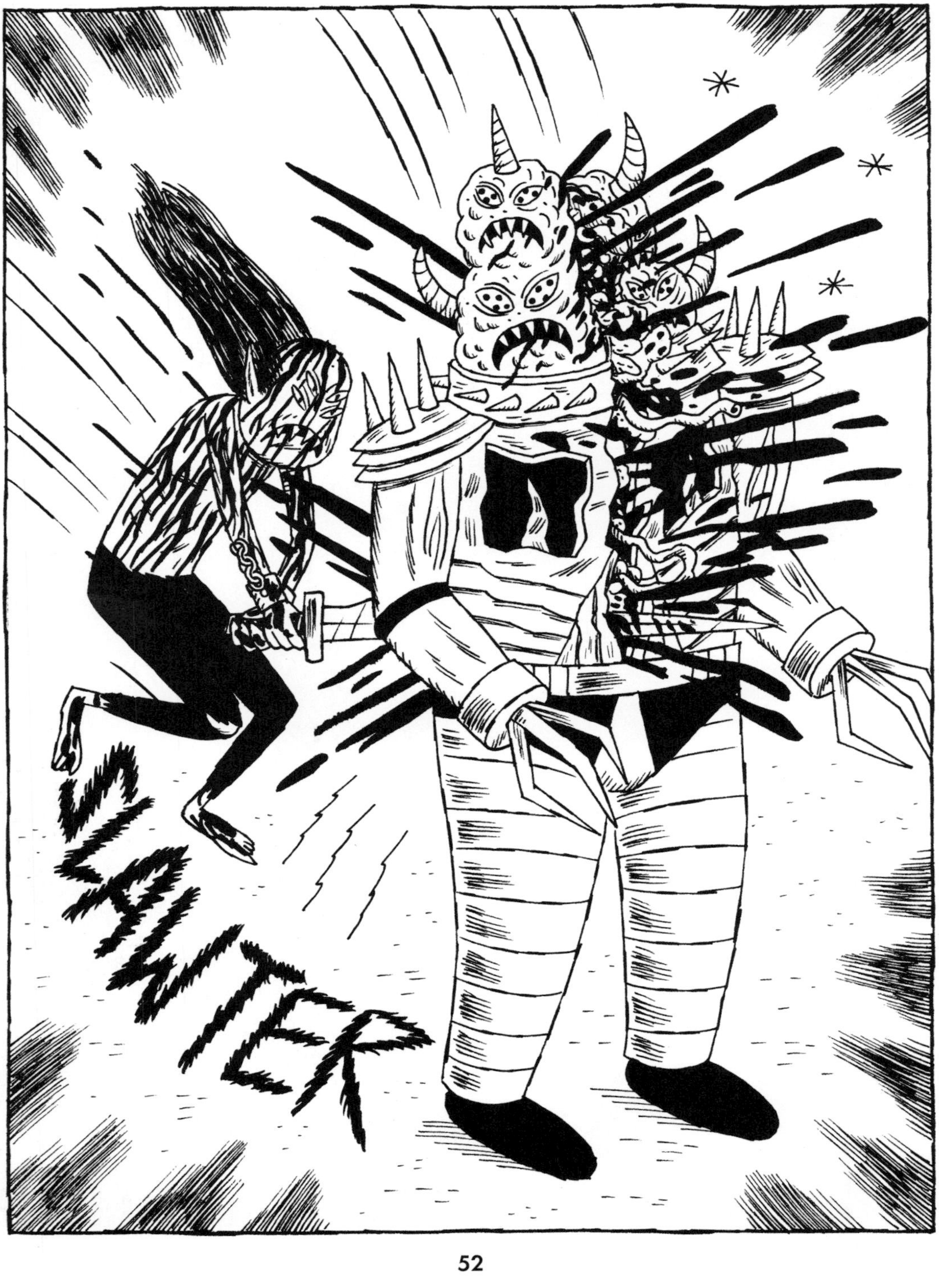
SLAWTER

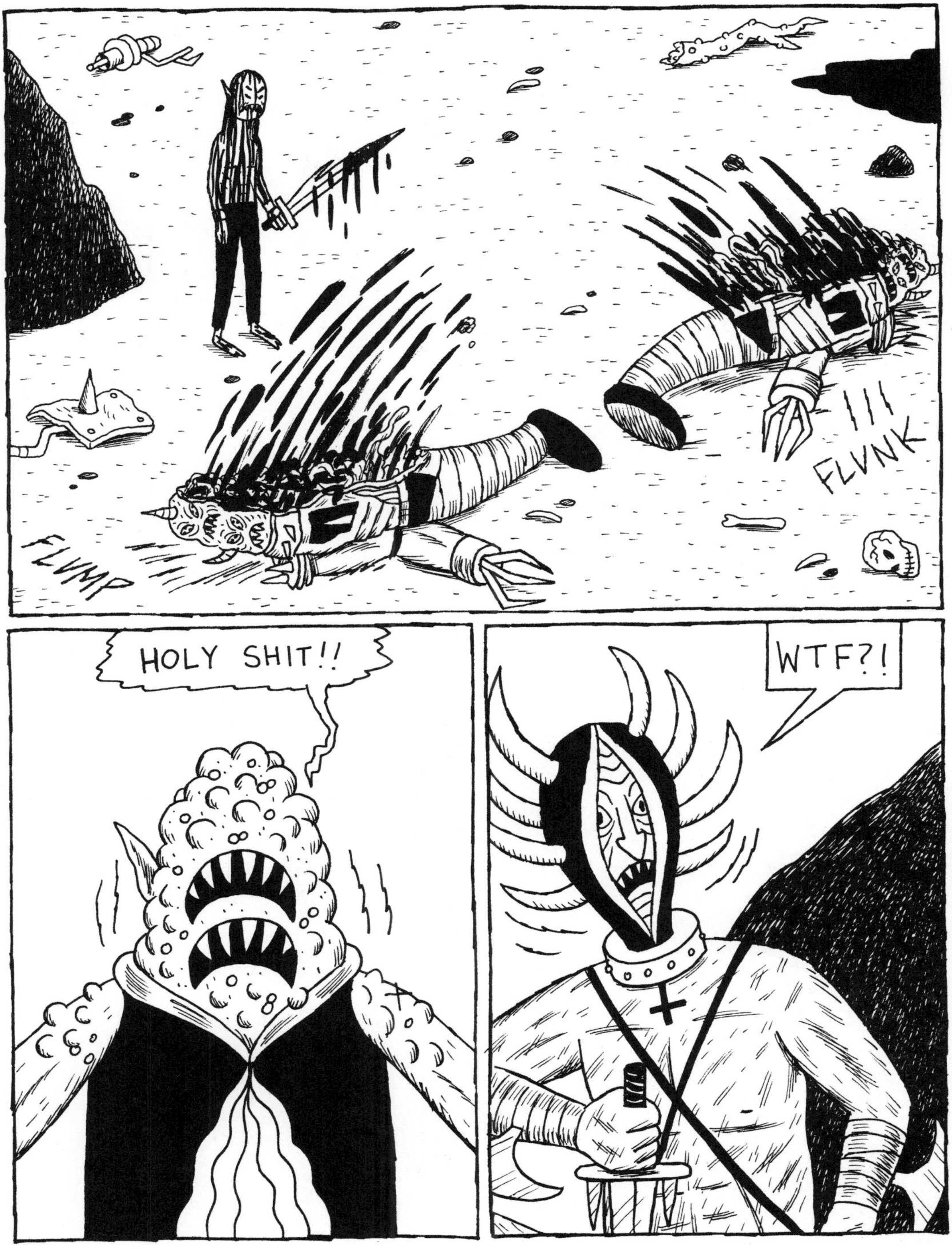

FLVNK
FLUMP
HOLY SHIT!!
WTF?!

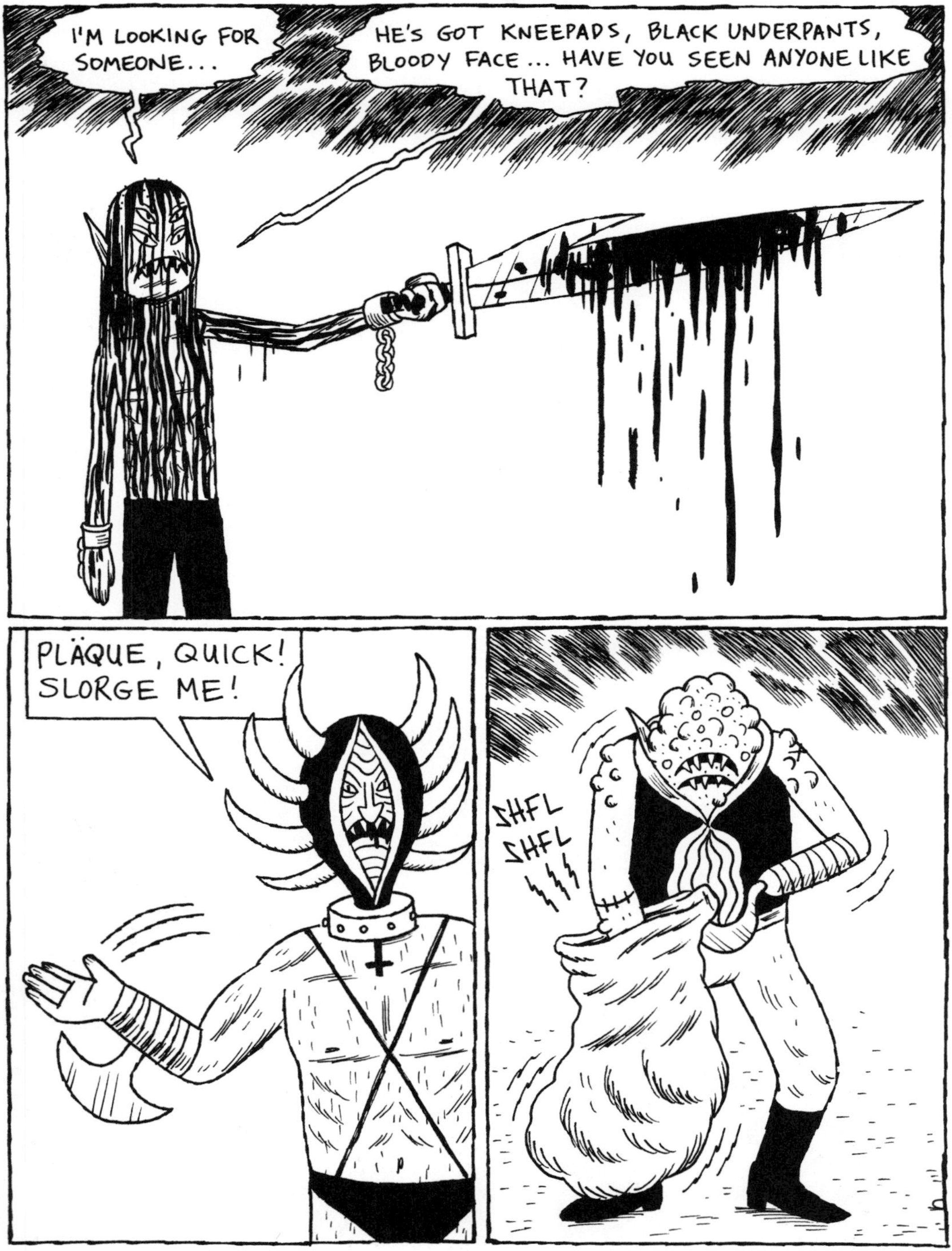
I'M LOOKING FOR SOMEONE...
HE'S GOT KNEEPADS, BLACK UNDERPANTS, BLOODY FACE... HAVE YOU SEEN ANYONE LIKE THAT?
PLÄQUE, QUICK! SLORGE ME!
SHFL SHFL

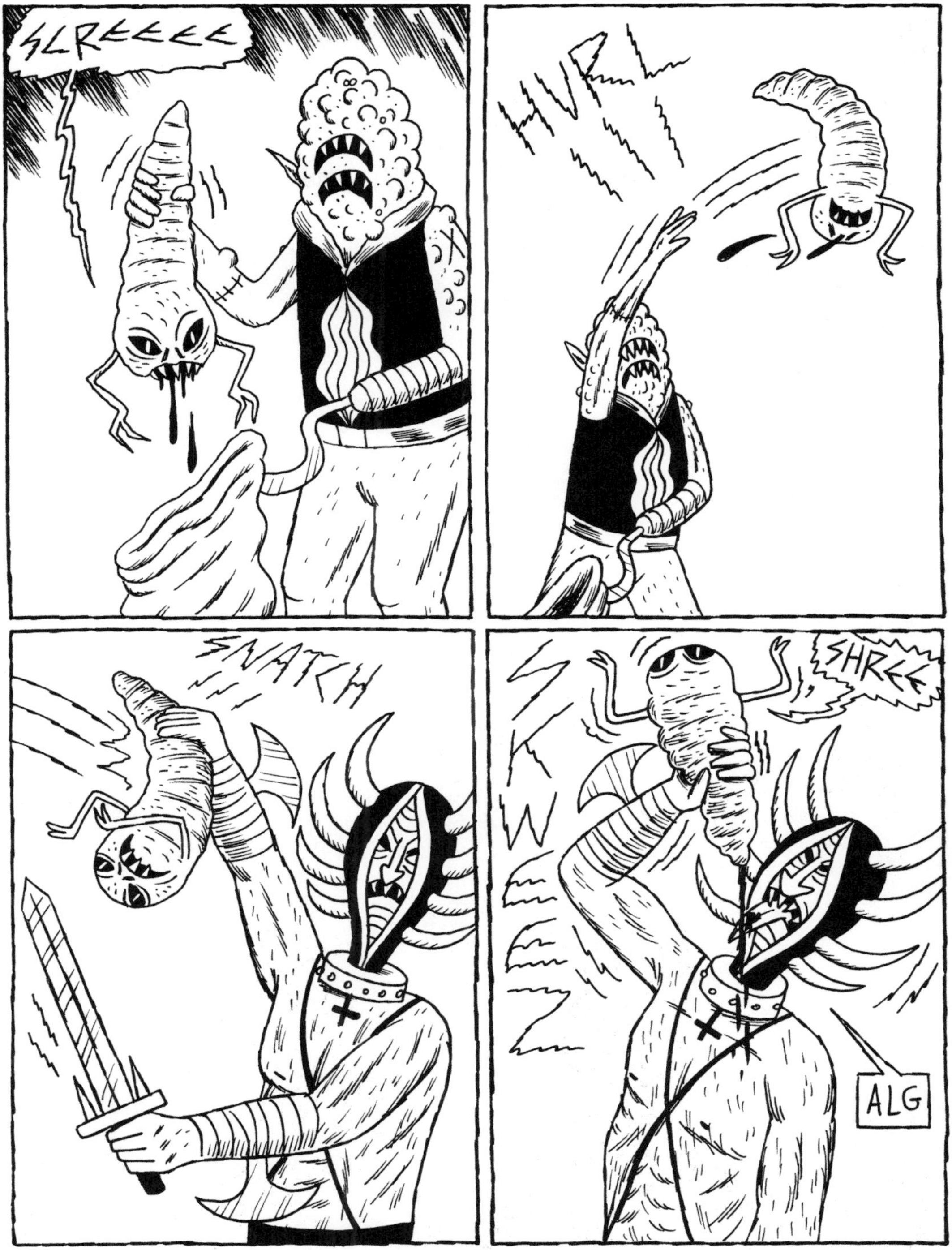
SCREEEEE
HURL
SNATCH
SHREEE
ALG

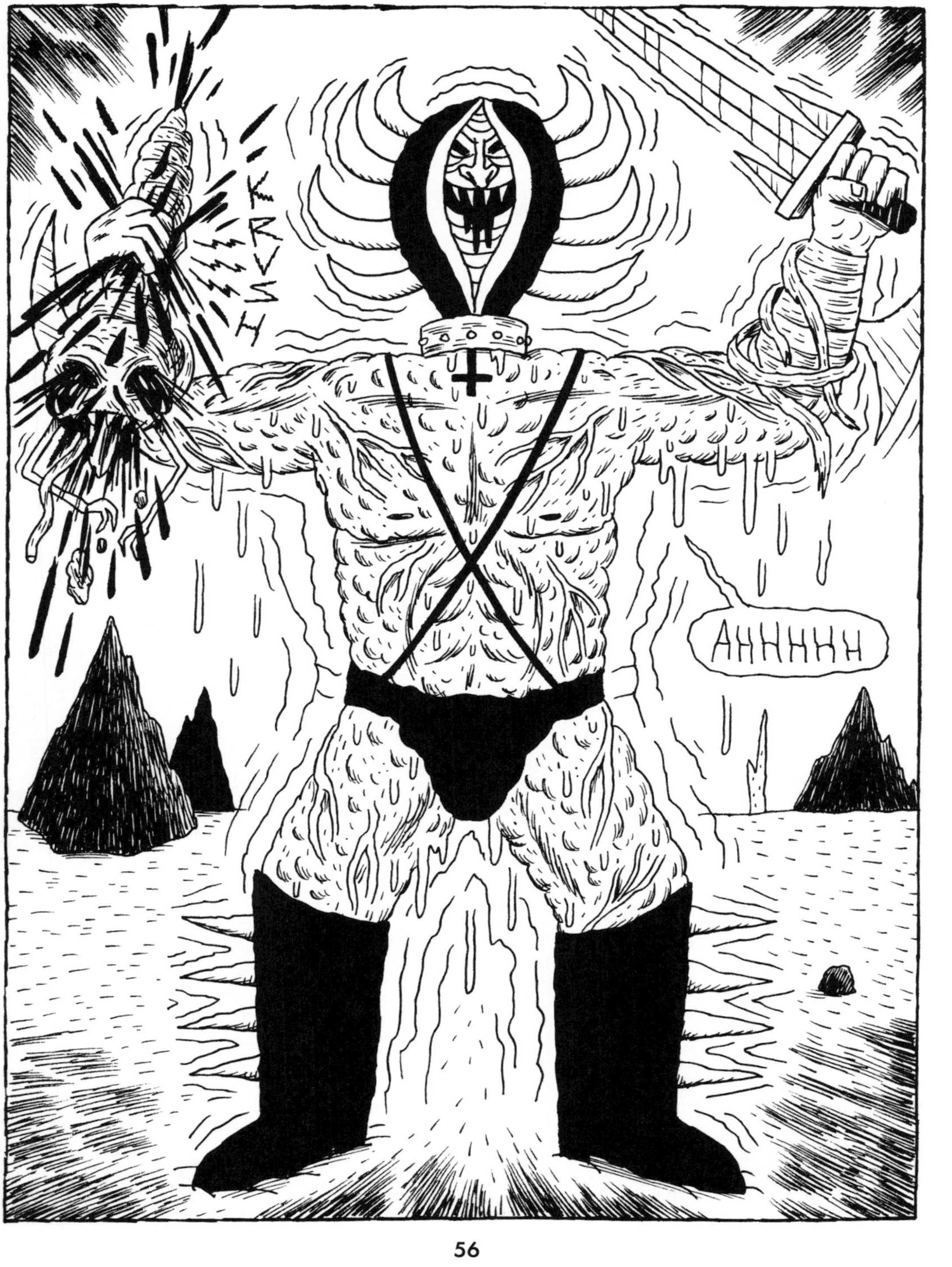
KRUSH
AHHHHH

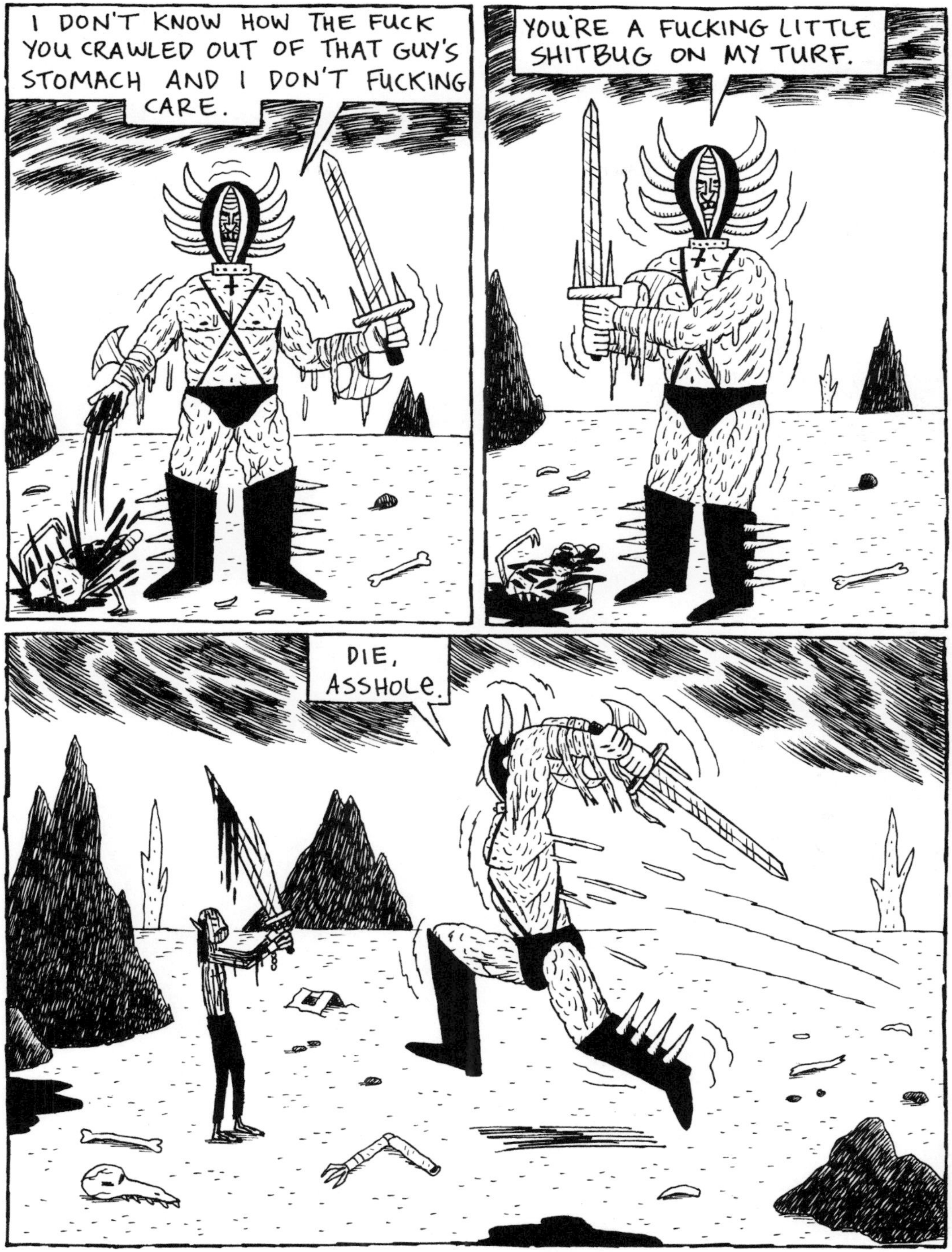
I DON'T KNOW HOW THE FUCK YOU CRAWLED OUT OF THAT GUY'S STOMACH AND I DON'T FUCKING CARE.
YOU'RE A FUCKING LITTLE SHITBUG ON MY TURF.
DIE, ASSHOLE.

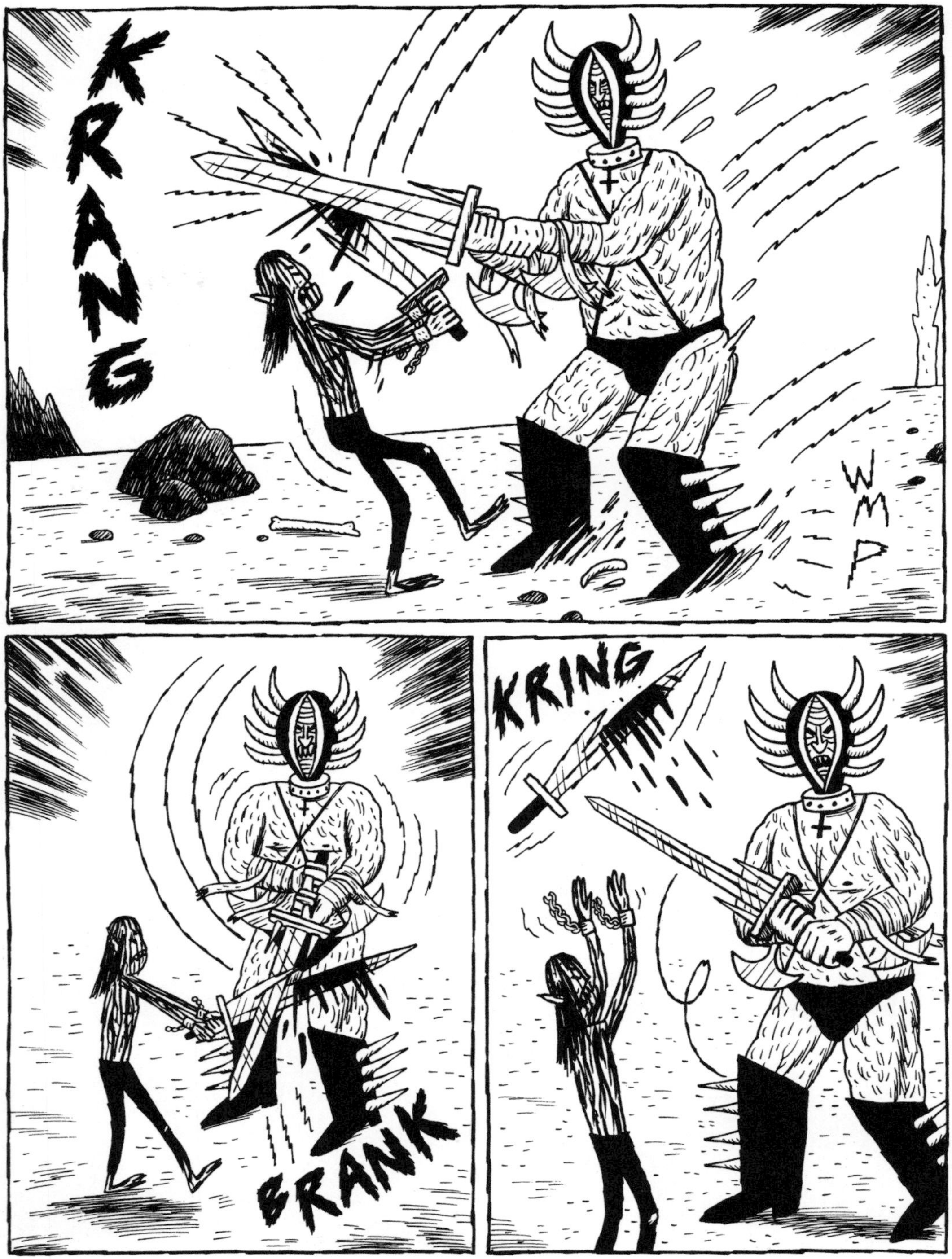
KRANG
WMP
BRANK
KRING

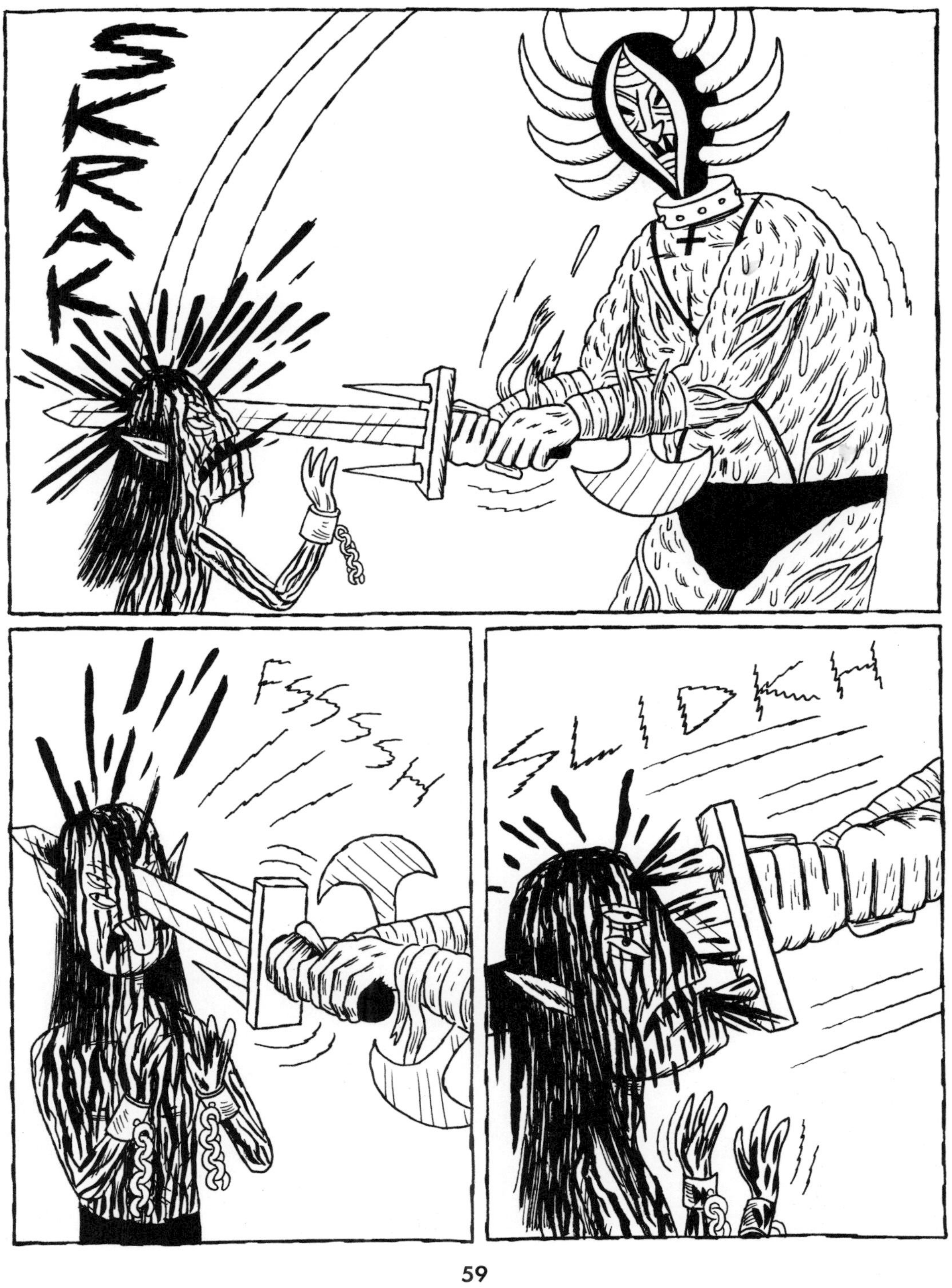
SKRAK
FSSSSH
SLIDKH

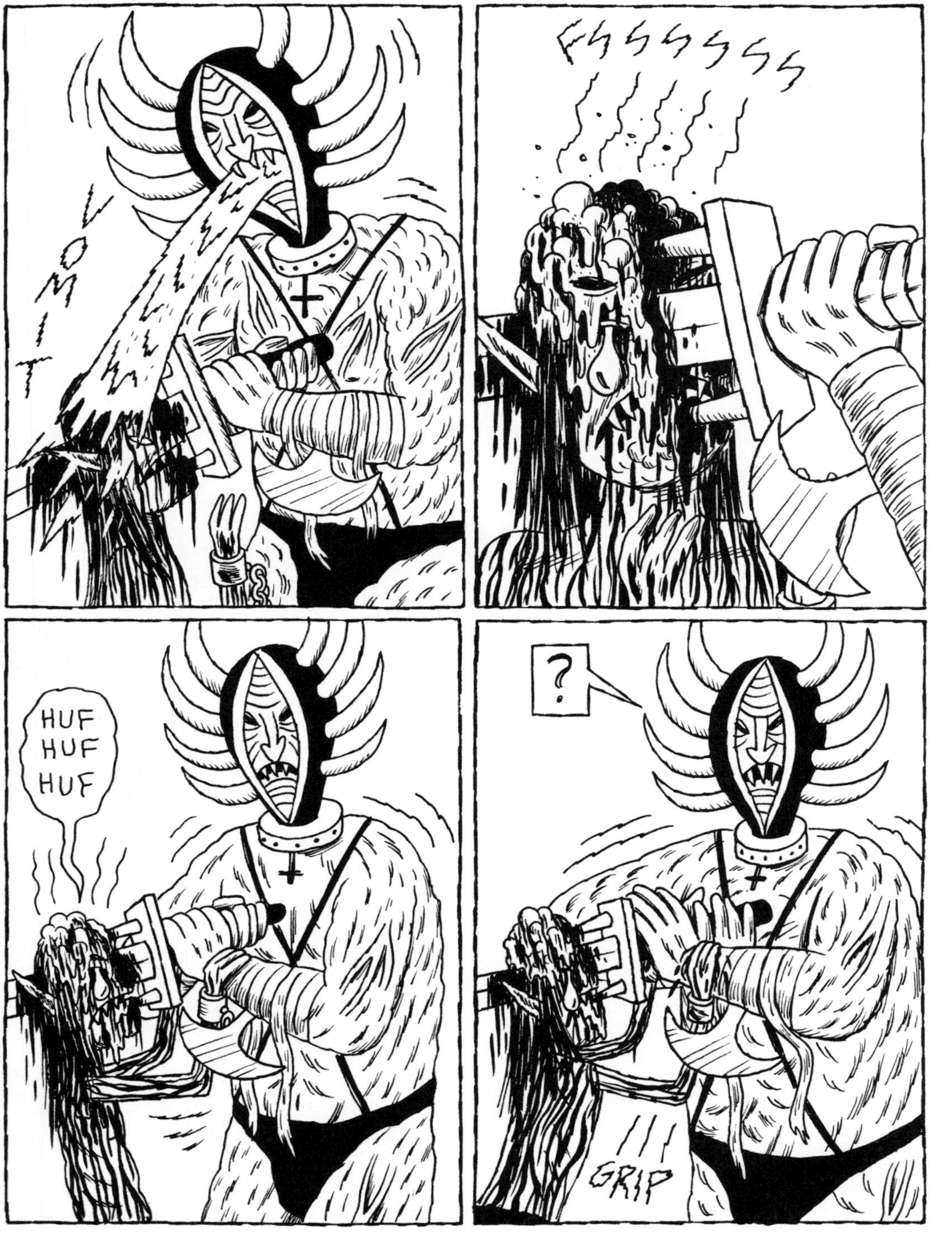
VOMIT
FSSSSSSS
HUF HUF HUF
?
GRIP

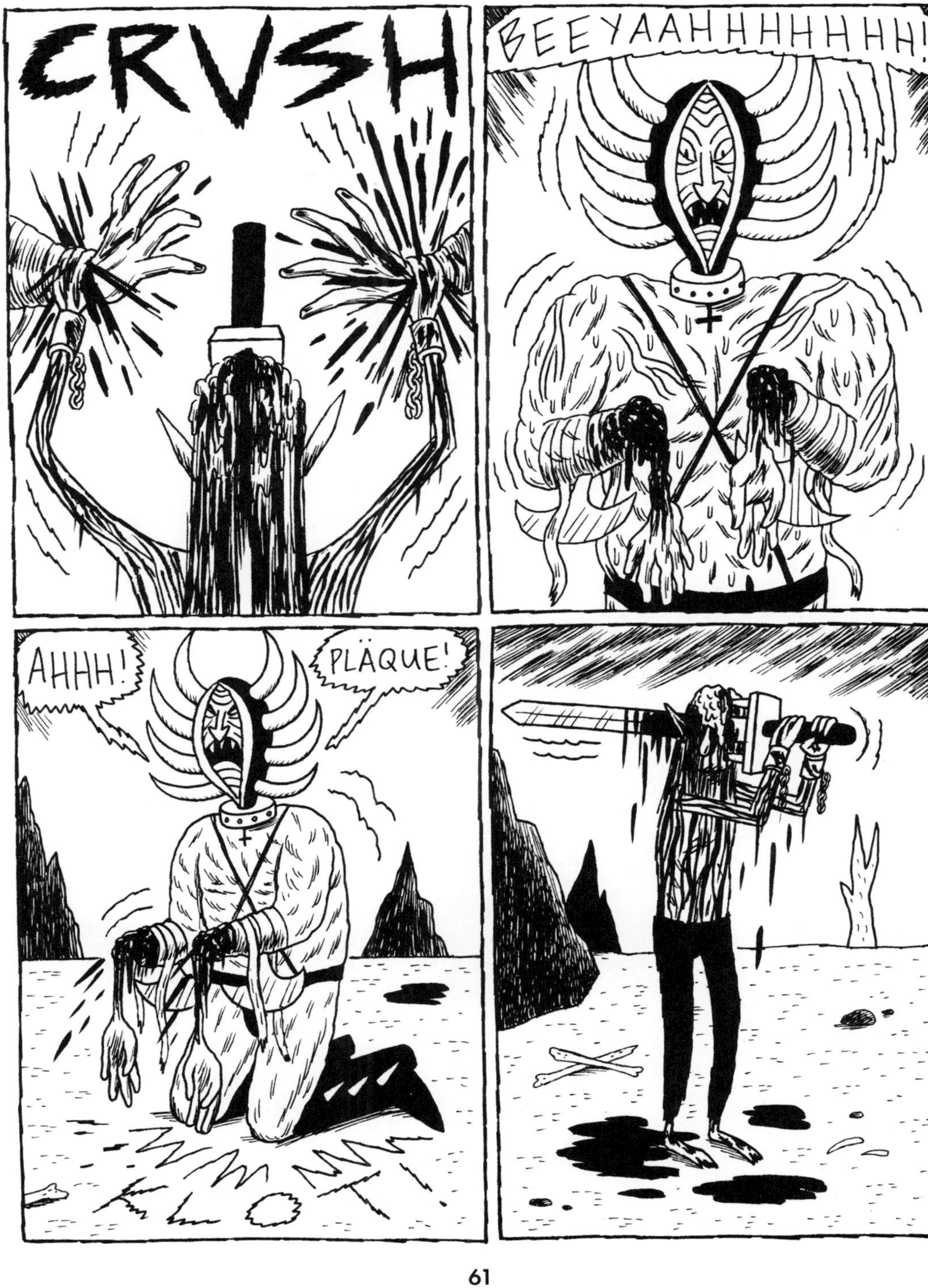
CRVSH
BEEYAAHHHHHHH!
AHHH!
PLÄQUE!
KLOST!

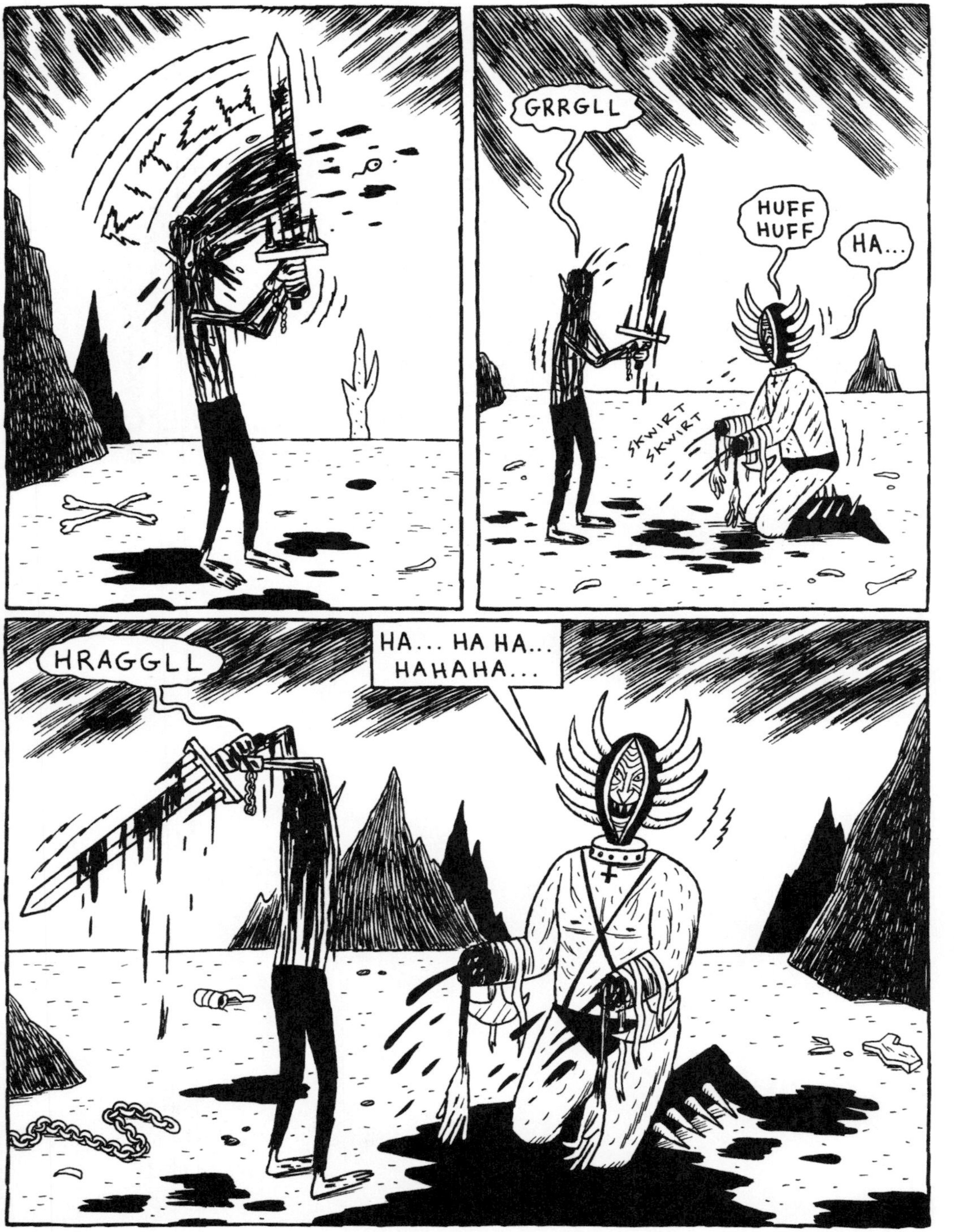
GRRGLL
HUFF HUFF
HA...
SKWIRT SKWIRT
HRAGGLL
HA... HA HA... HAHAHA...

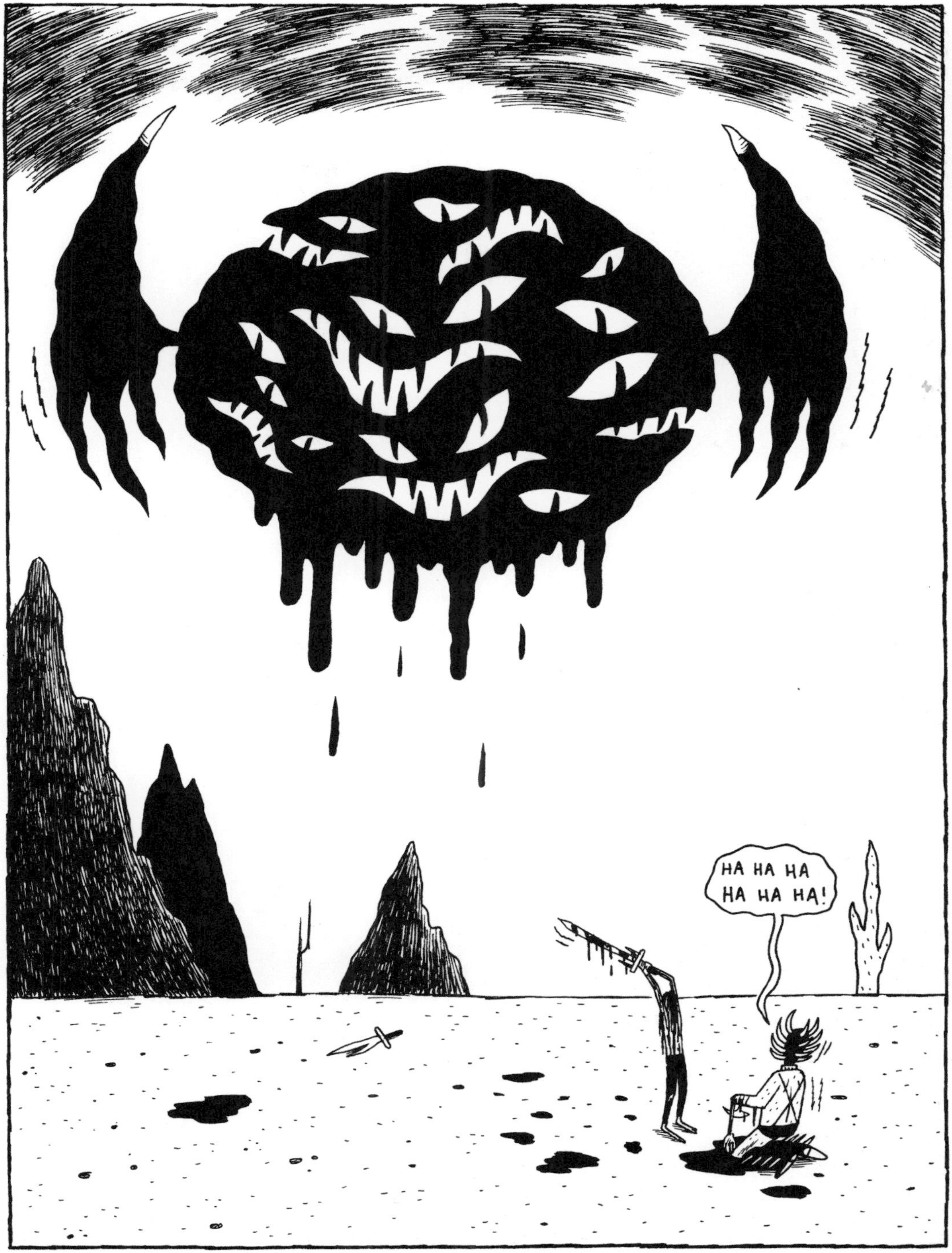
HA HA HA
HA HA HA!

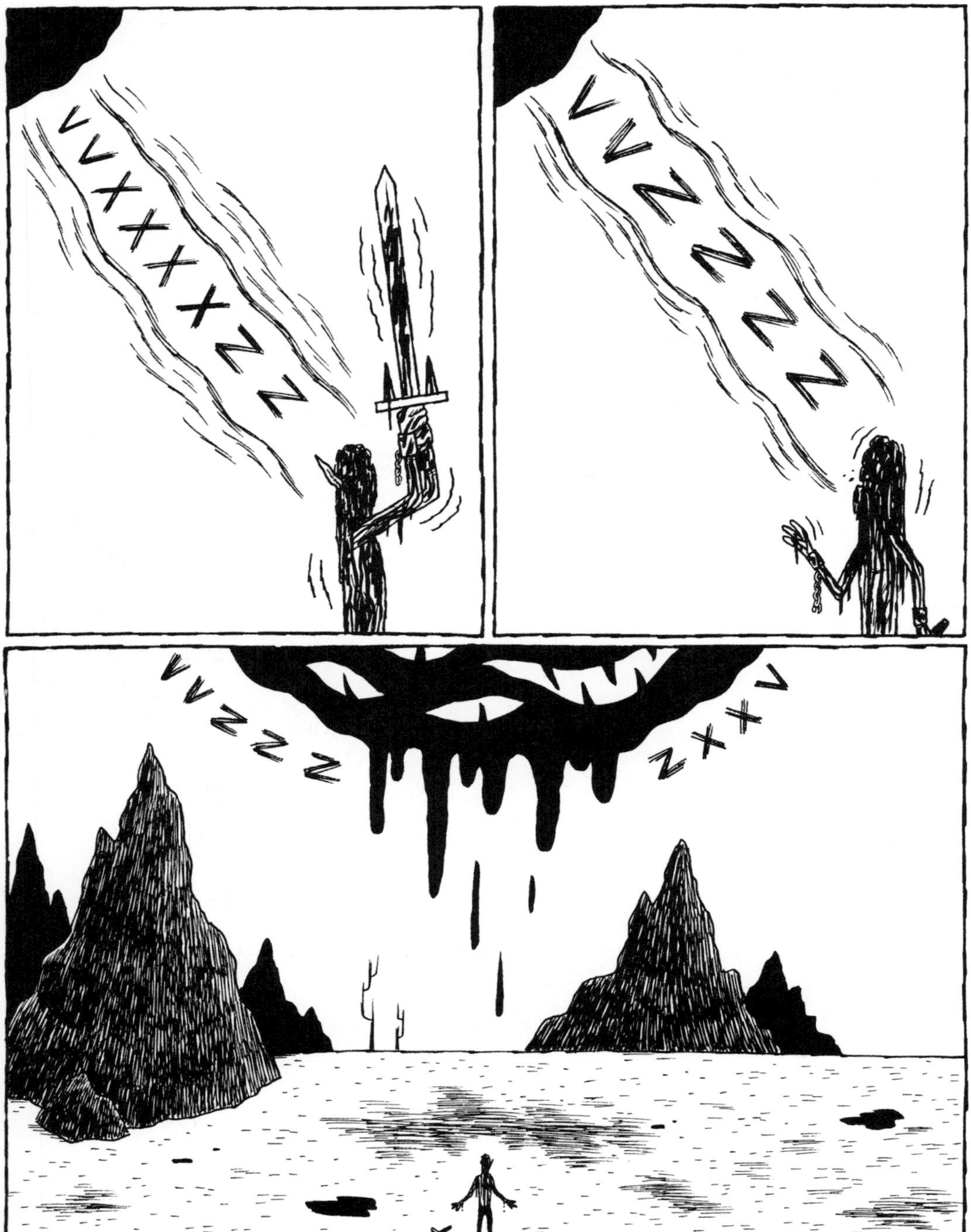
VVXXXXXZZ
VVZZZZ
VVZZZZ
ZXXV

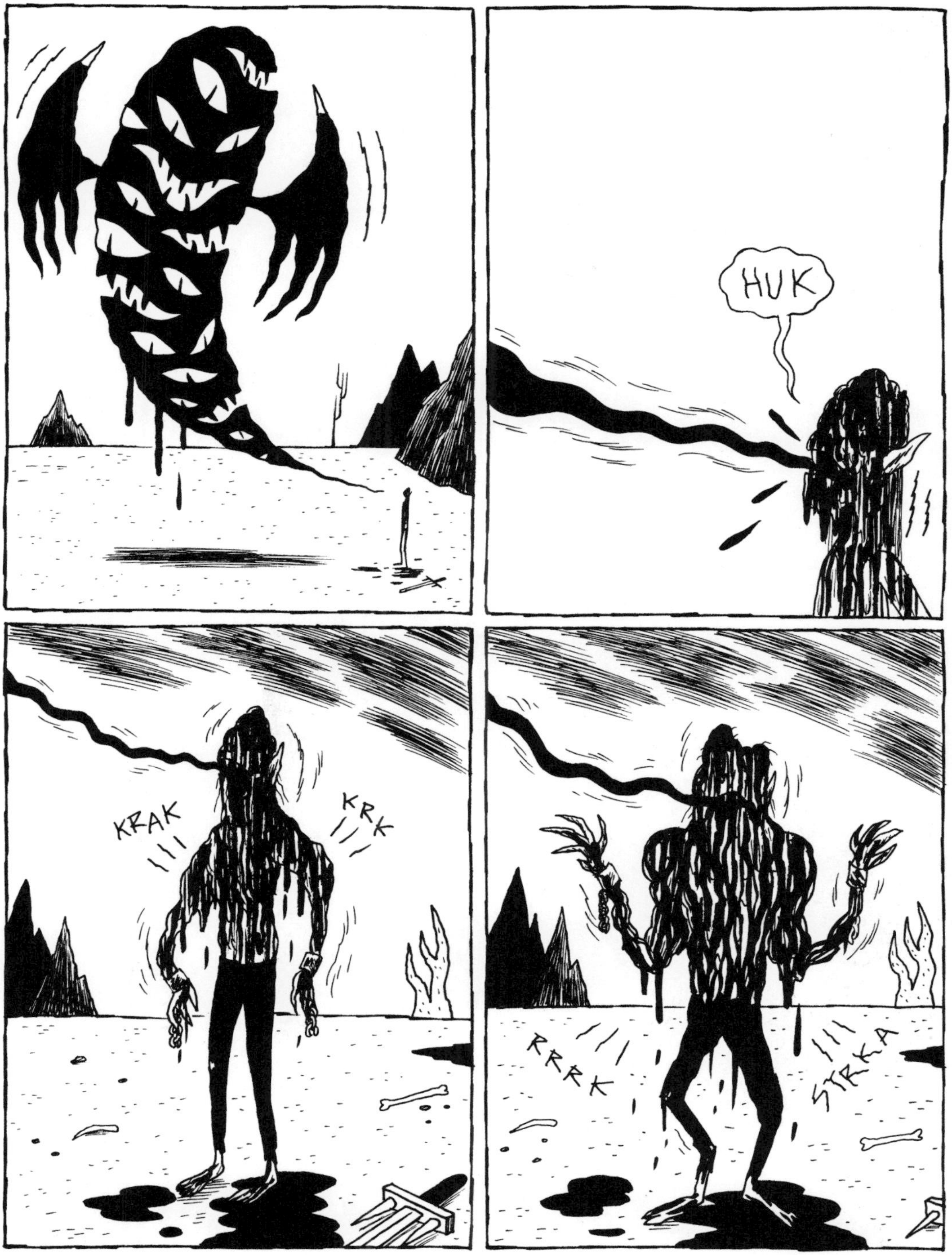
HUK
KRAK
KRK
RRRK
STRKA

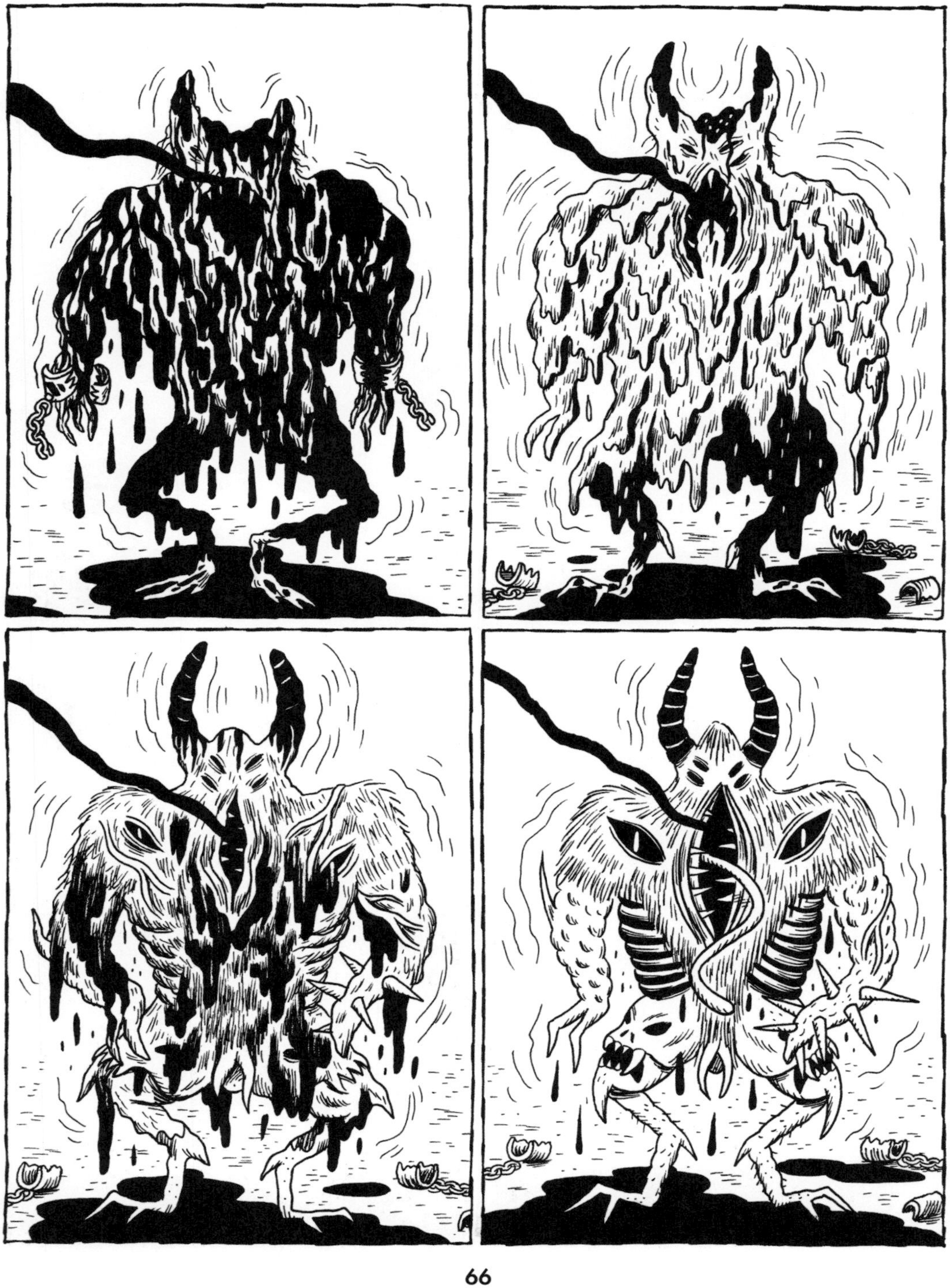

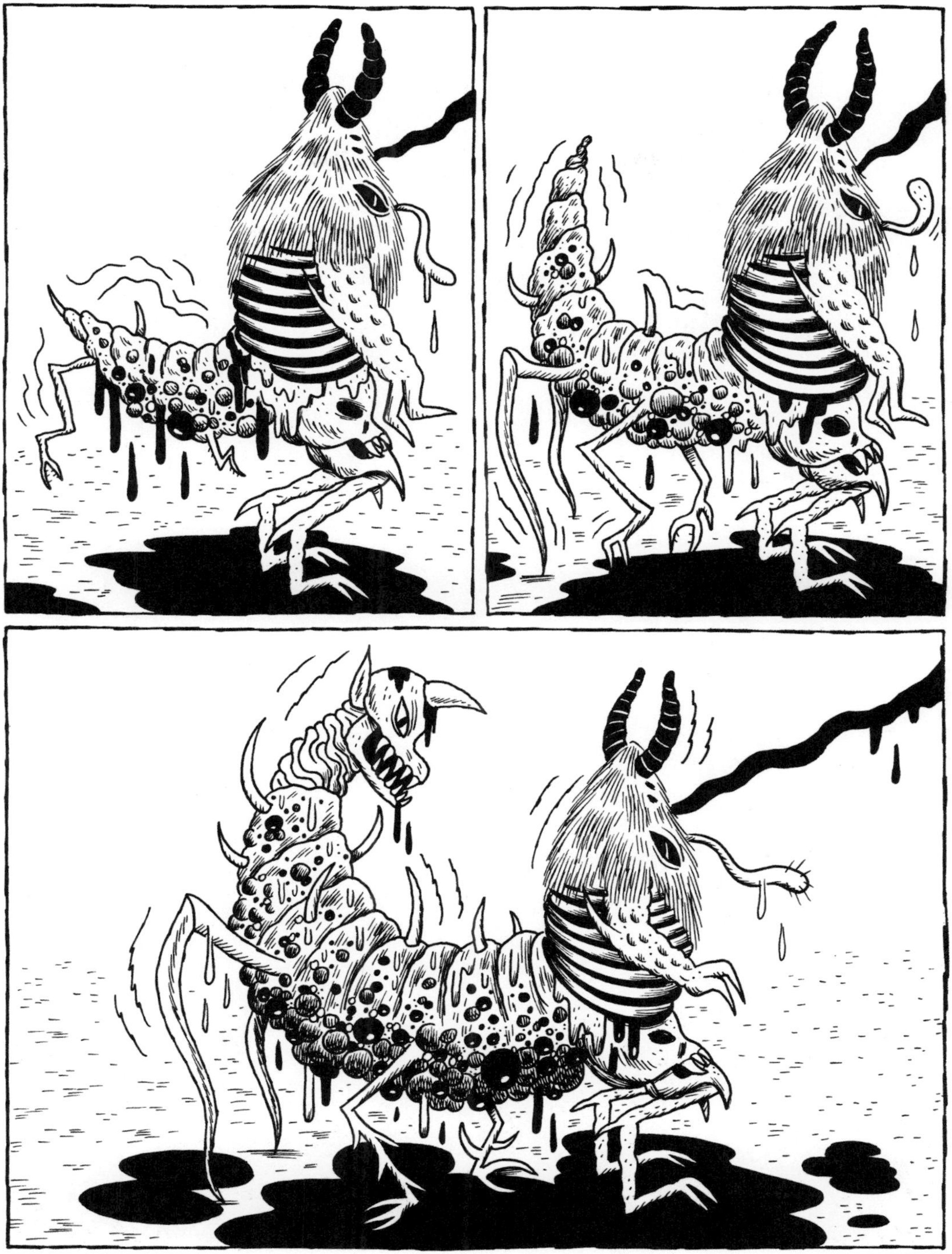

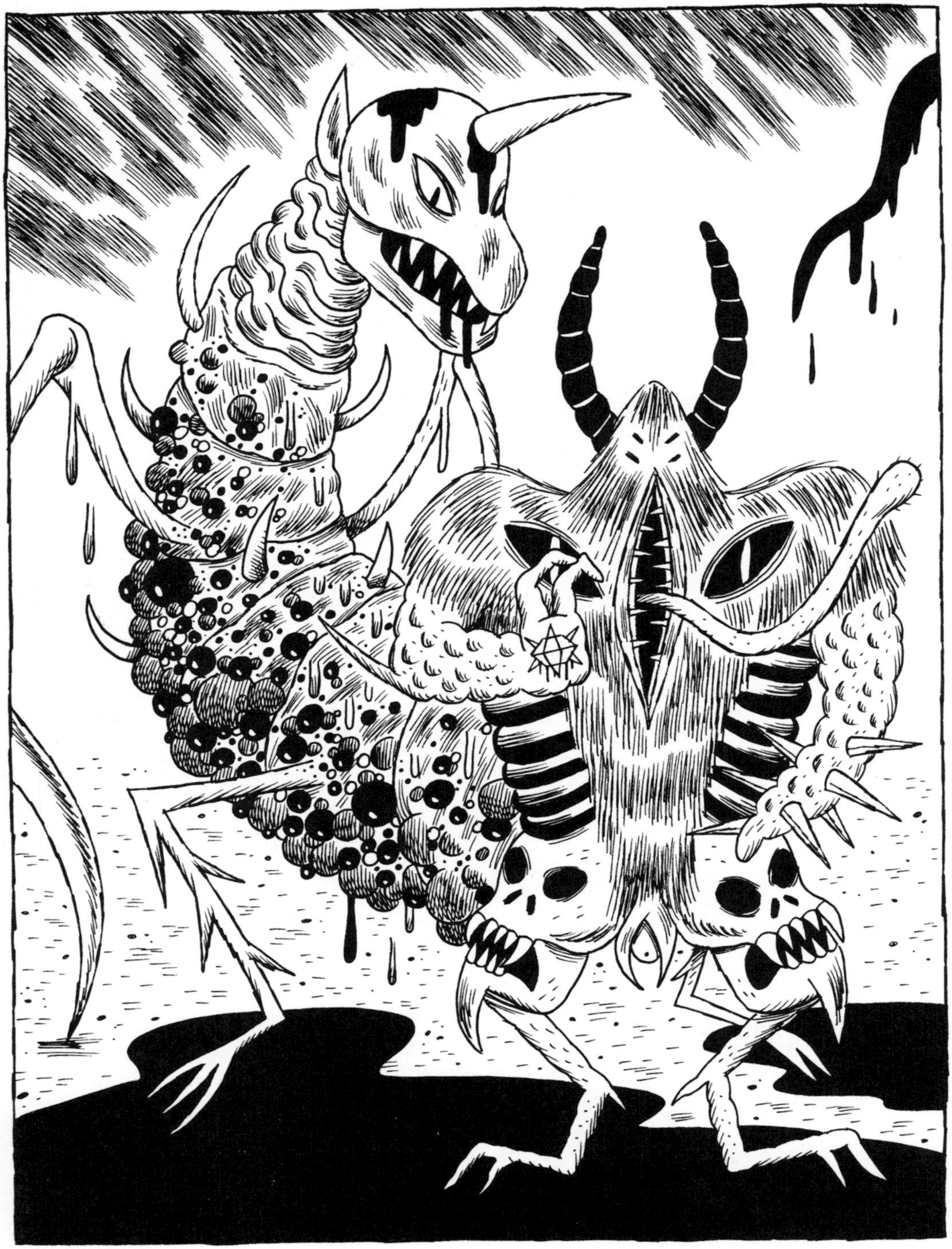

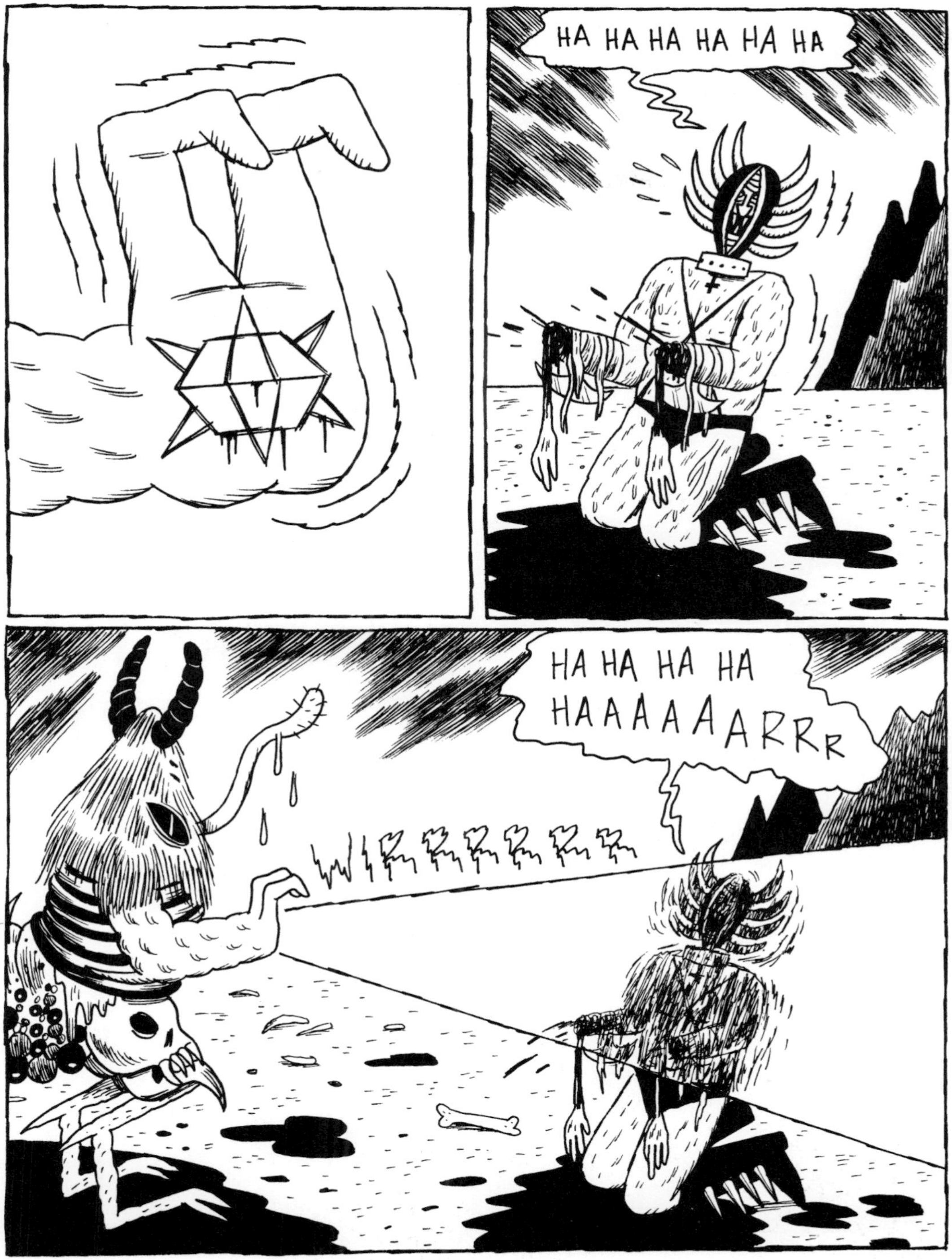
HA HA HA HA HA HA
HA HA HA HA
HAAAAAARRRR

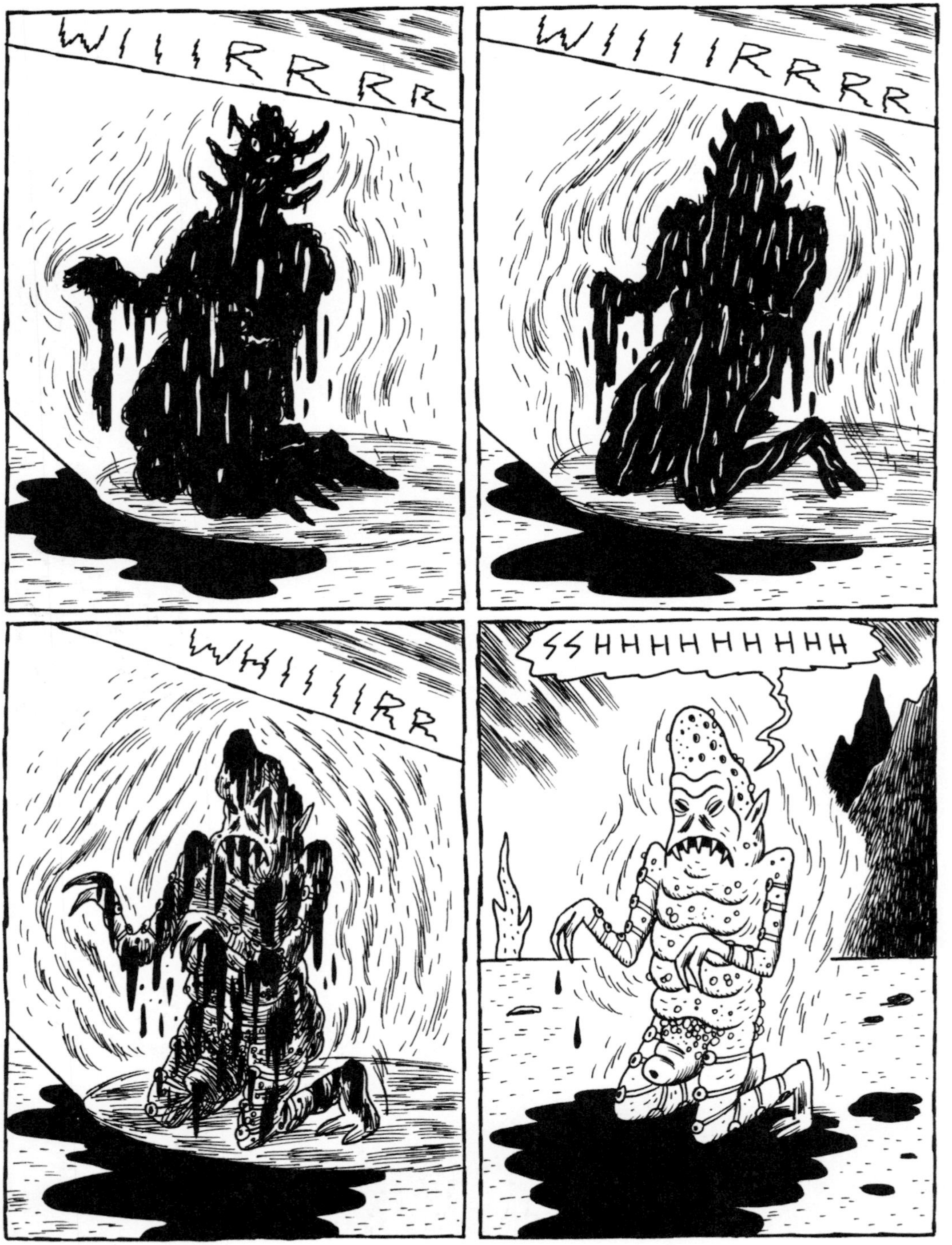
WIIIRRRR
WIIIIRRRR
WHIIIIRR
SSHHHHHHHHH

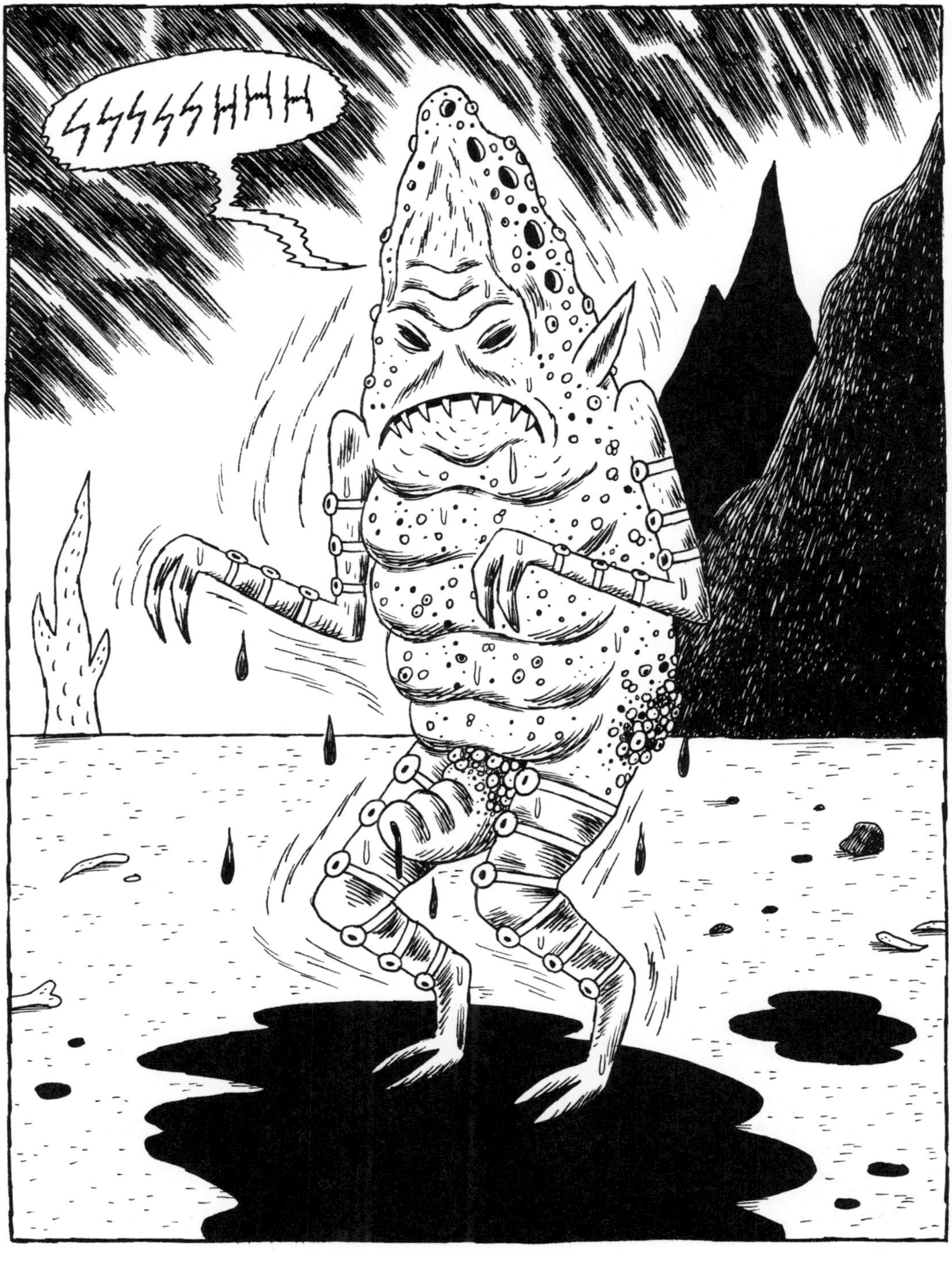
SSSSSHHHH

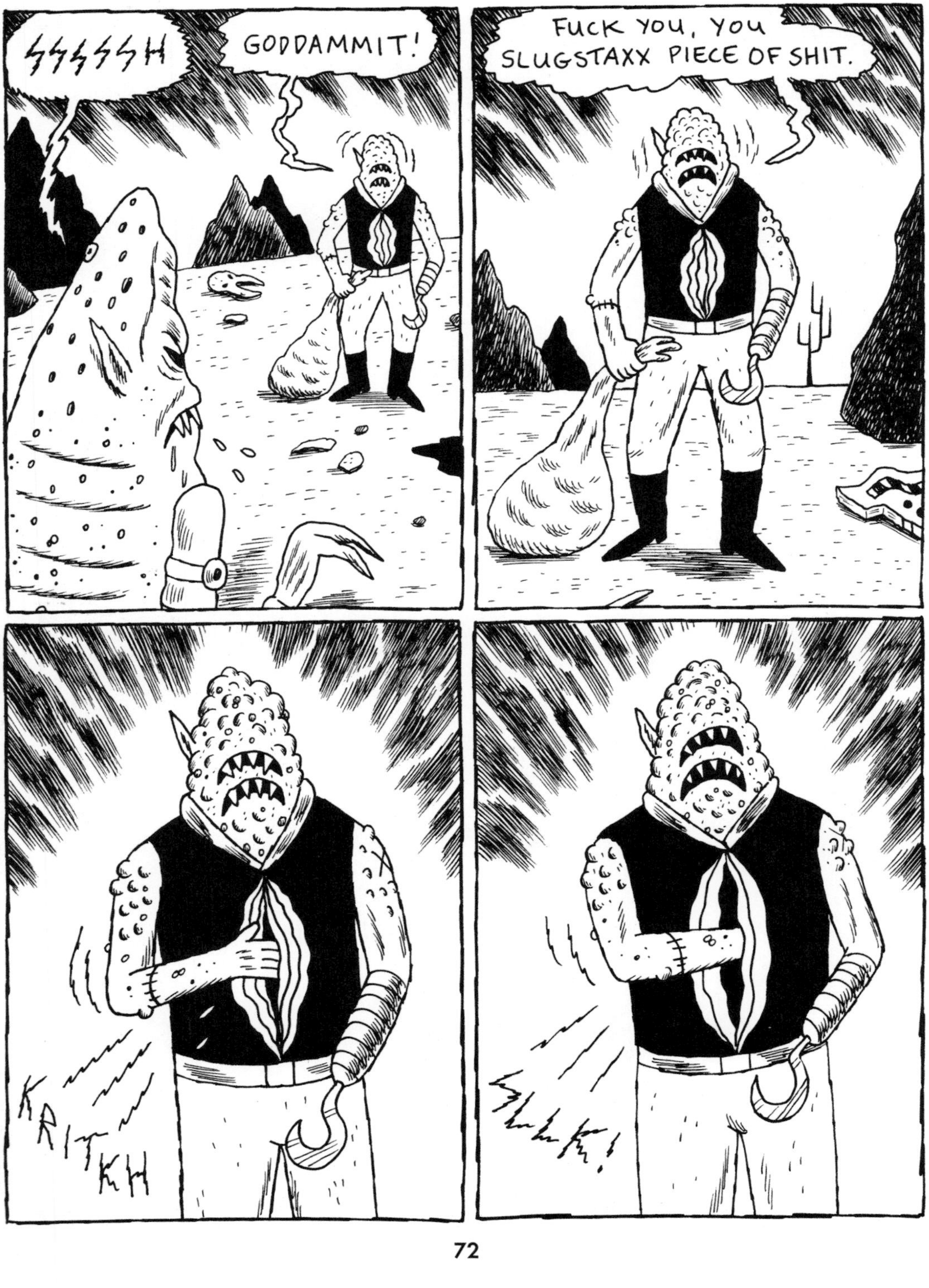
SSSSSH
GODDAMMIT!
FUCK YOU, YOU SLUGSTAXX PIECE OF SHIT.
KRITKH
SHLKK!

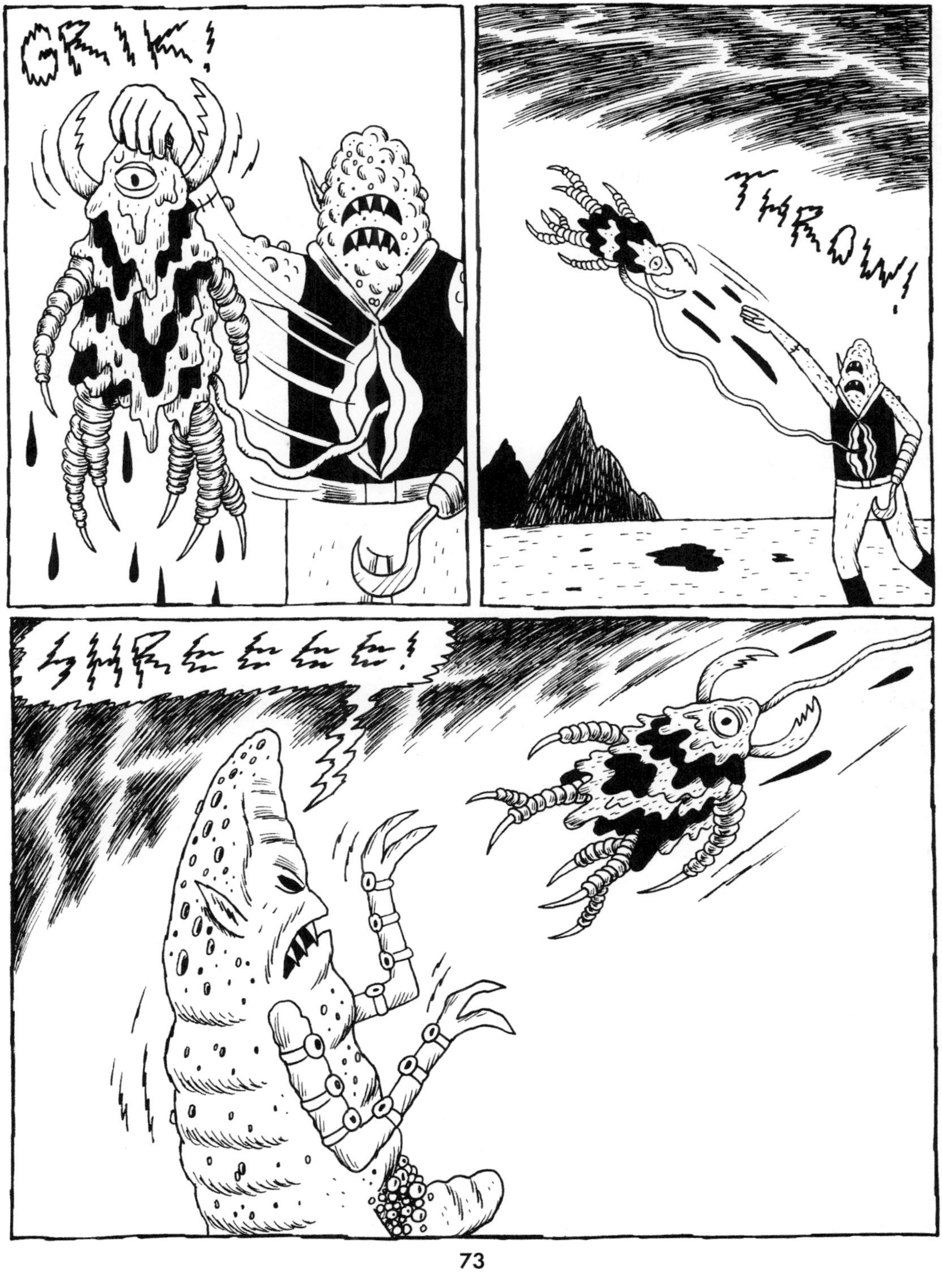
GRIK!
THROW!
SHREEEE!

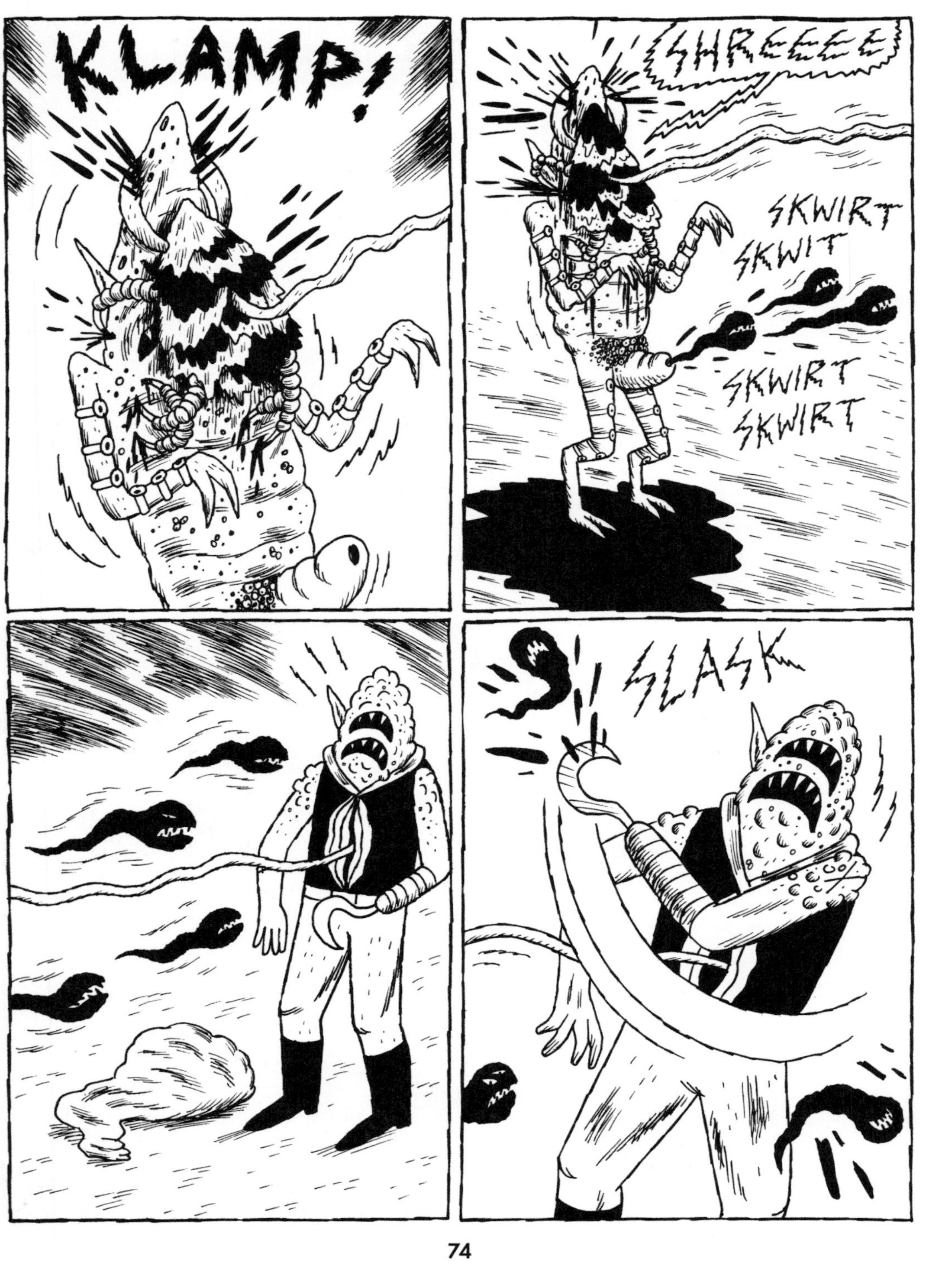
KLAMP!
SHREEEE
SKWIRT
SKWIT
SKWIRT
SKWIRT
SLASK

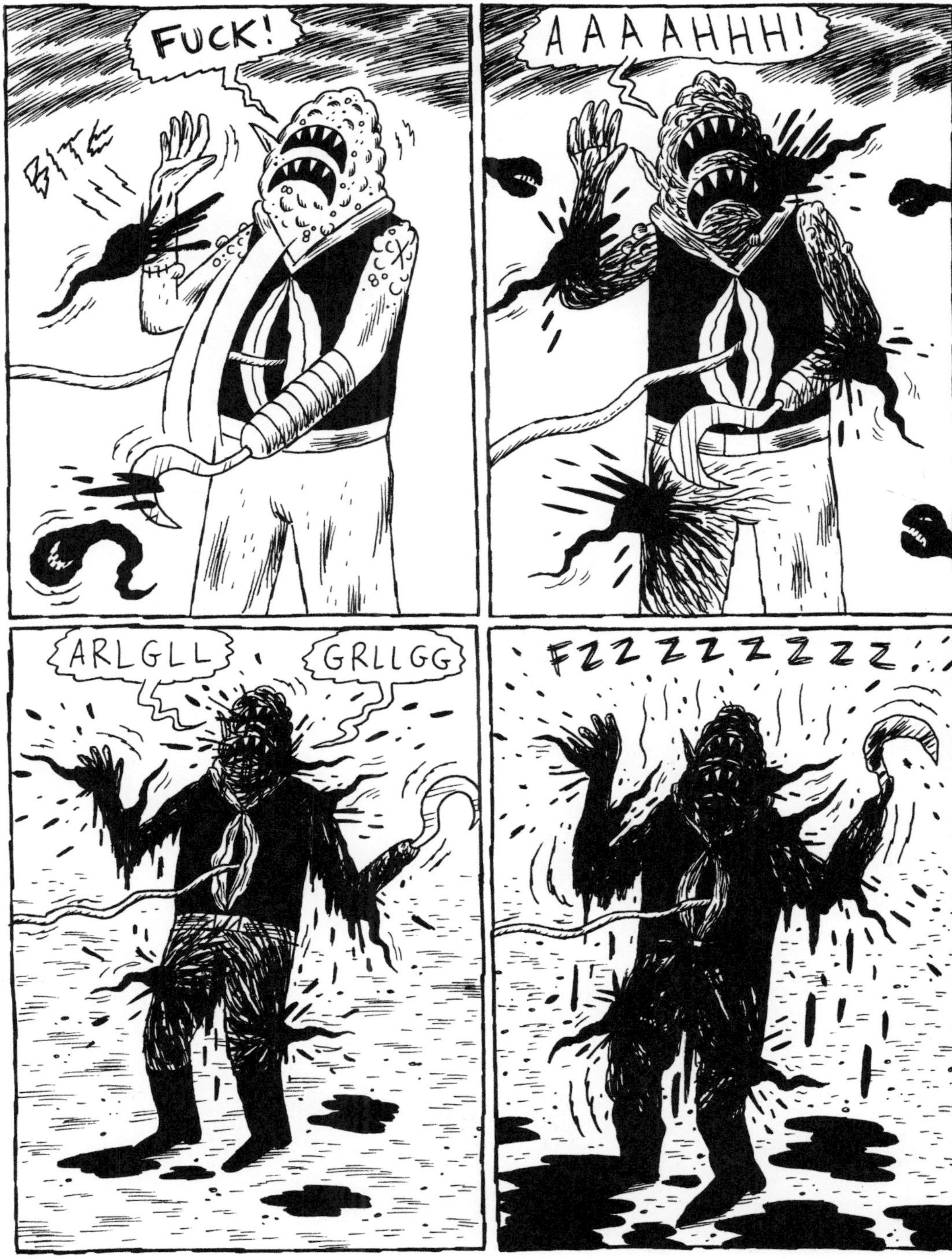
FUCK!
BITE
AAAAHHH!
ARLGLL
GRLLGG
FZZZZZZZZZ

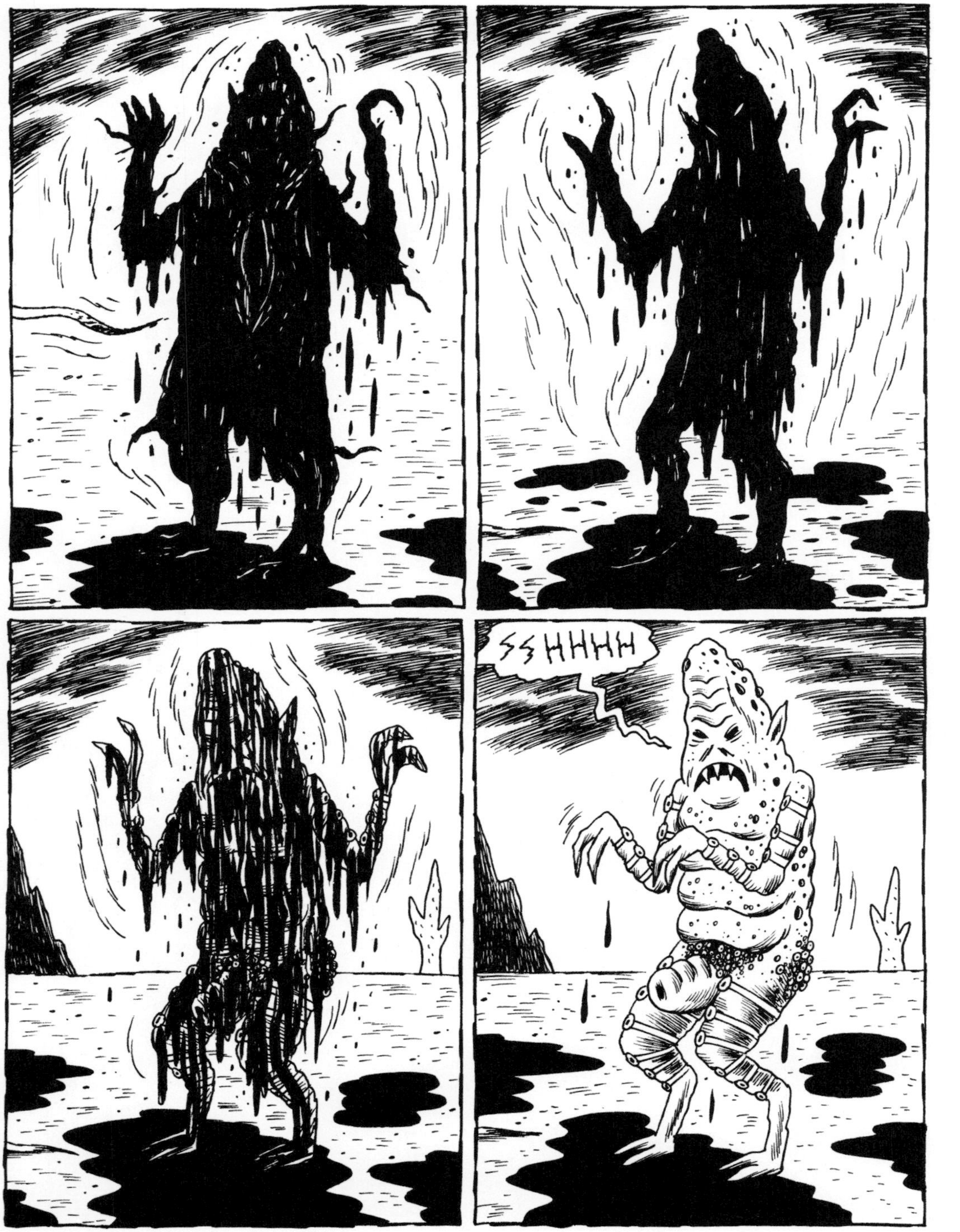
SSHHHHH

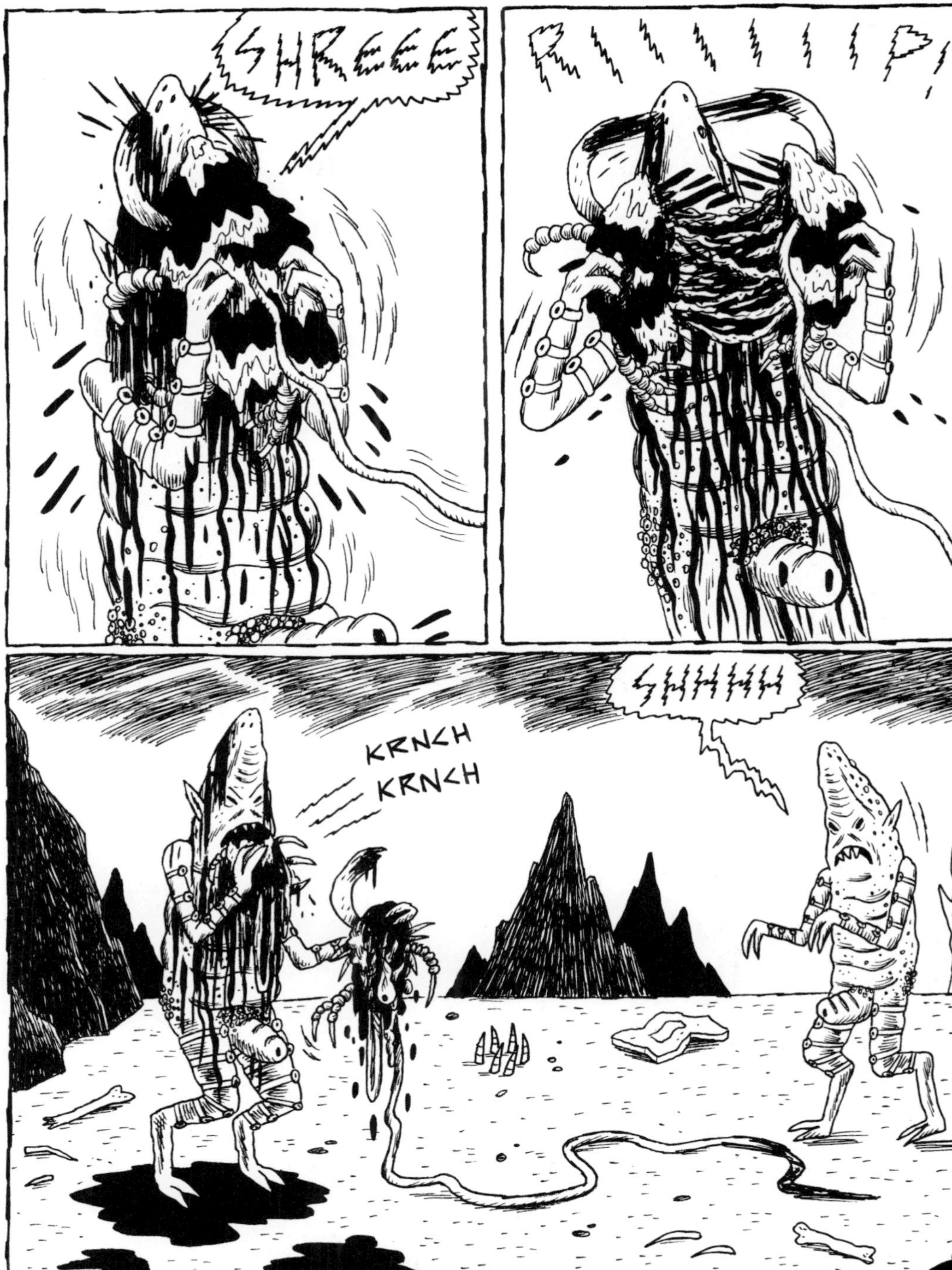
SHREEE
RIIIIIIP!
KRNCH
KRNCH
SHHHHH

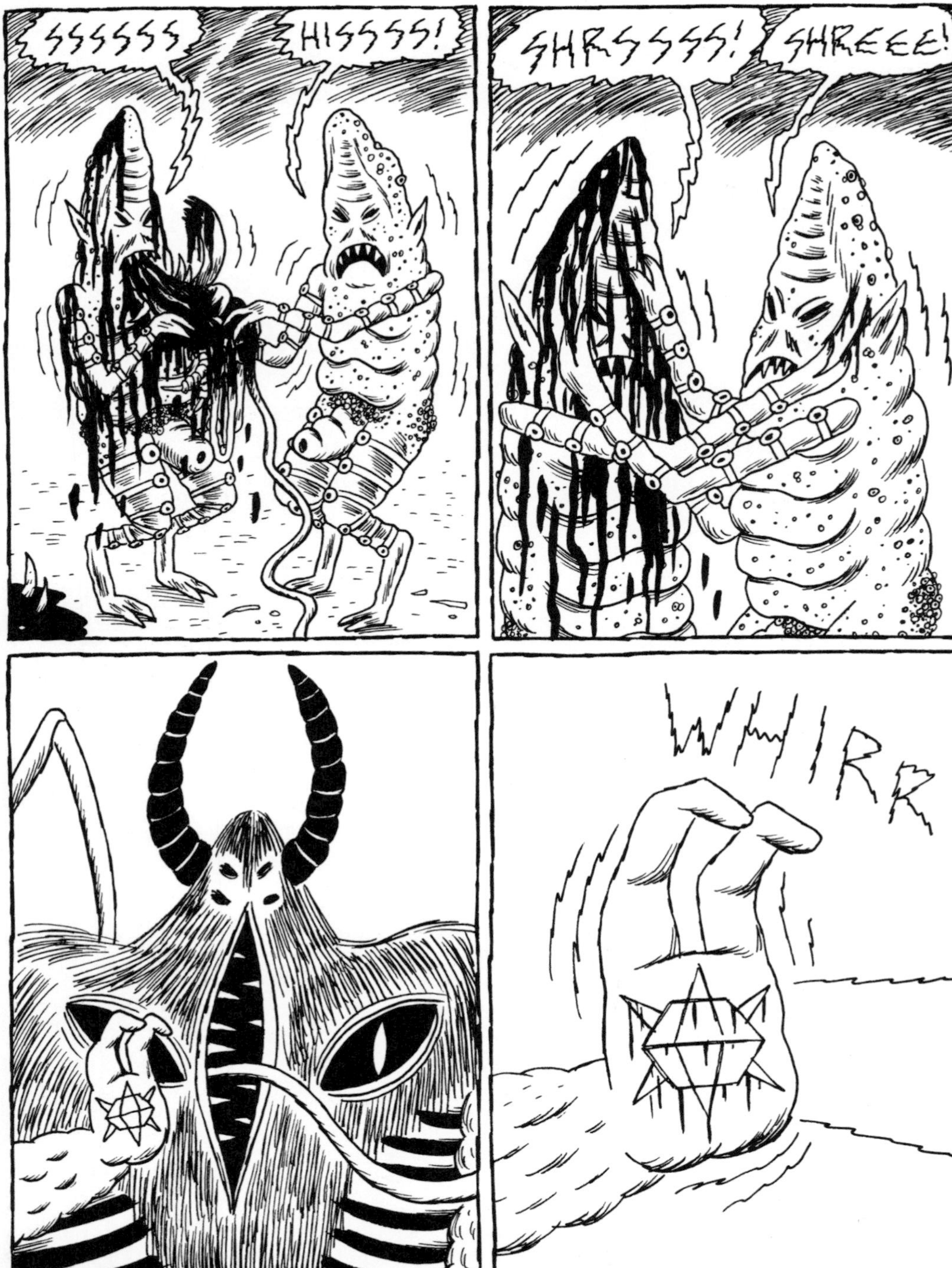
SSSSSS
HISSSS!
SHRSSSS!
SHREEE!
WHIRR

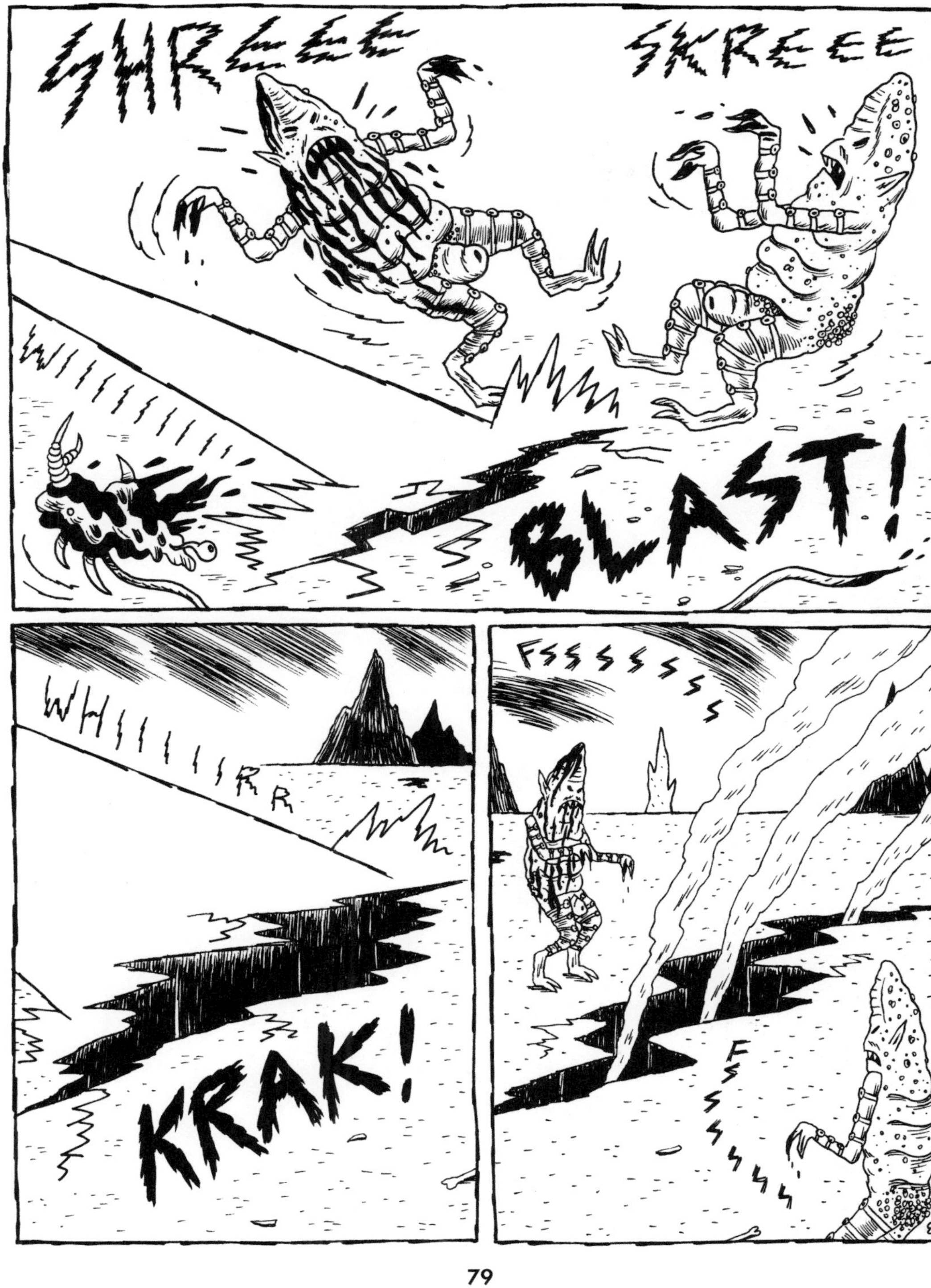
SHREEE
SKREEE
WHIIIIII
BLAST!
WHIIIIIIRR
KRAK!
FSSSSSSSS
FSSSSSSS

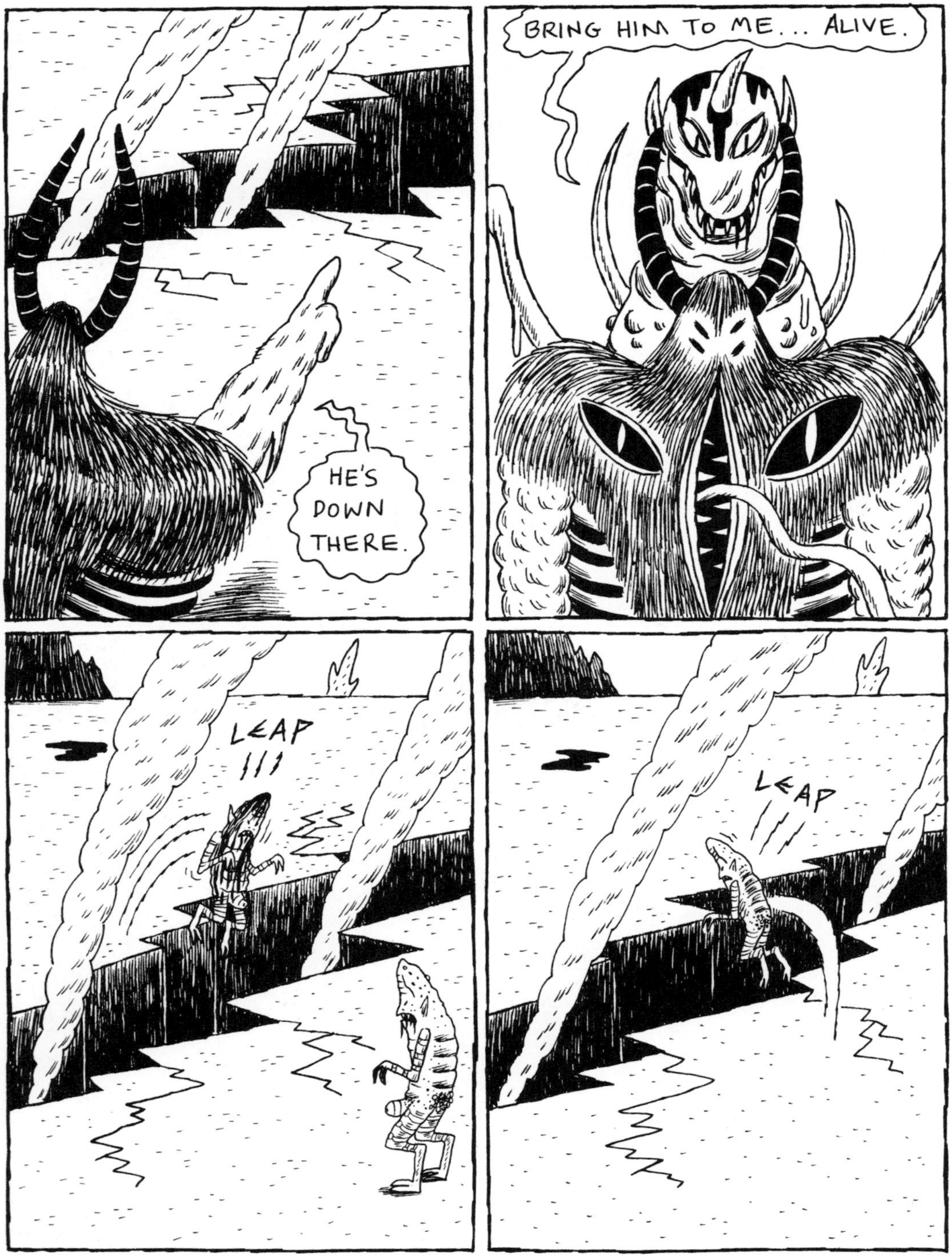
HE'S DOWN THERE.
BRING HIM TO ME... ALIVE.
LEAP
LEAP

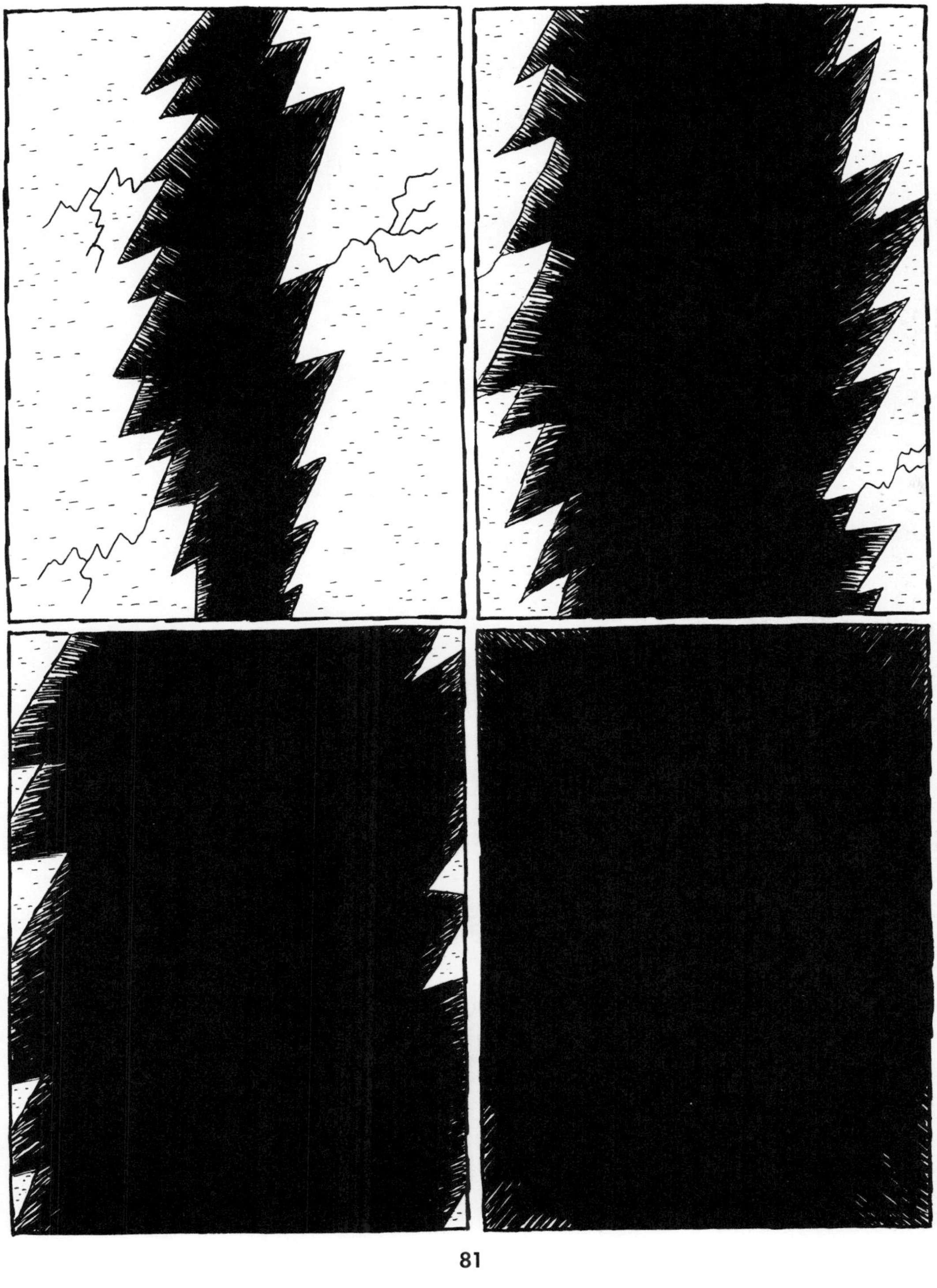

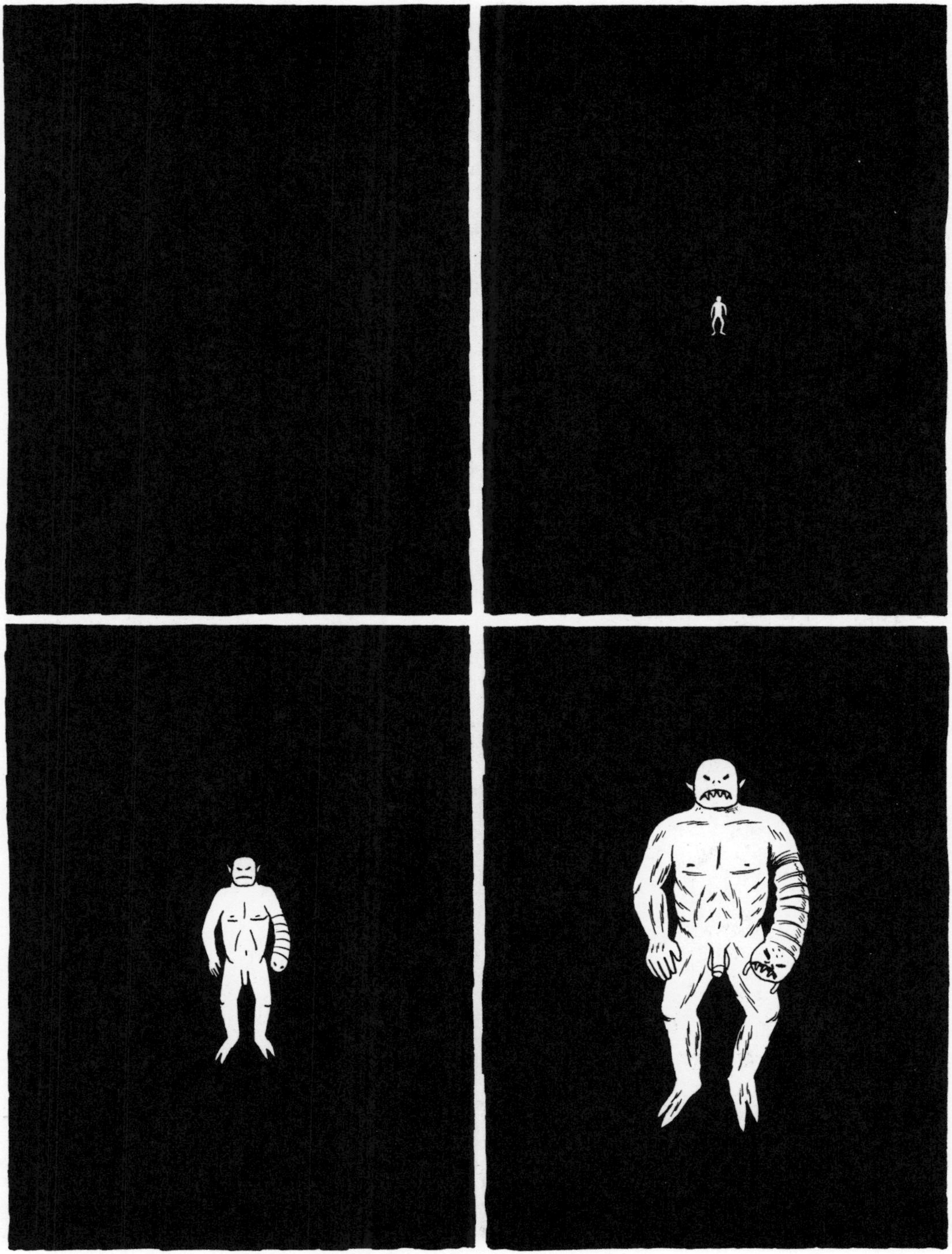

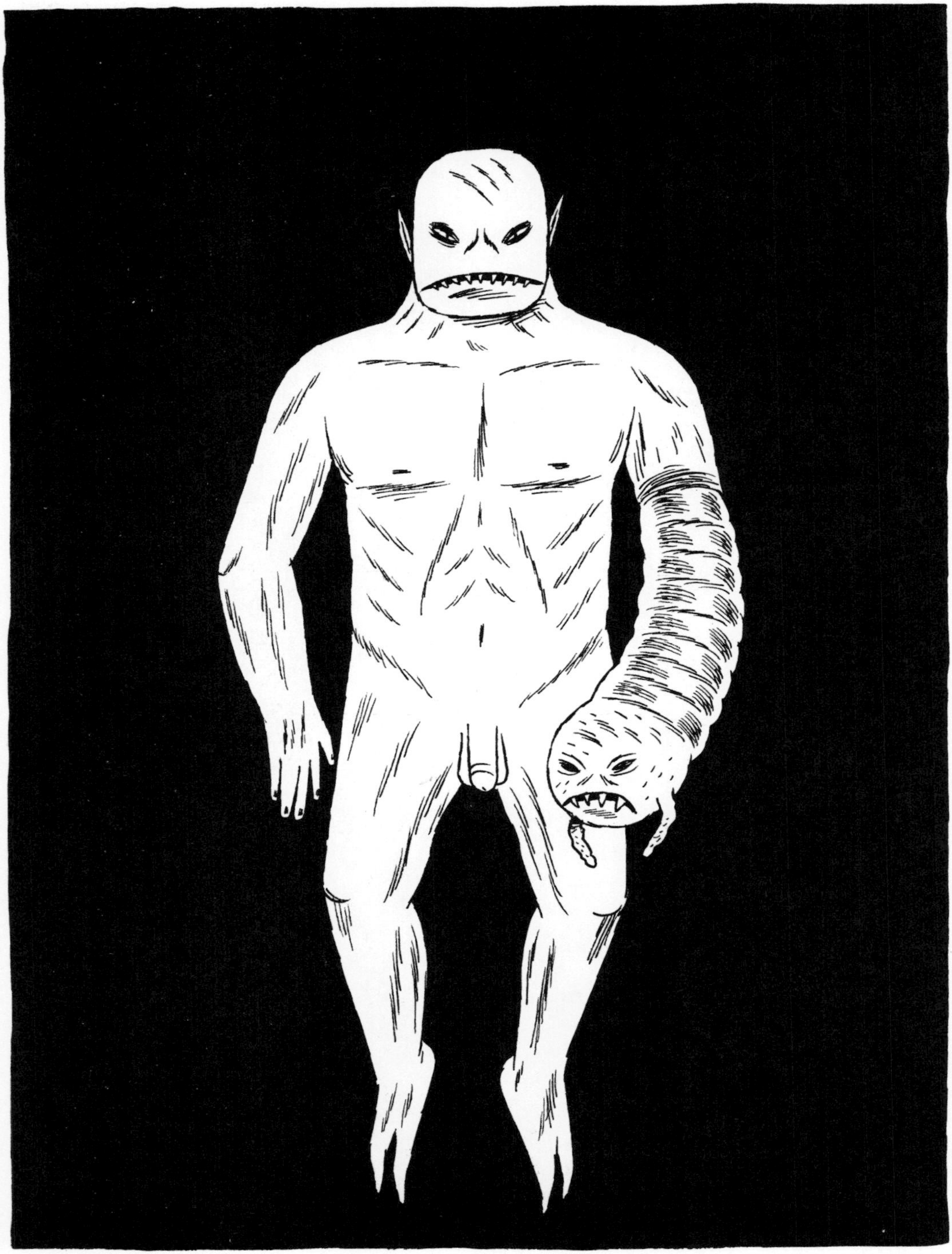

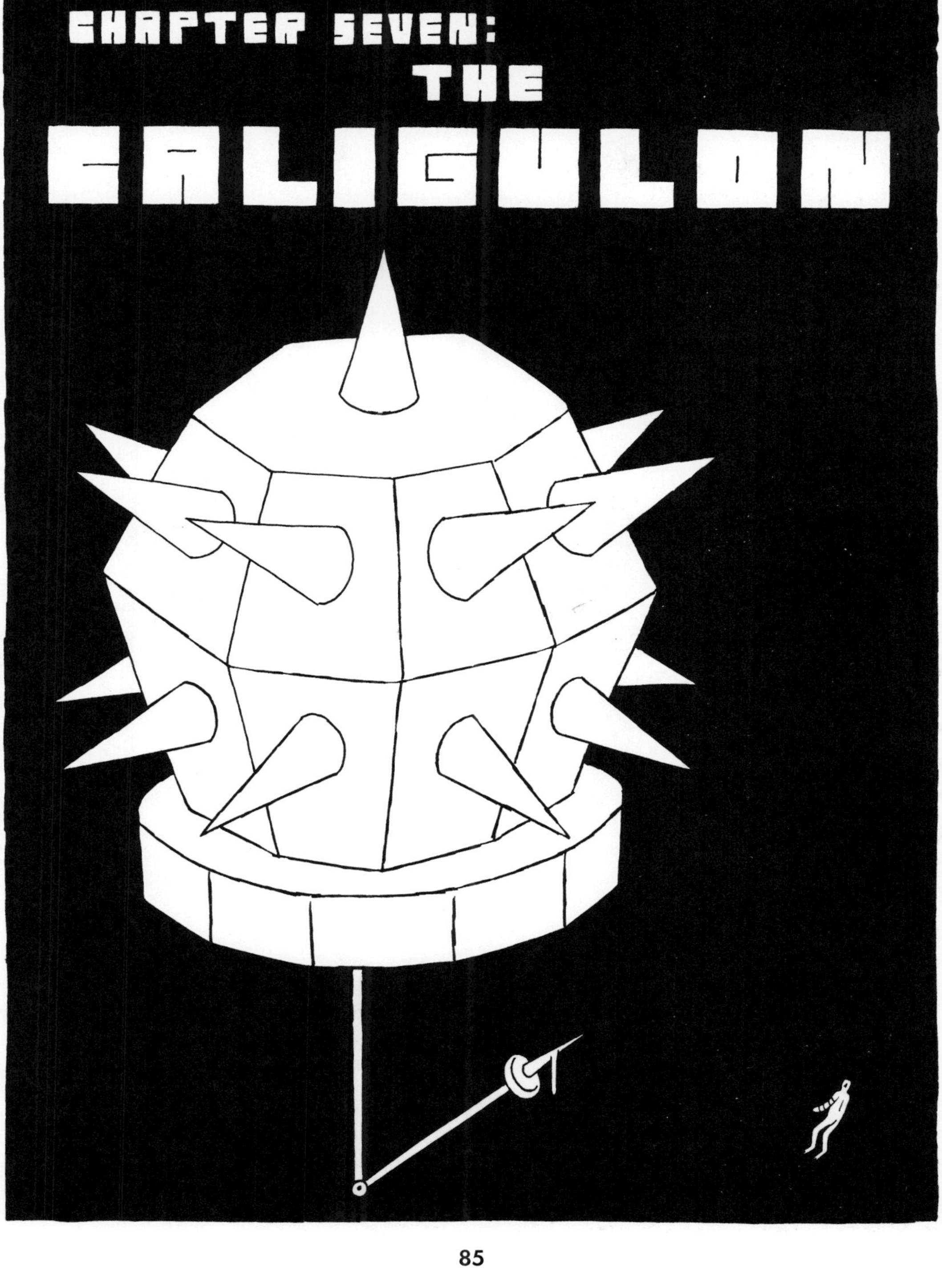
CHAPTER SEVEN:
THE
CALIGULON

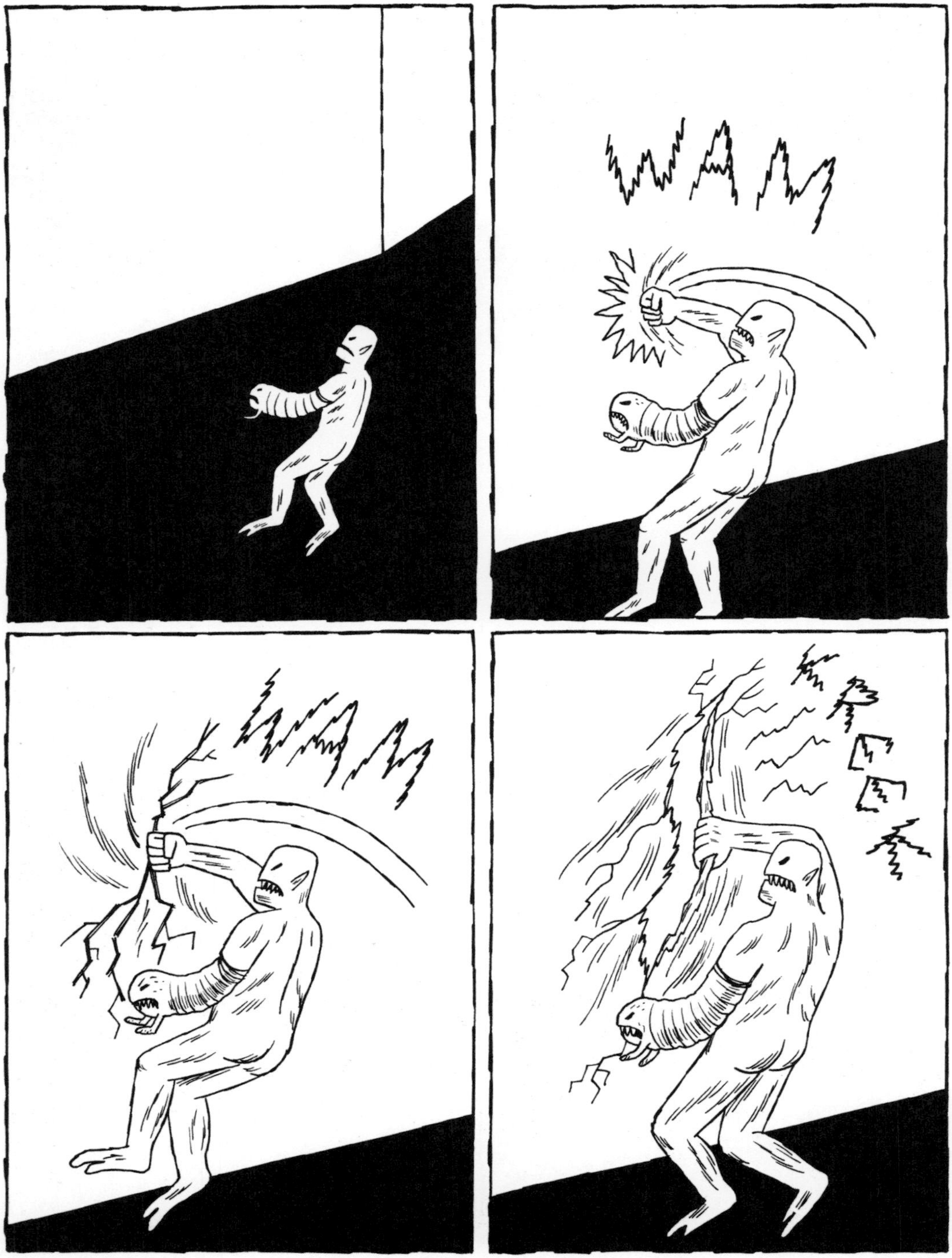
WAM

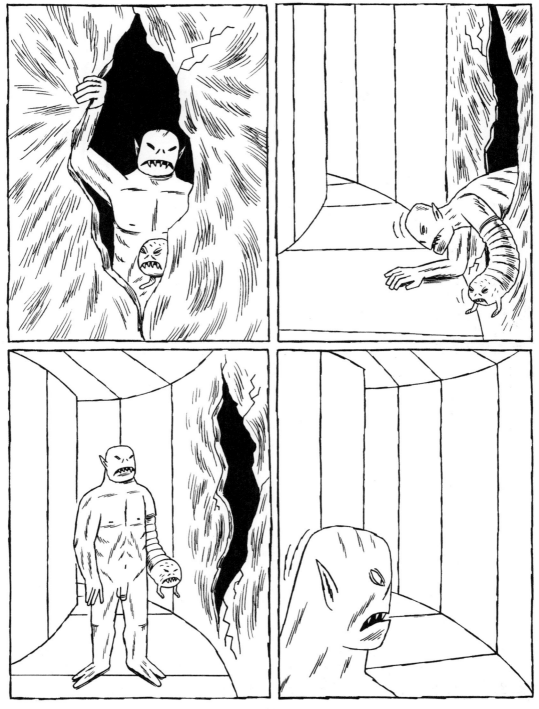

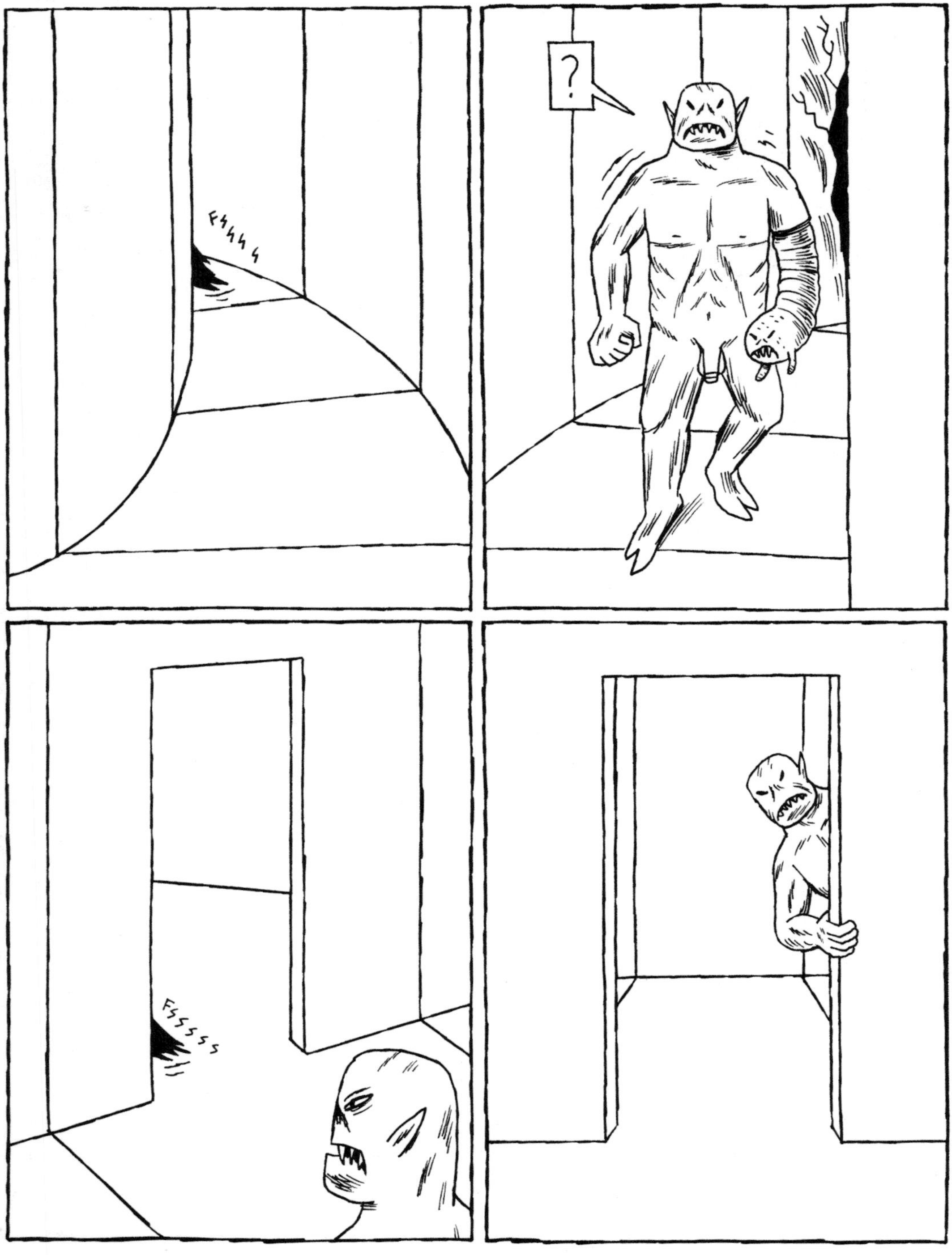
FSSSSS
?
FSSSSS

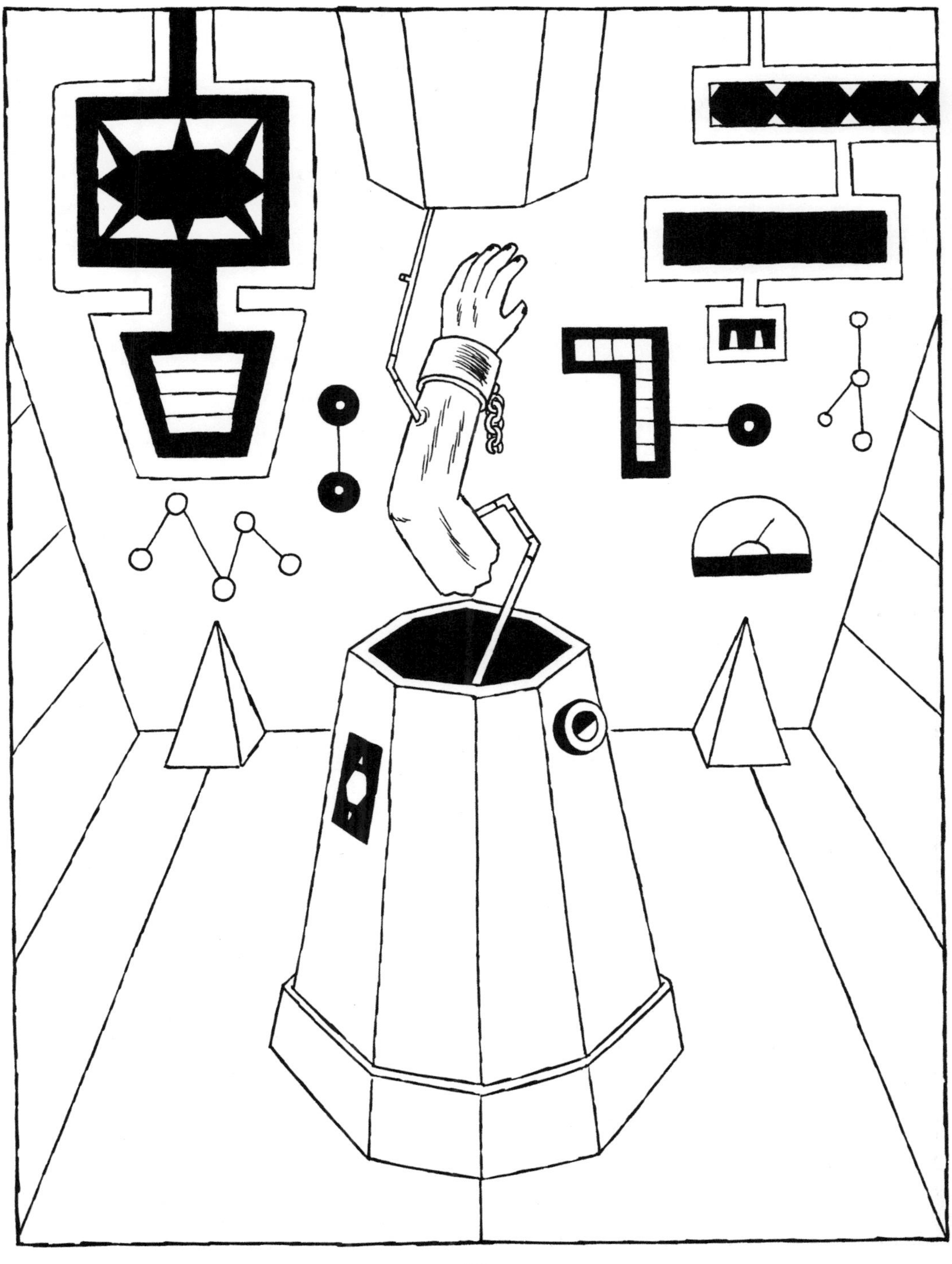

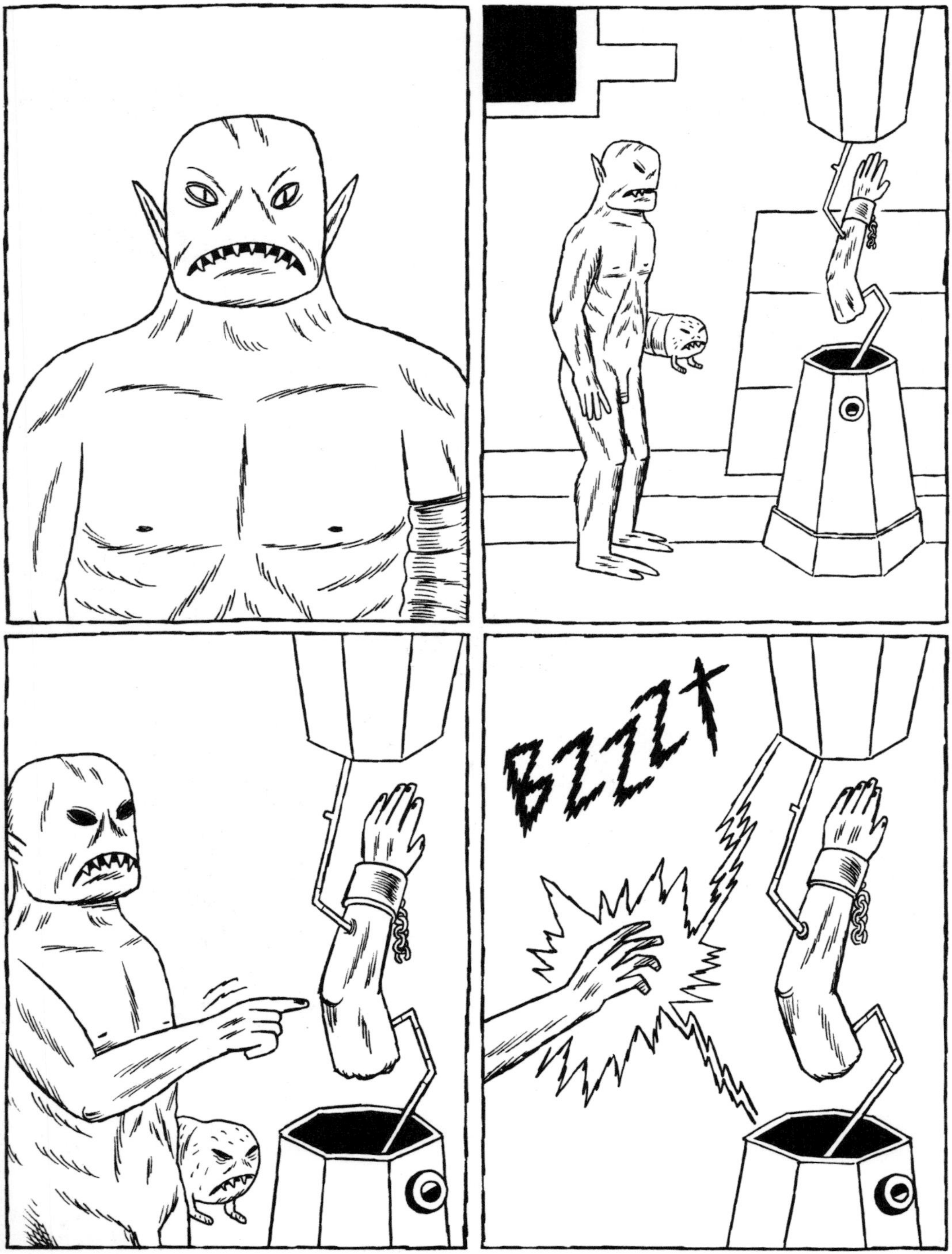
BZZZT

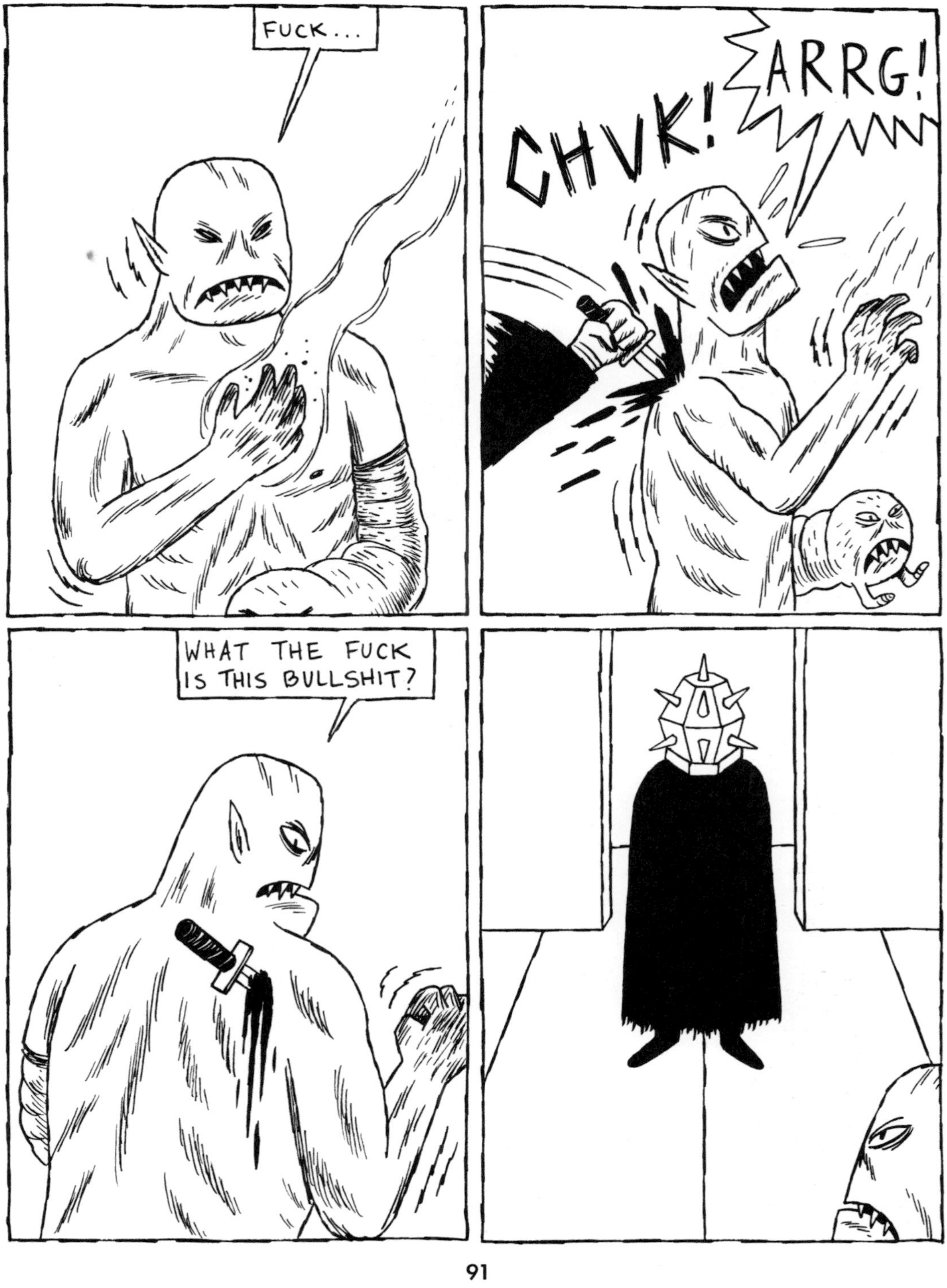
FUCK...
CHVK!
ARRG!
WHAT THE FUCK IS THIS BULLSHIT?

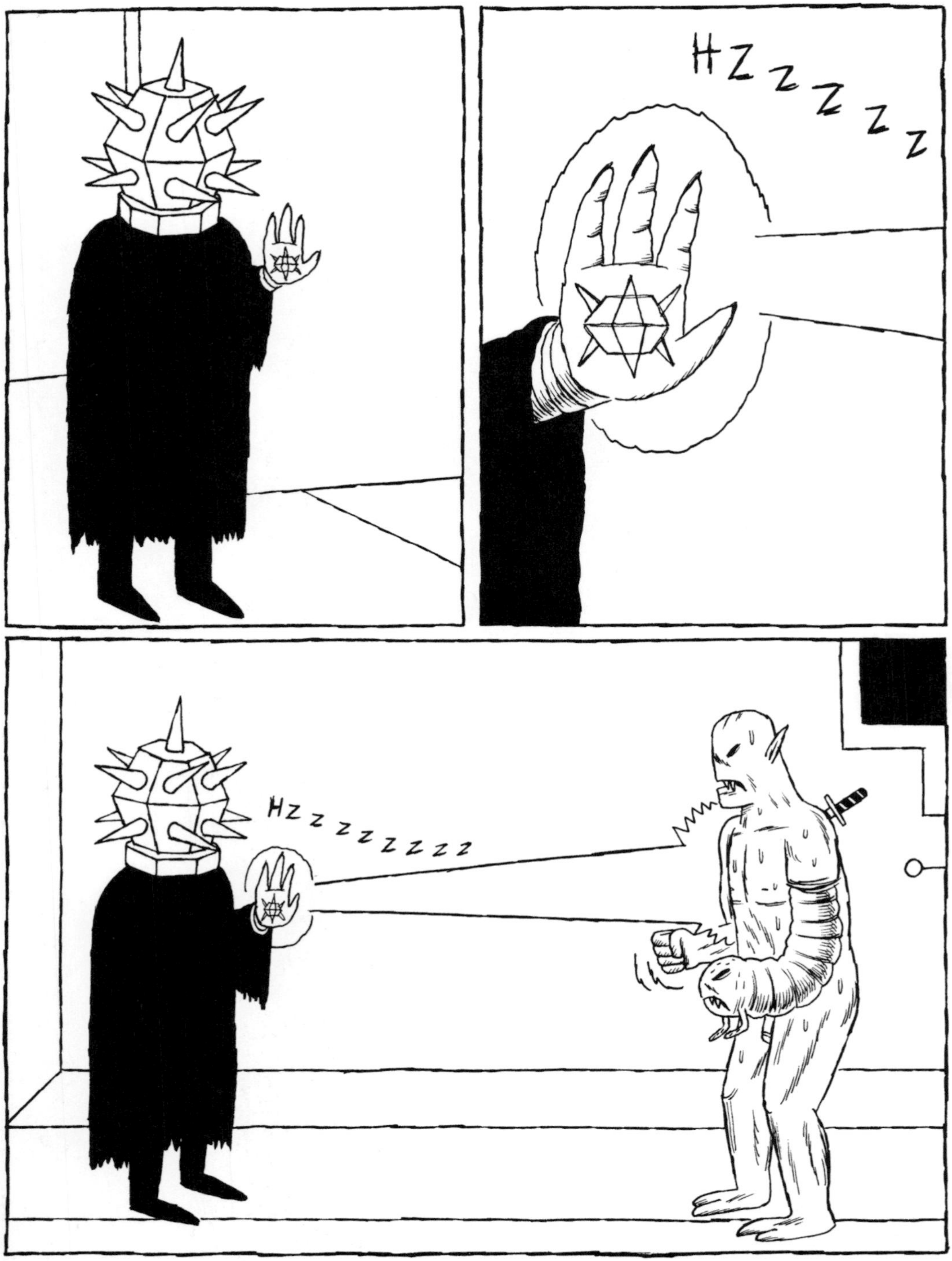
HZZZZZZ
HZZZZZZZZZ

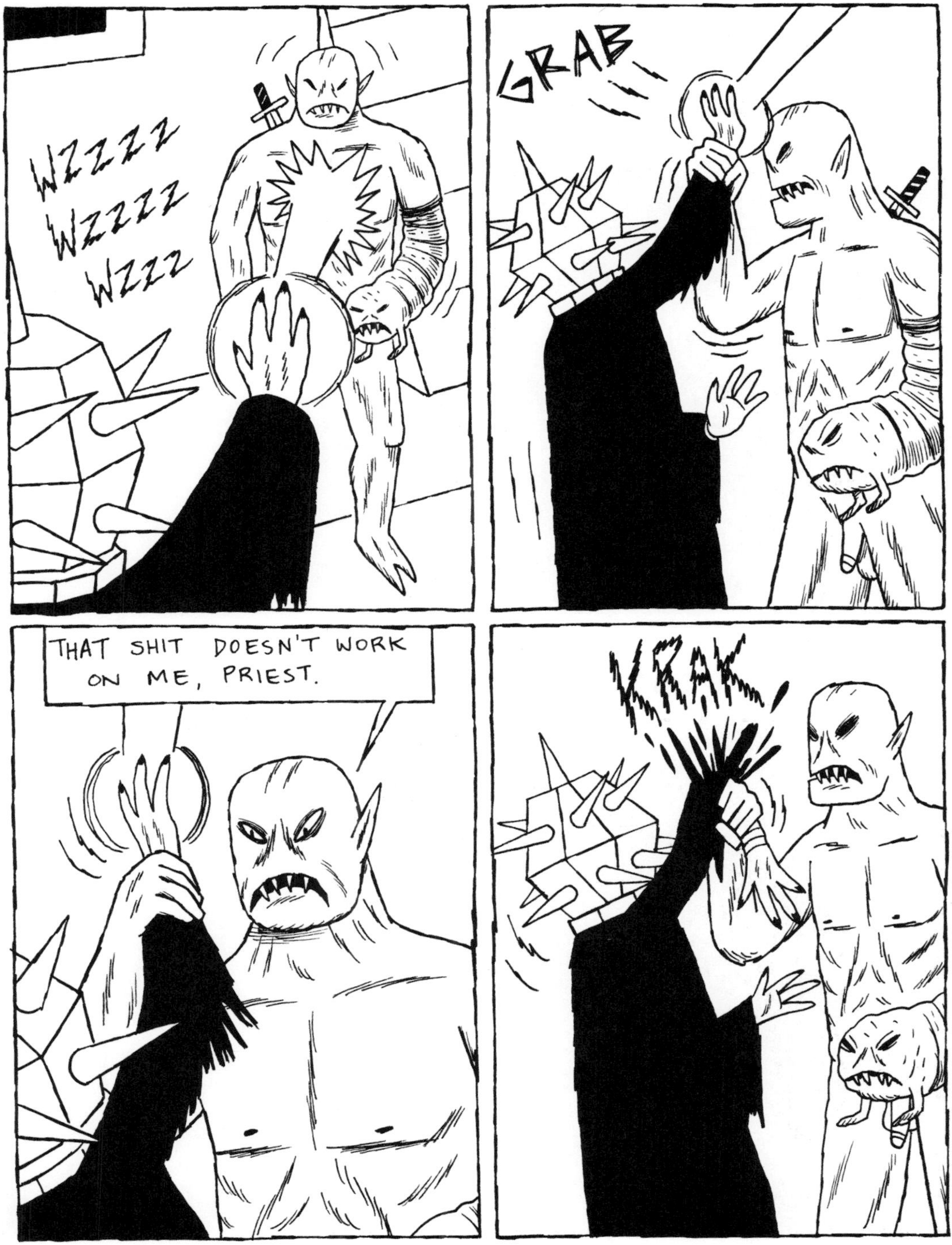
WZZZZZ
WZZZZZ
WZZZZ
GRAB
THAT SHIT DOESN'T WORK ON ME, PRIEST.
KRAK!

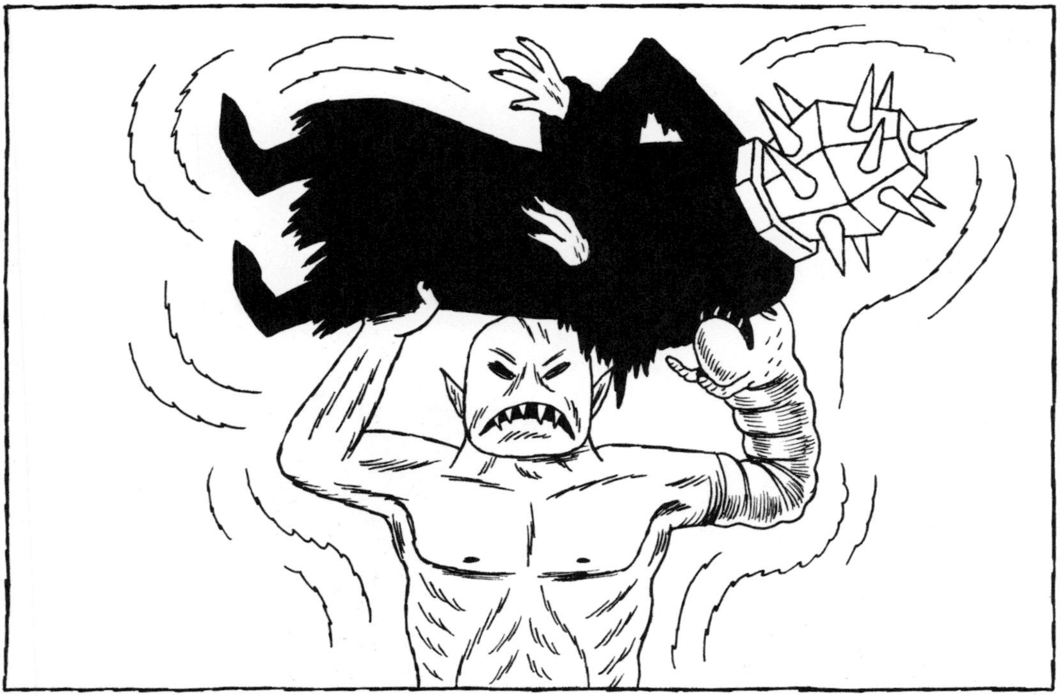

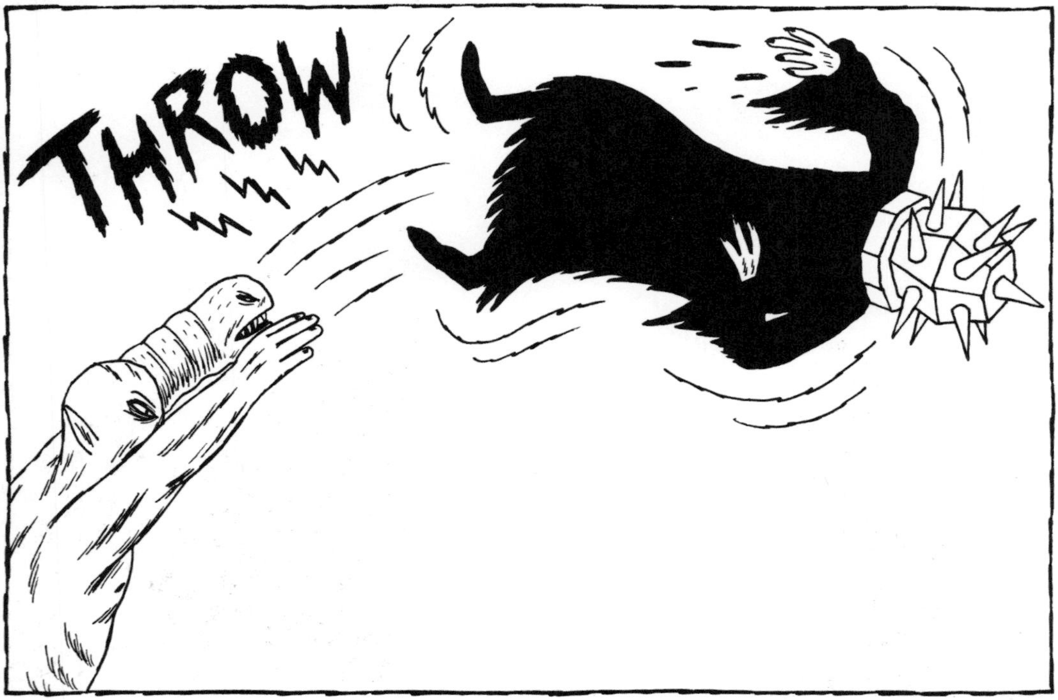
THROW

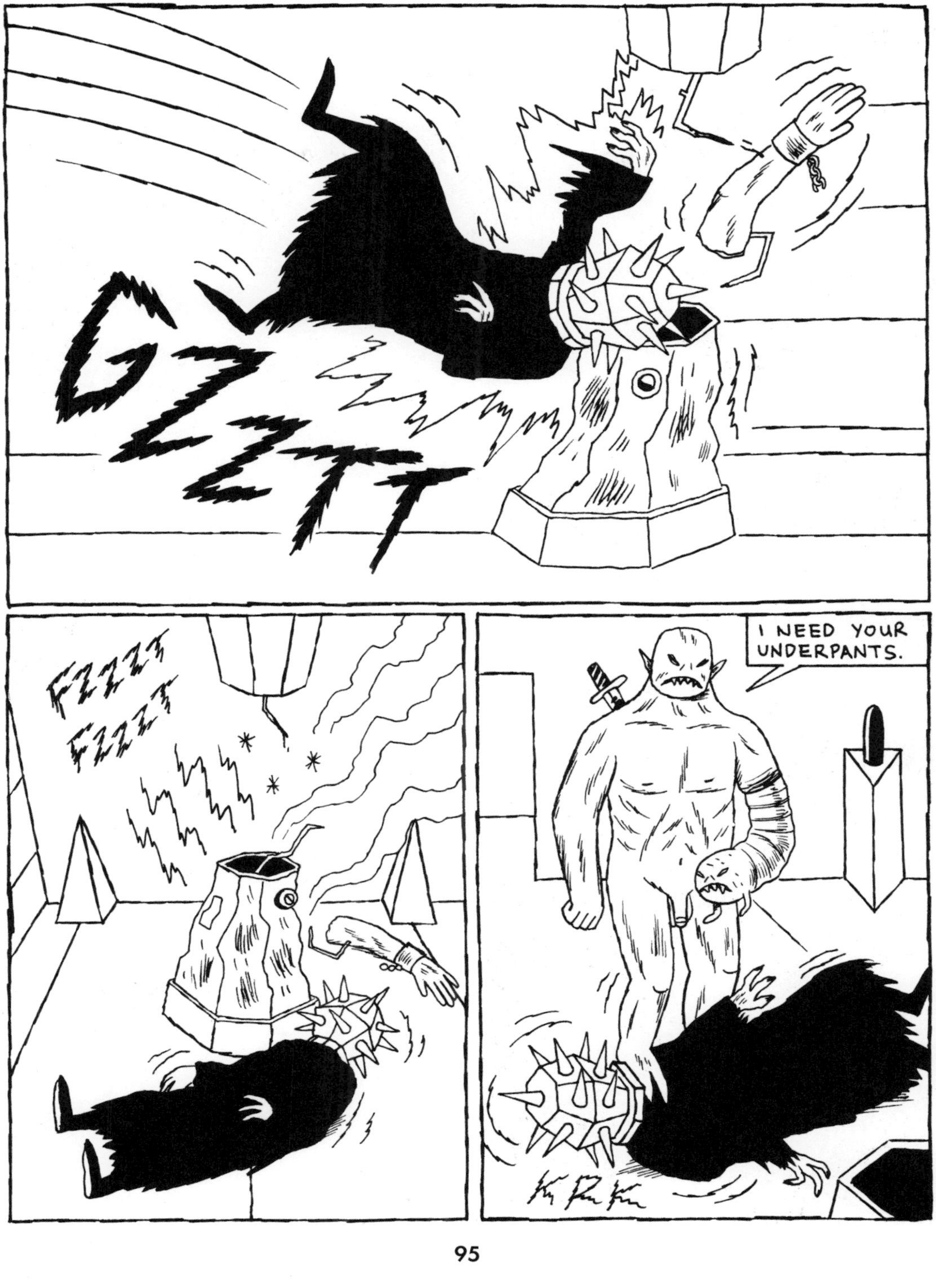
GZZTT
FZZZT
FZZZT
I NEED YOUR UNDERPANTS.

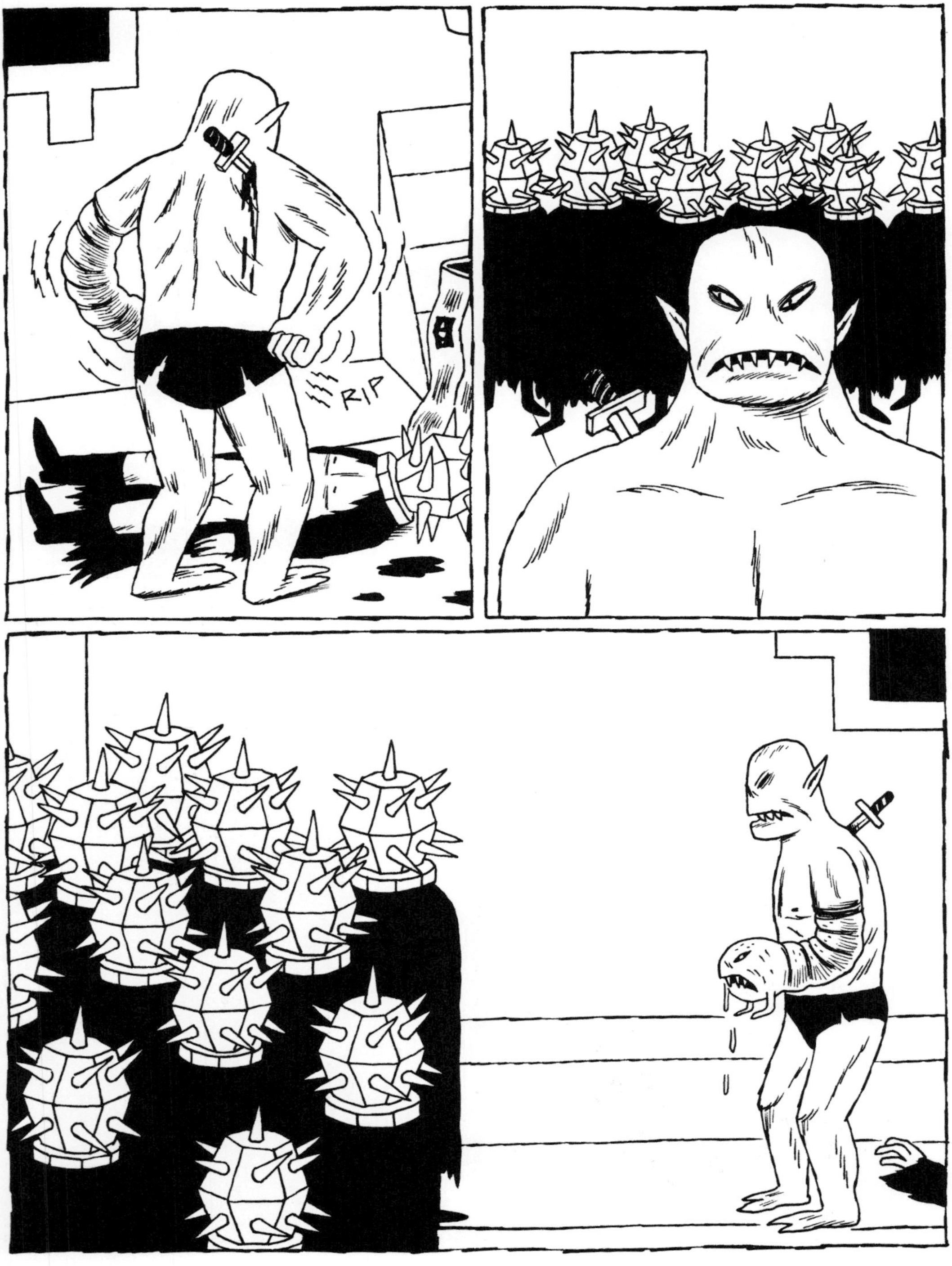
RIP

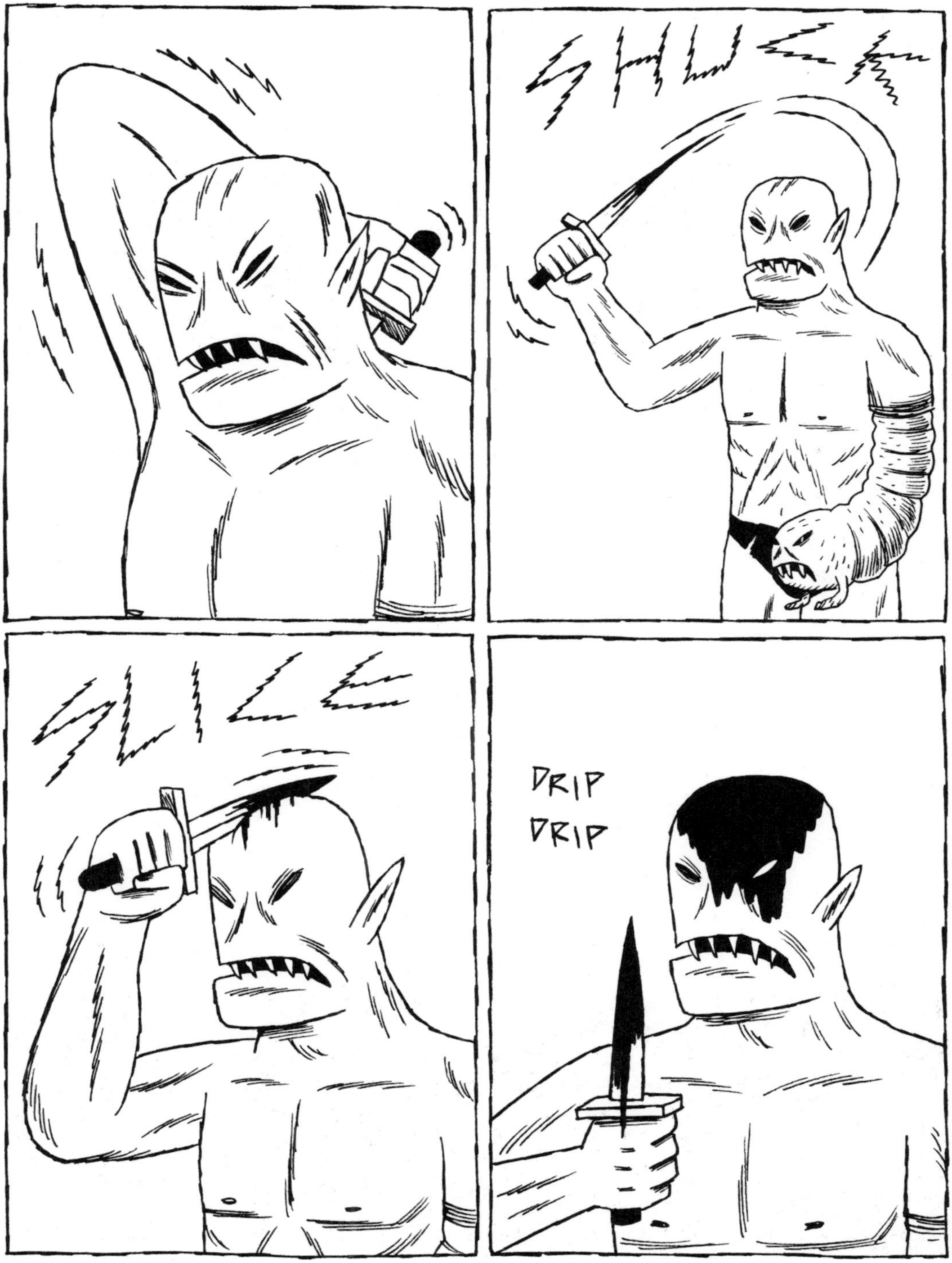
SLICE
DRIP
DRIP

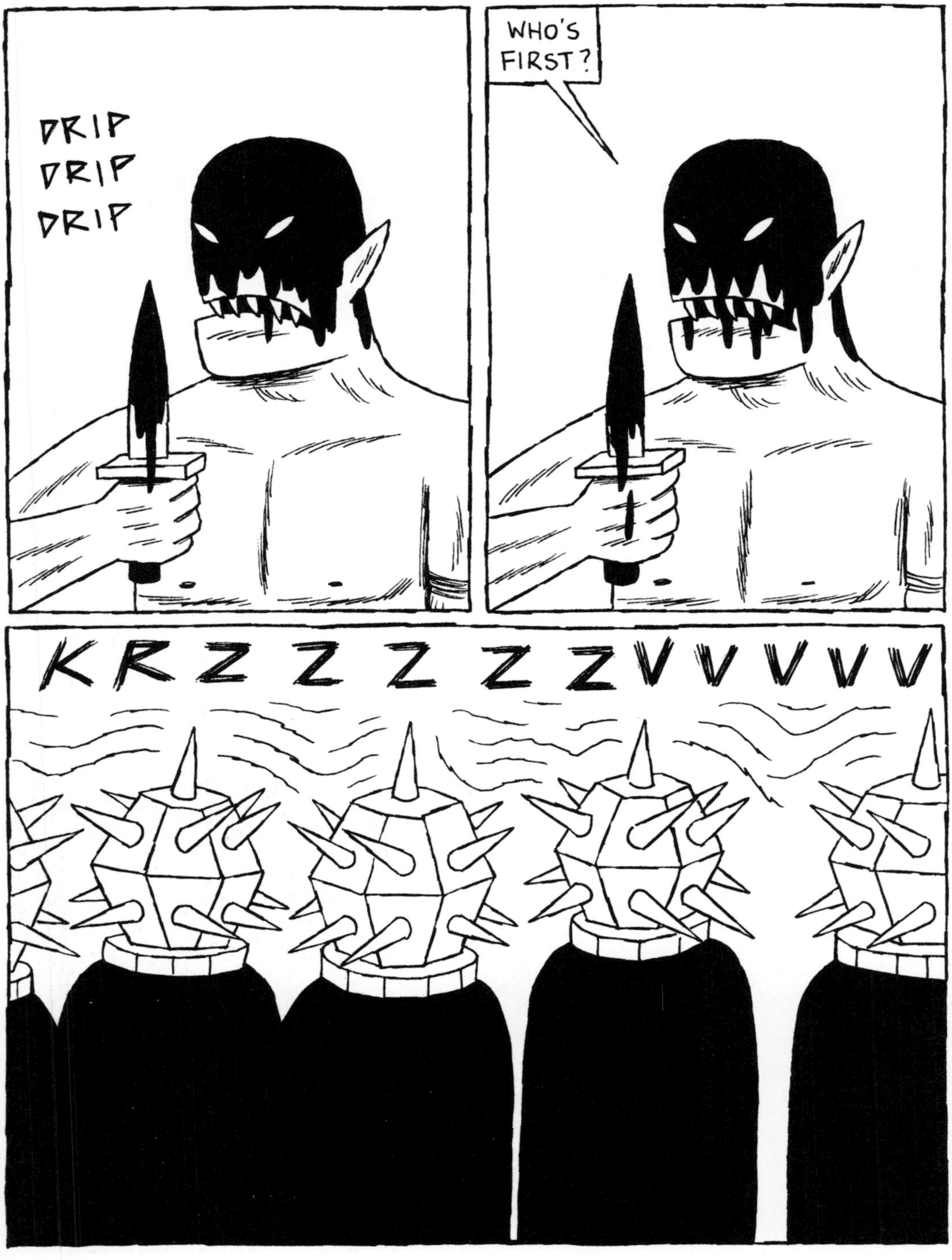
DRIP
DRIP
DRIP
WHO'S FIRST?
KRZZZZZVVVVV

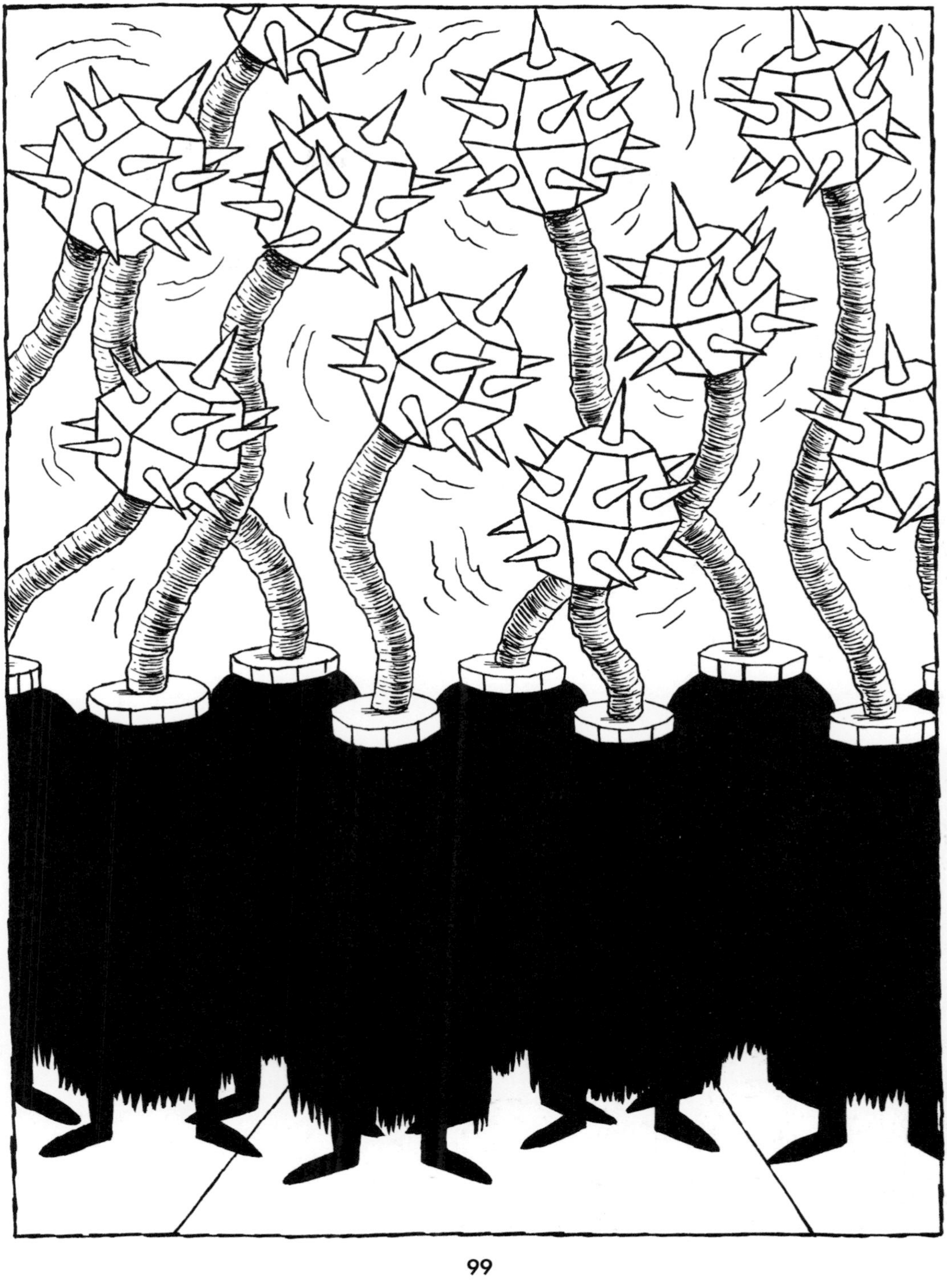

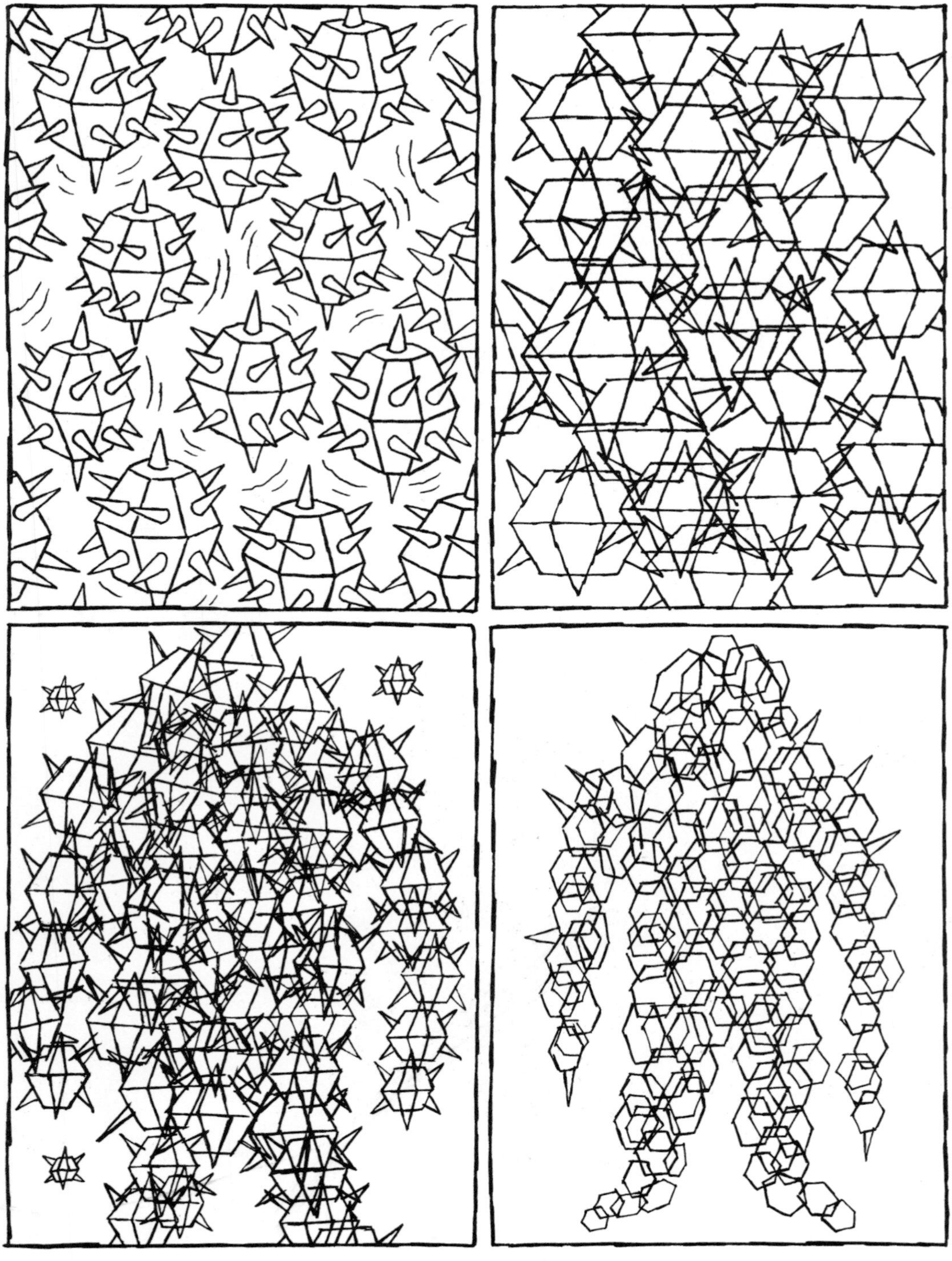

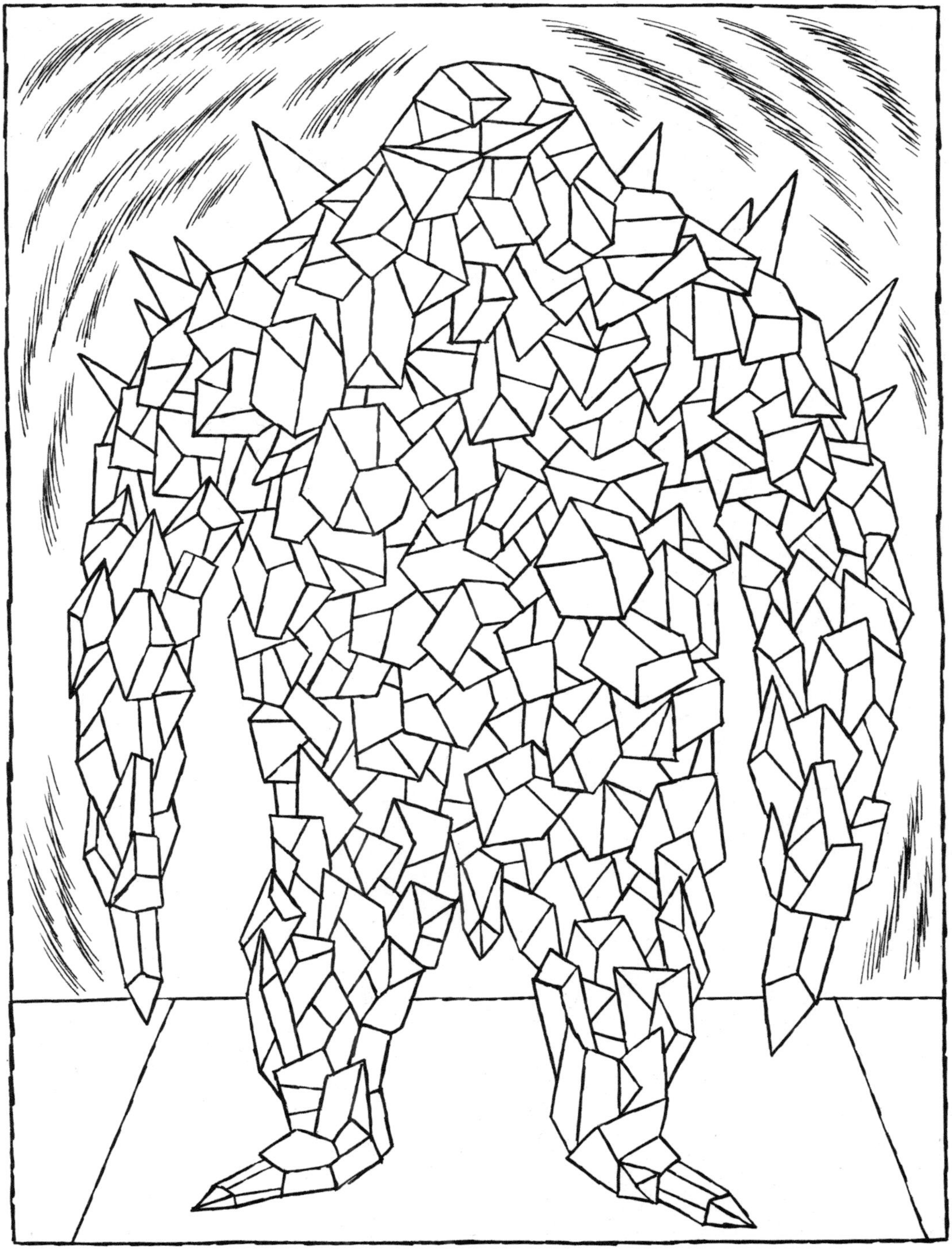

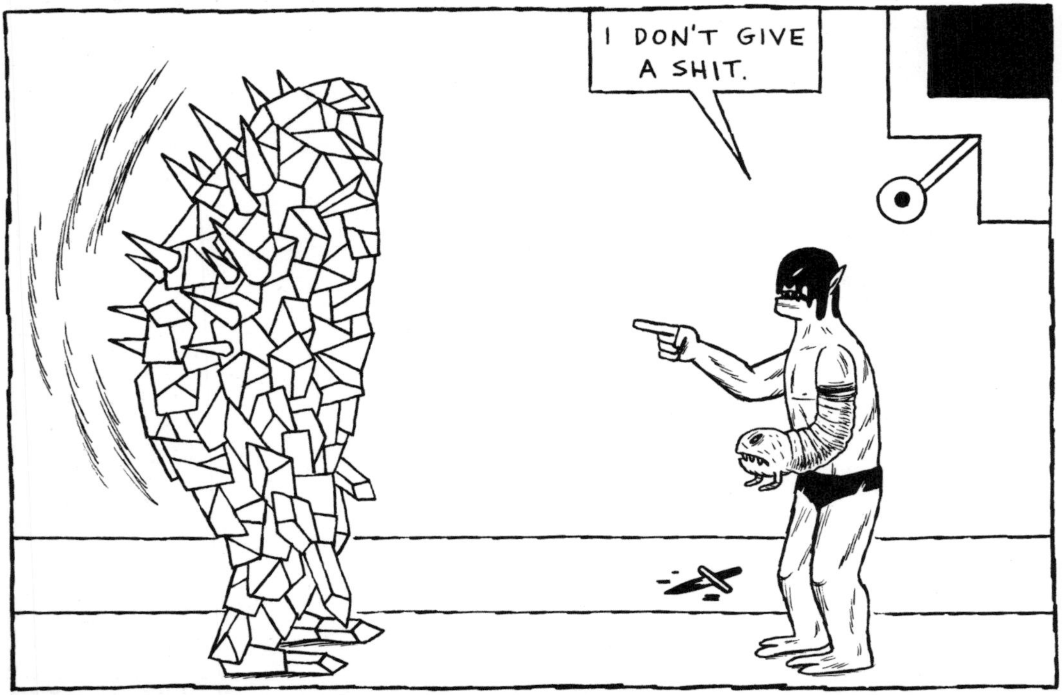
I DON'T GIVE A SHIT.

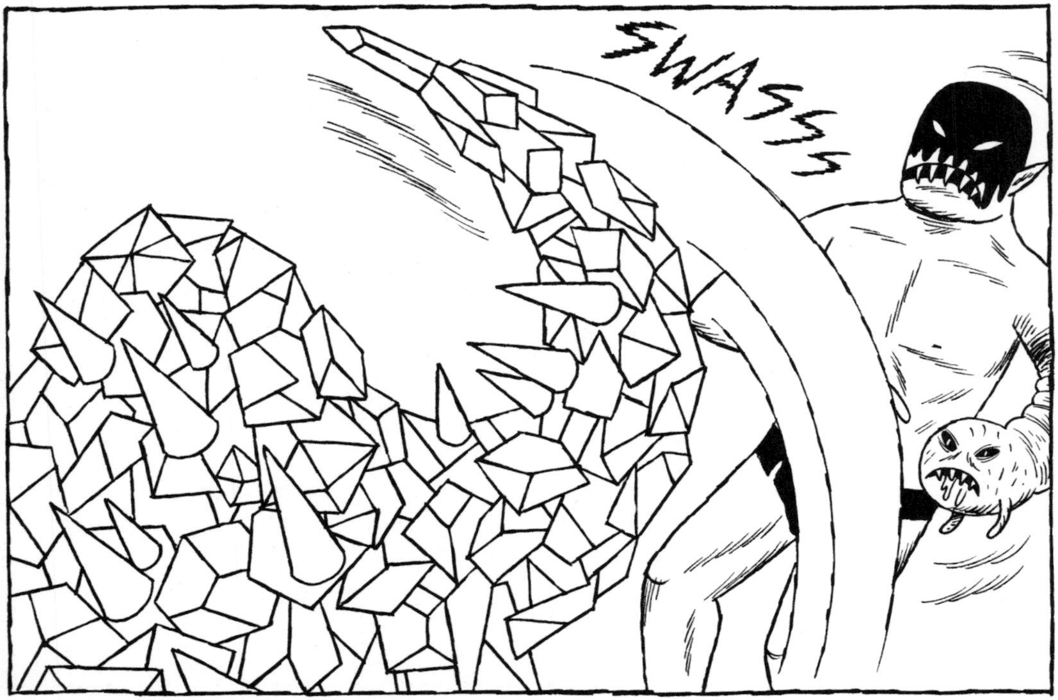
SWASSS

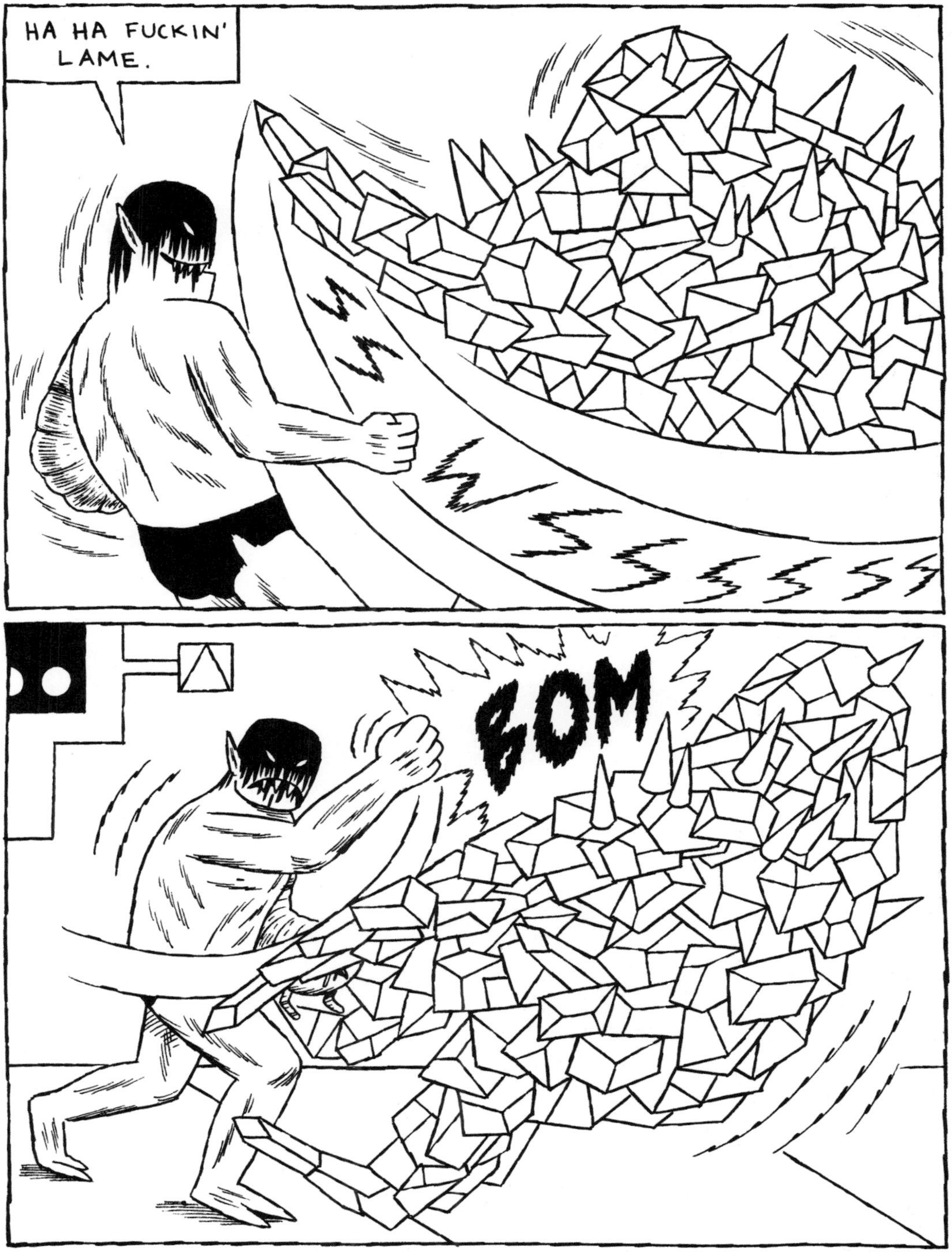
HA HA FUCKIN' LAME.
BOM

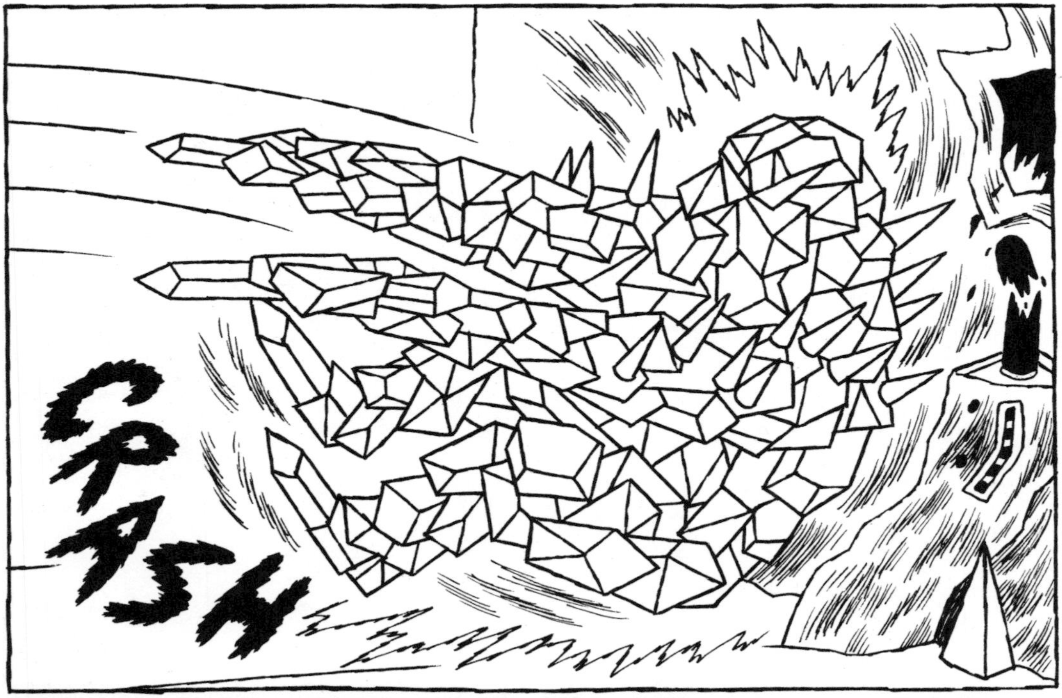
CRASH

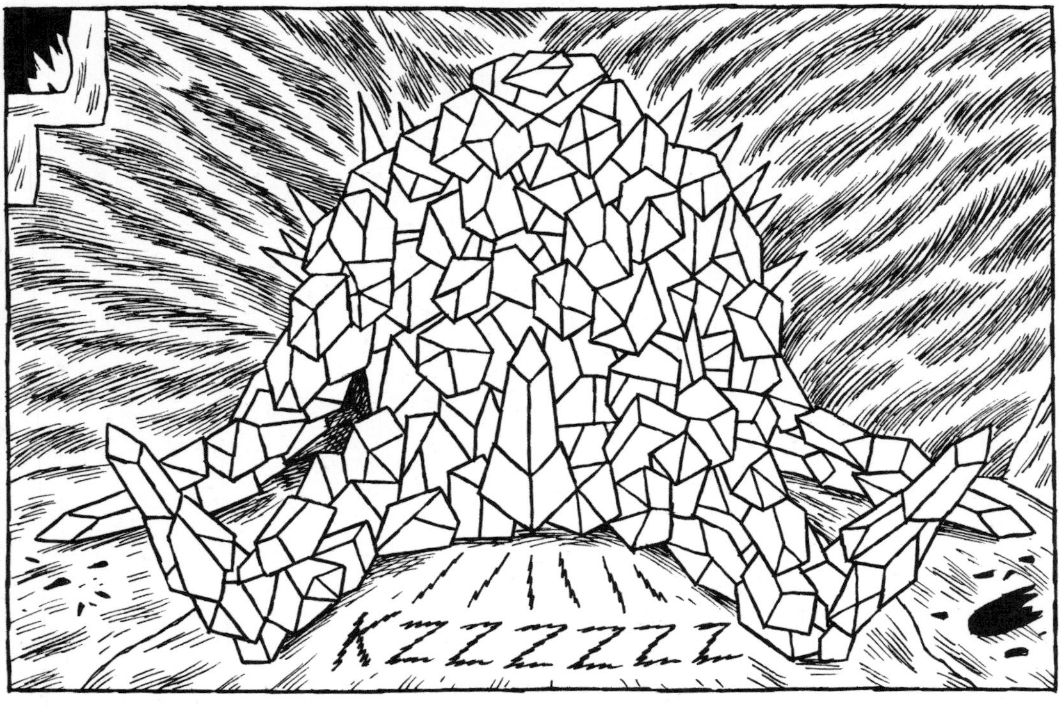
KZZZZZZ

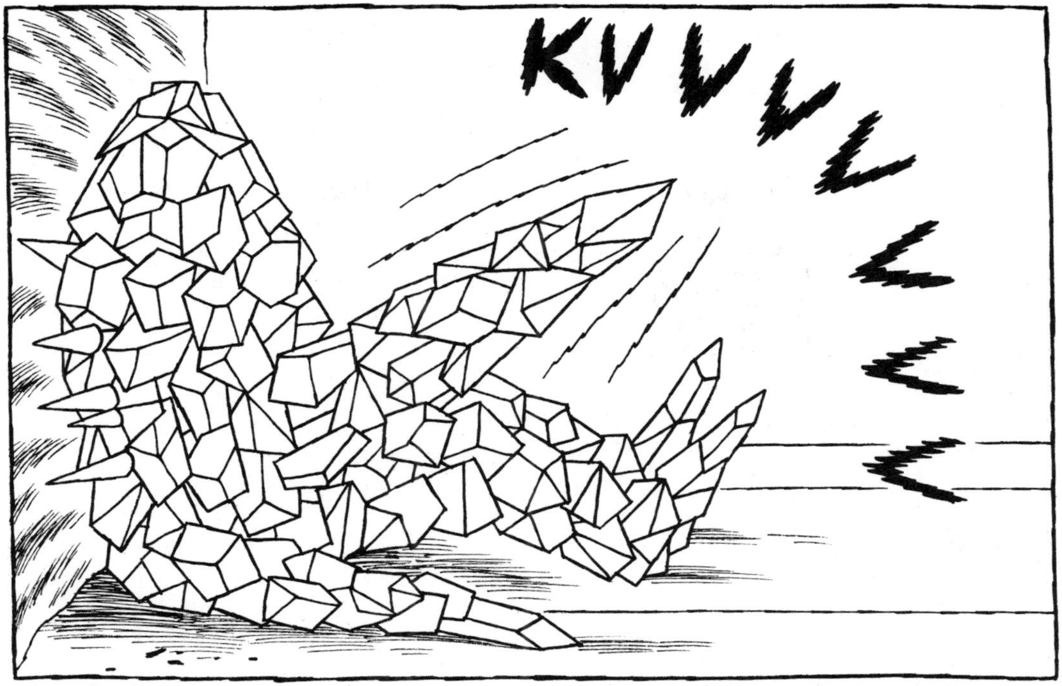
KVVVVVVVVV

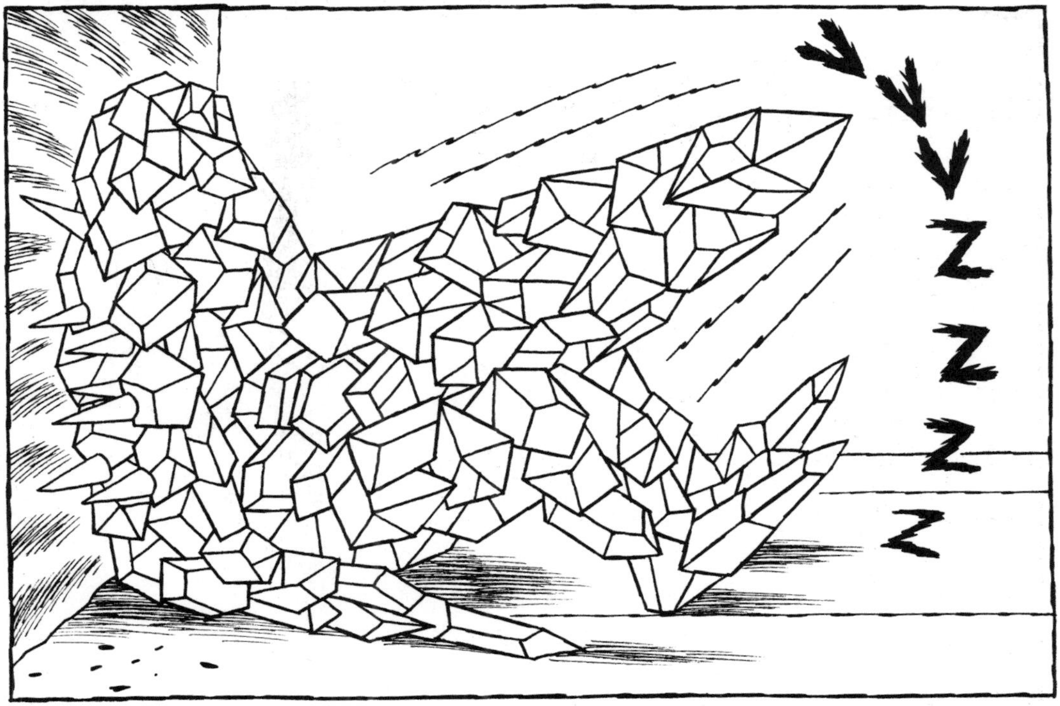
VVVZZZZ

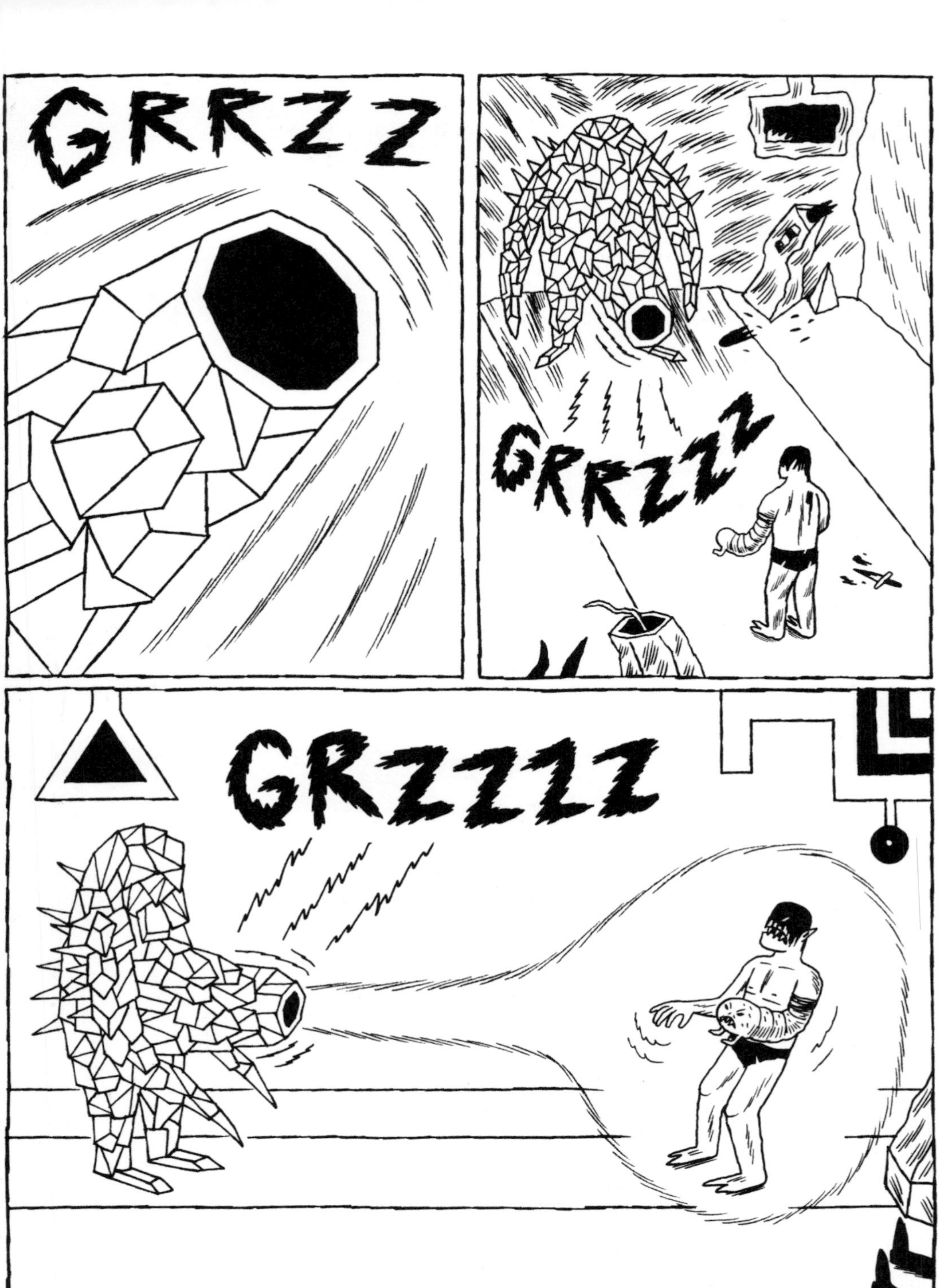
GRRZZZ
GRRZZZ
GRZZZZZ

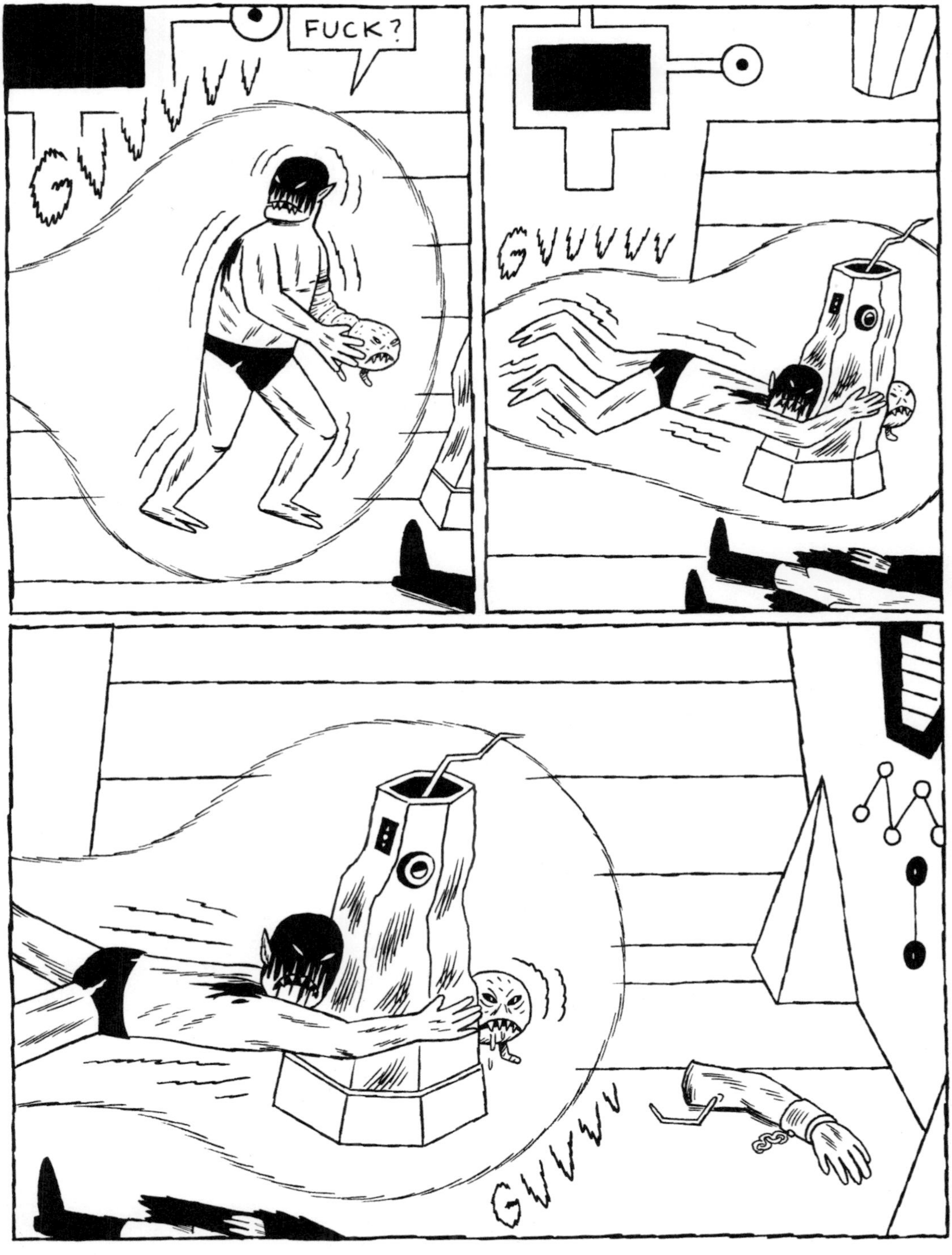
GUUUUV
FUCK?
GUUUUV
GUUUV

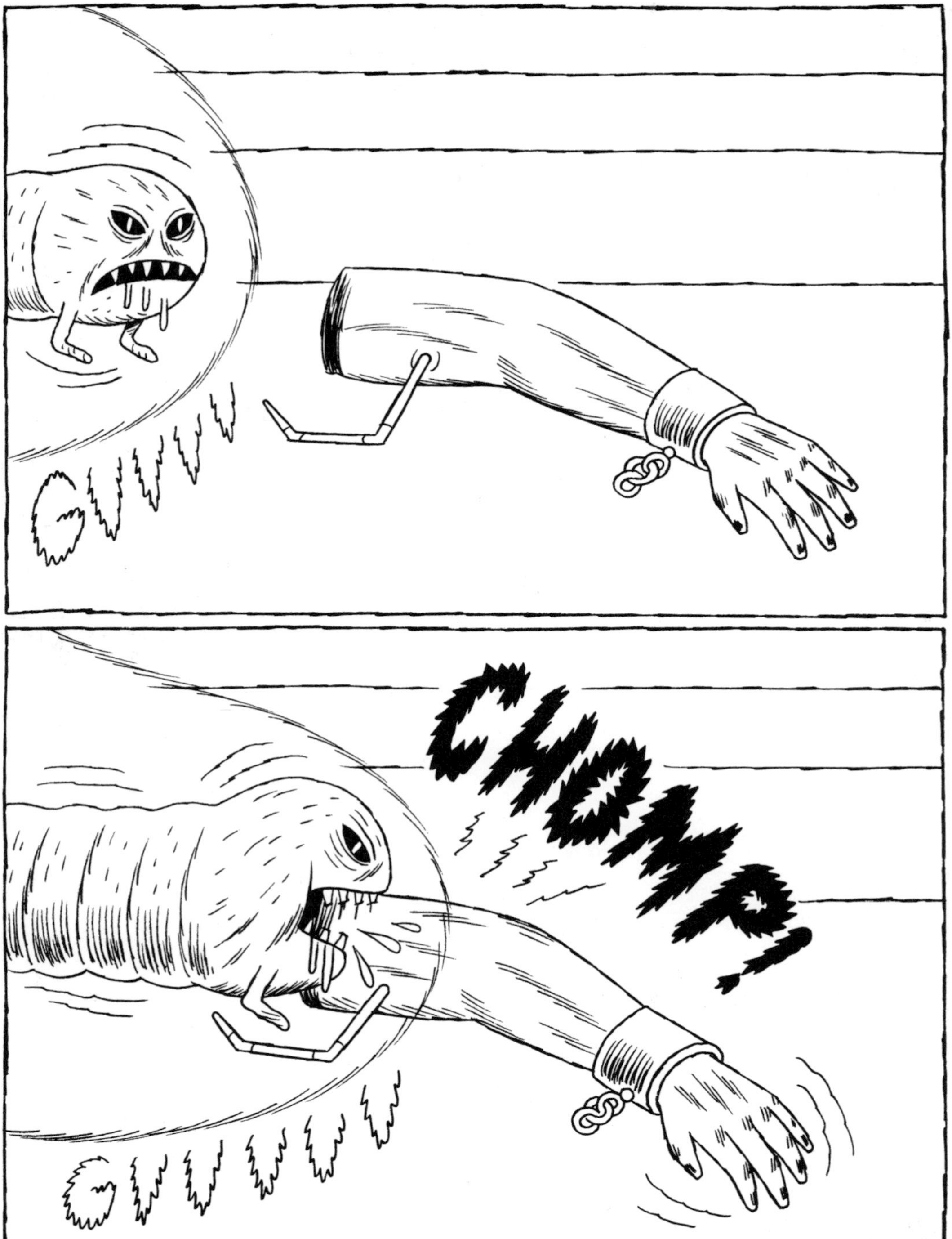
GUUUU
CHOMP!
GUUUUU

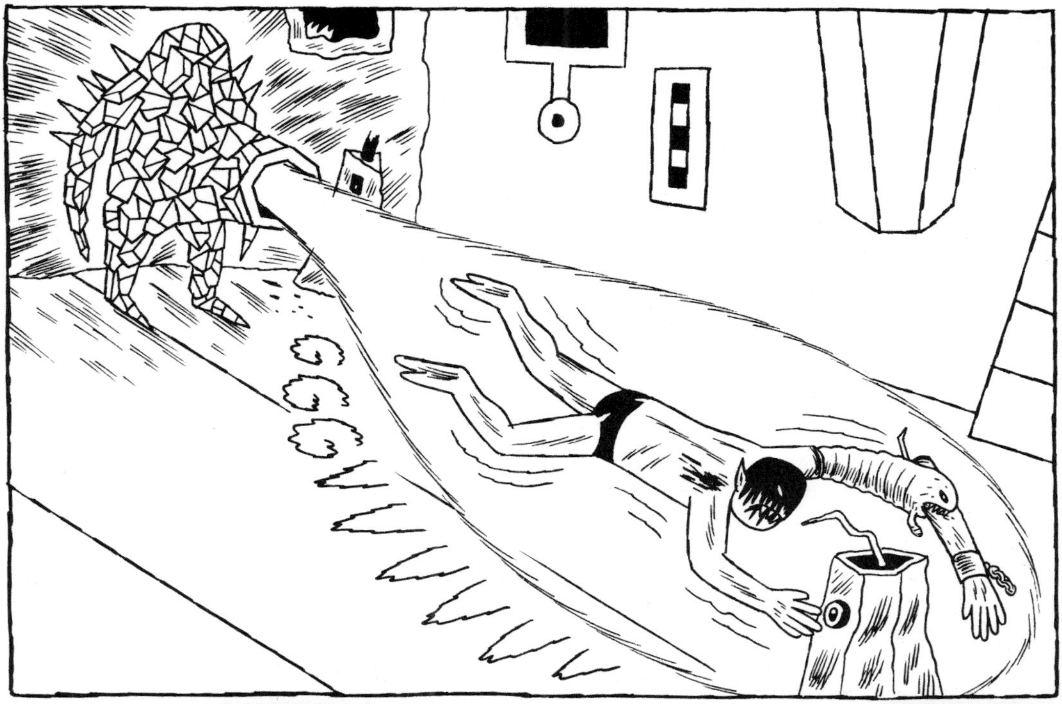

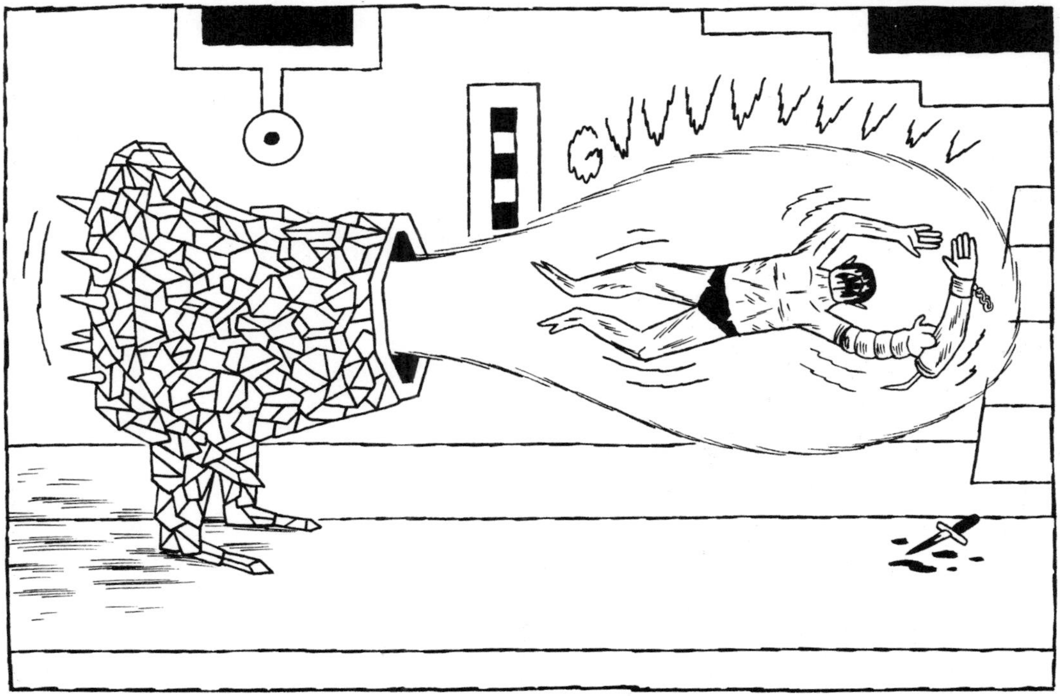

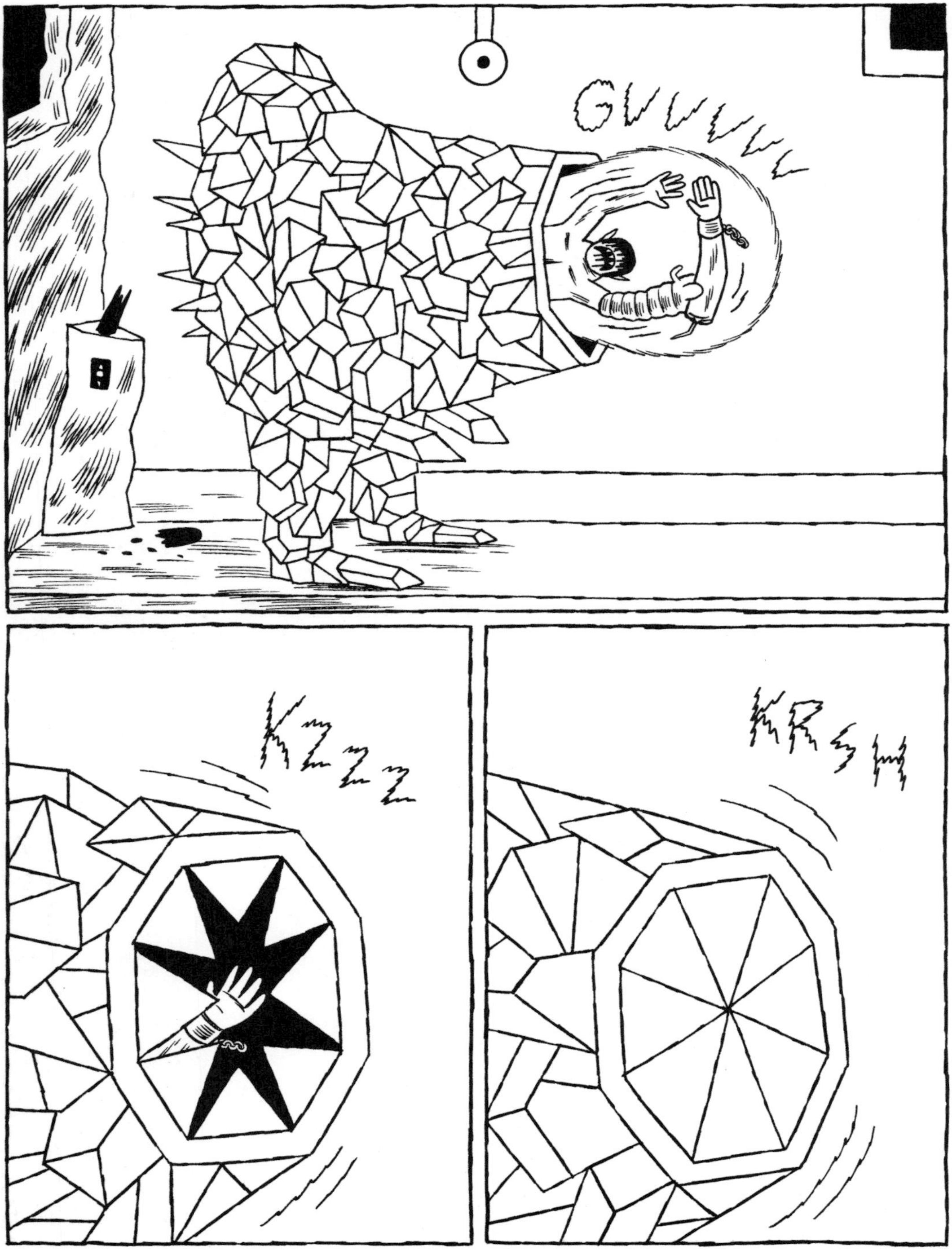
GVUUUUU
KZZZ
KRSH

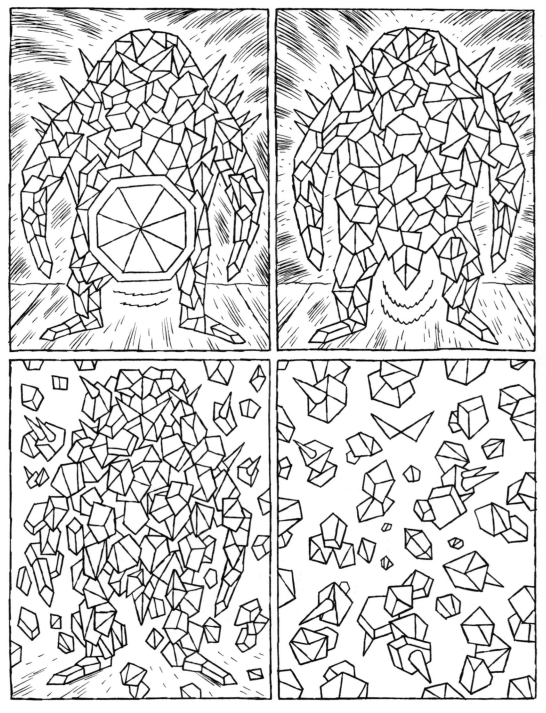

111

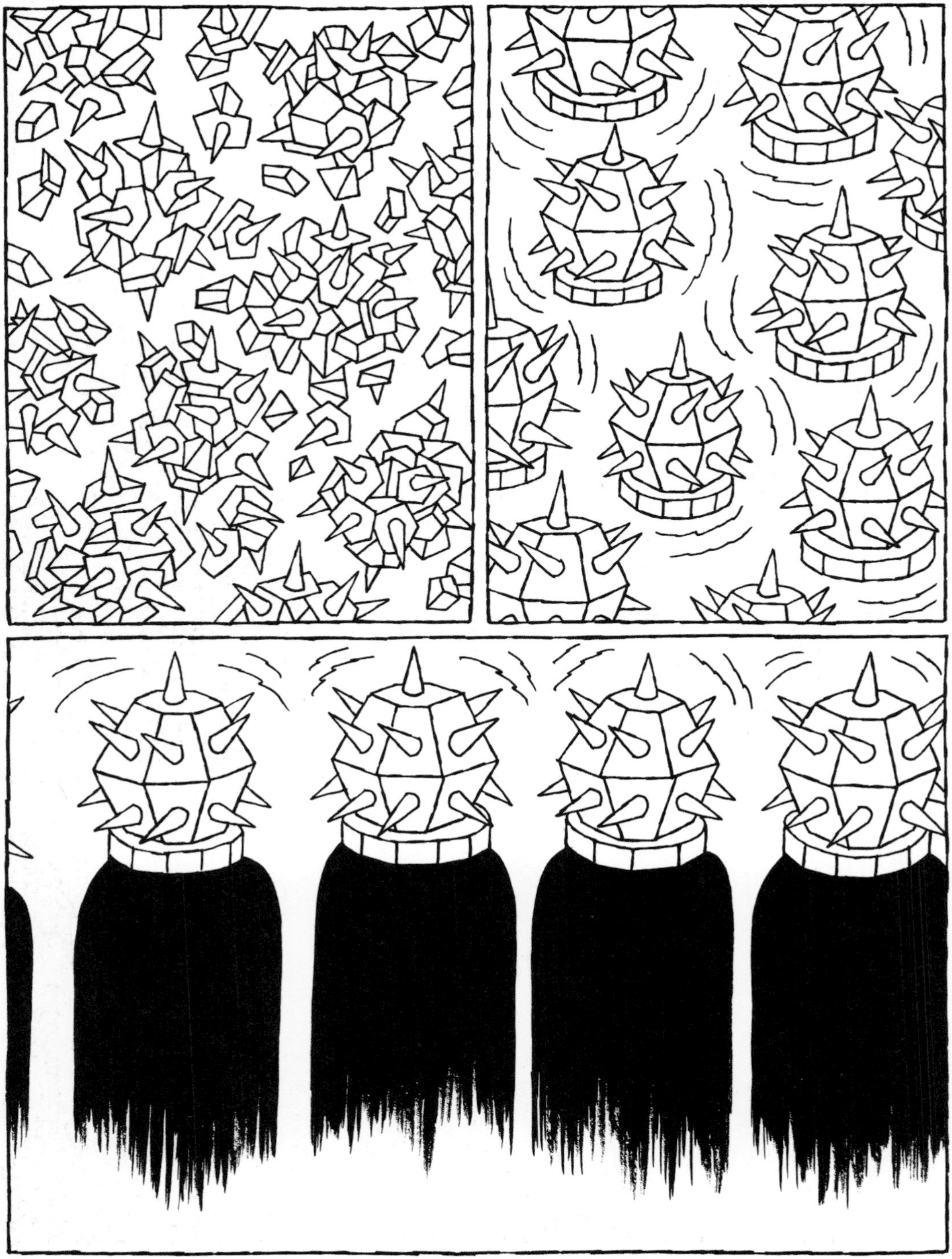

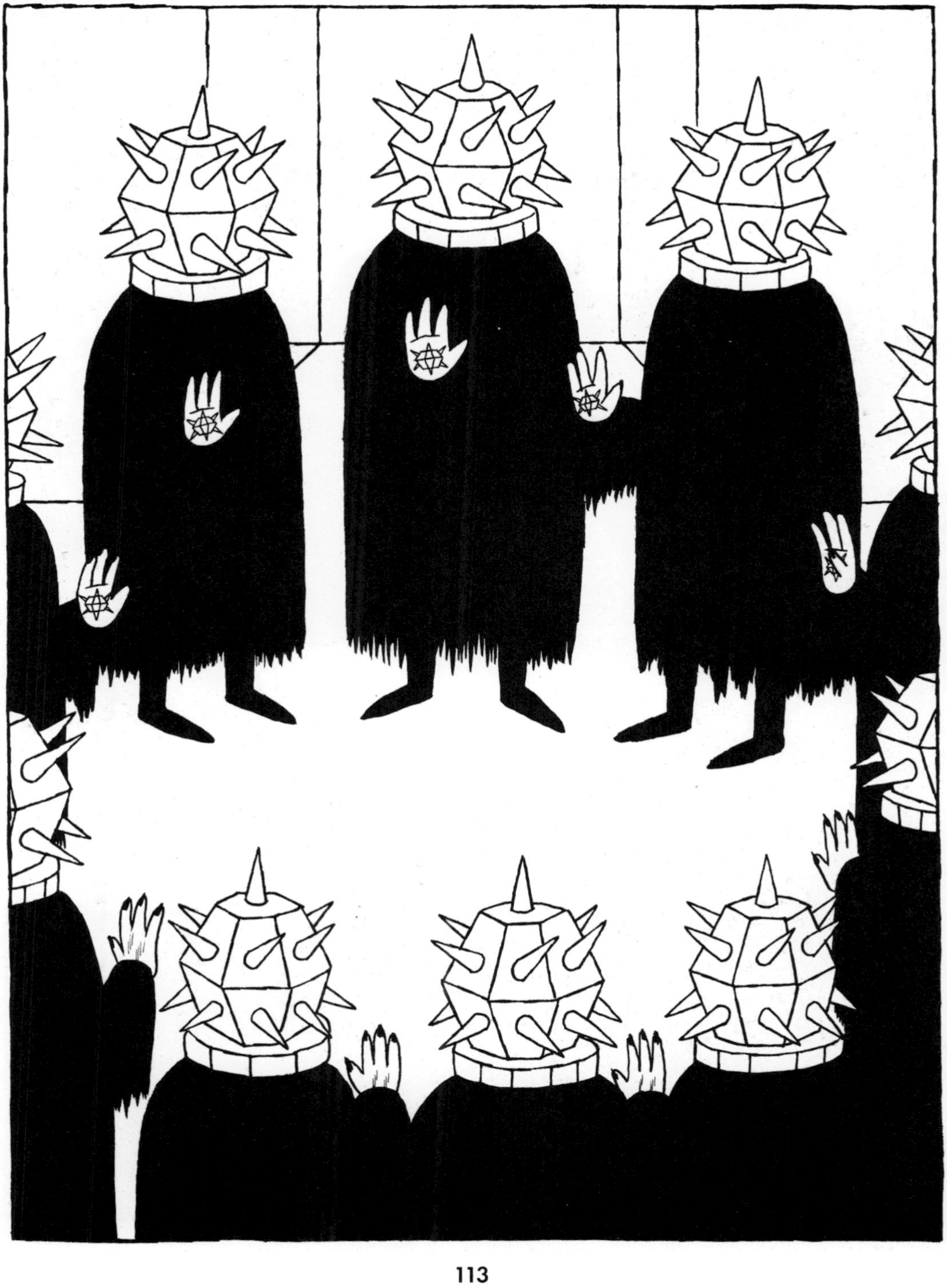

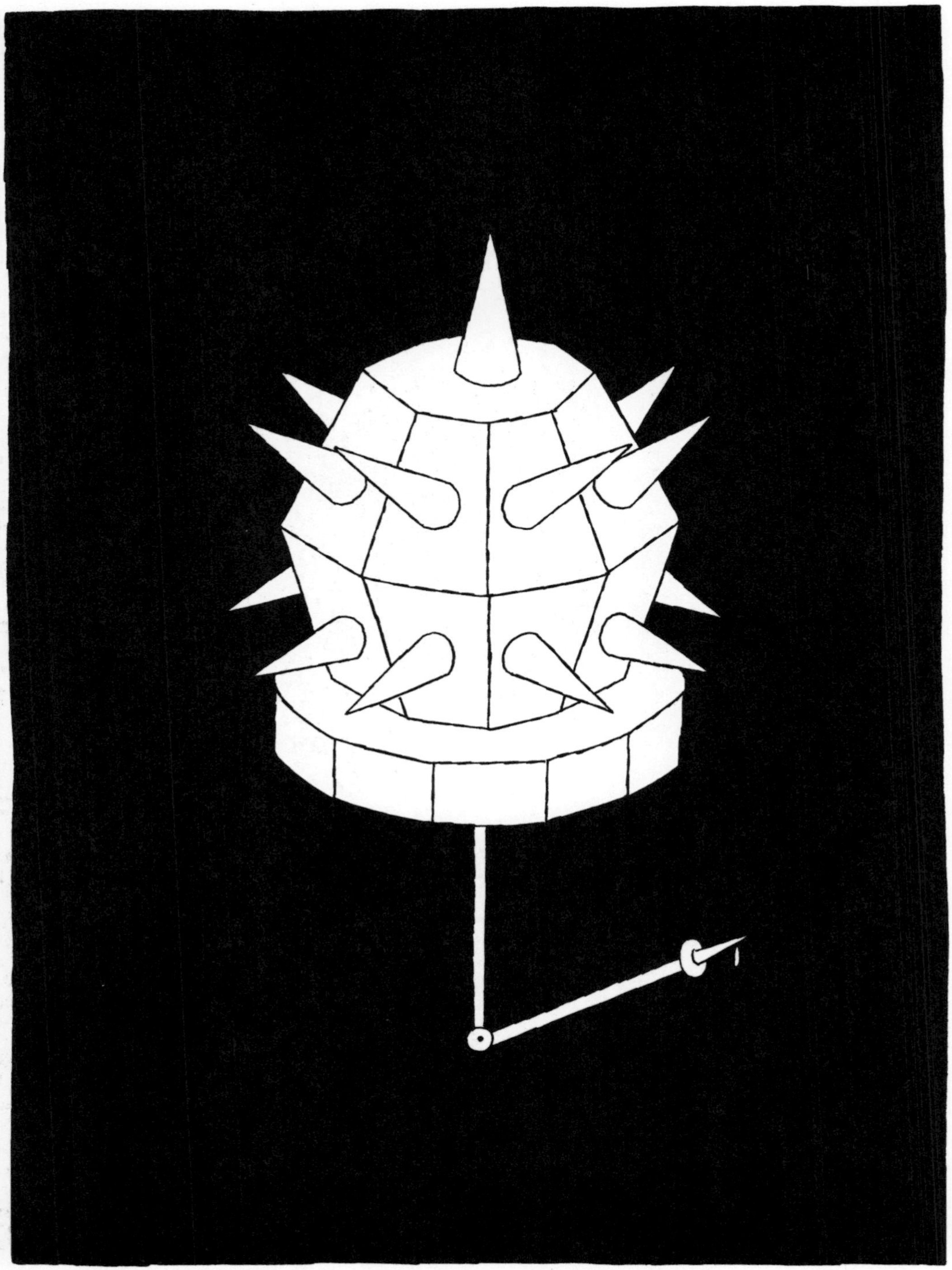

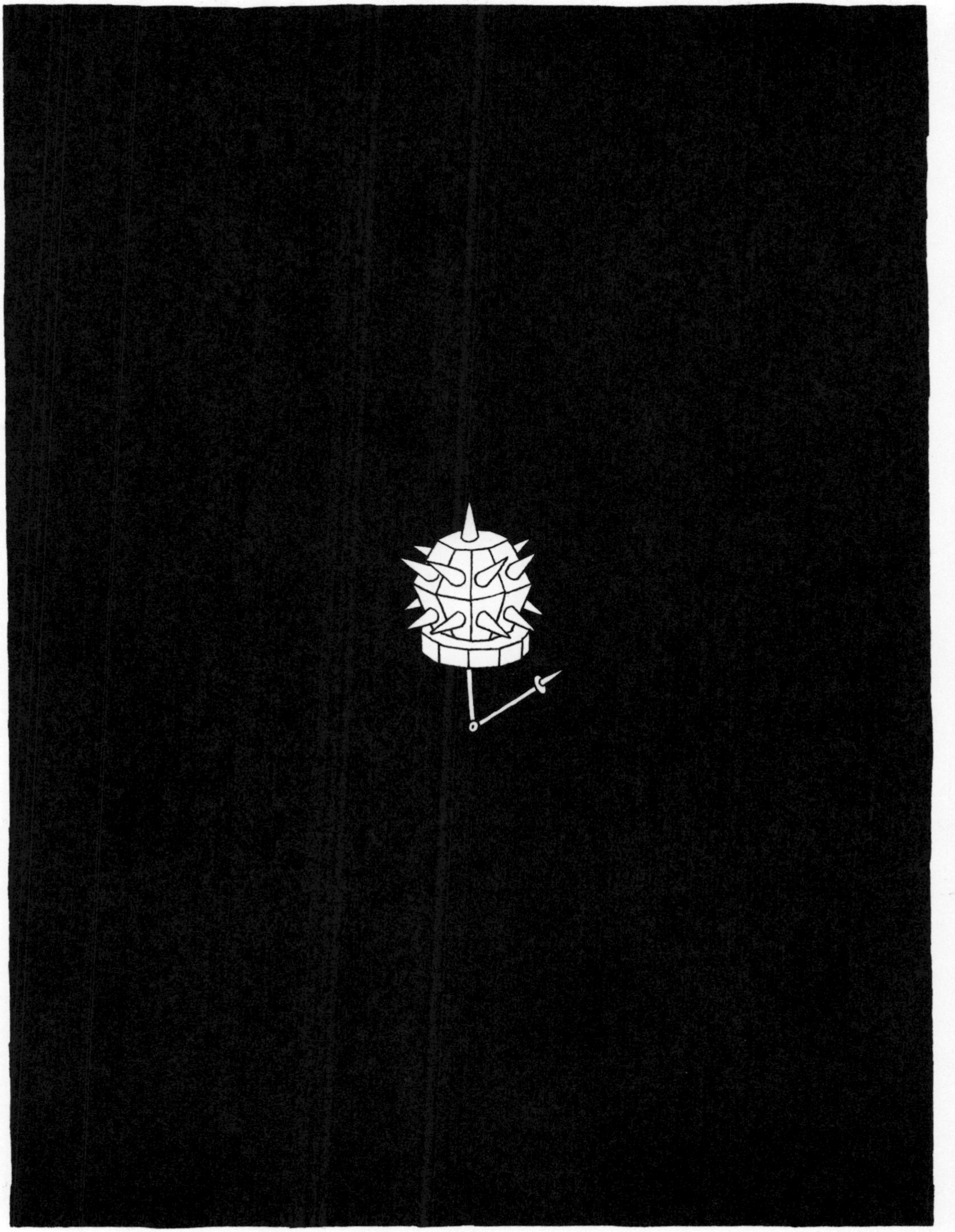